PLAYING TO WIN

PLAYING TO WIN

Dave Whelan

FOREWORD BY STEVE BRUCE

urum

First published in Great Britain
2009 by Aurum Press Ltd
7 Greenland Street
London NW1 0ND
www.aurumpress.co.uk

Picture section designed by David Fletcher Welch

A catalogue record for this book is available from the British Library.

ISBN 978 1 84513 461 7

1 3 5 7 9 10 8 6 4 2

2009 2011 2013 2012 2010

Typeset in Garamond by SX Composing DTP, Rayleigh, Essex
Printed by MPG Books, Bodmin, Cornwall

CONTENTS

All the author's profits from this book will go to the establishment of the new Wigan Boys and Girls Club

FOREWORD

Often when I was having a cup of tea with an opposing manager before a match at the JJB Stadium, the chairman, Dave Whelan, would come down for five minutes to wish me luck and pay his respects to the other team. In my two stints at Wigan I lost count of the number of times he'd leave the room and the other manager would say, 'He seems a decent geezer to work for.'

And they were absolutely right.

When I first went to Wigan in April 2001, I'd been out of football for six months. More importantly, I think I was out of love with the game as well.

Dave Whelan changed all that.

The club had just let Bruce Rioch go and Dave asked me to come in for the last eight weeks of the season. I said I'd give it a go, but after my experiences of managing Huddersfield and Sheffield United I can't say my heart was in it. With no disrespect to those clubs today, I have to say that at the top level it was horrific. Every day there seemed to be boardroom squabbles or management buyouts – at Sheffield I had six chief executives in a year. At Huddersfield a major investor asked for his money back when we were top of the league. There were so many problems and none of them had anything to do with what went on on the pitch. It got to the point where I looked at my options and, for the first time in my adult life, imagined a life outside football.

My first eight weeks at Wigan transformed me. I got the bug back.

At Wigan everything worked as it should do all the time. No promises were broken, no lies were told. Everything was exactly as it appeared in the brochure which, after the couple of years I'd had, was a new experience for me. And I really enjoyed working with Dave.

But even though we managed to reach the League One (as it is now known) play-offs, when I got an offer to manage in London with Crystal Palace I couldn't turn it down. It was nothing to do with Wigan and it was definitely nothing to do with Dave. I just felt I needed to be away from the Manchester area – I wanted a fresh start away from the North West.

I eventually ended up at Birmingham for six years but I never forgot those two months at Wigan.

In November 2007 I got a call from Dave.

'Wigan are in trouble. We're in the relegation zone. Will you come and save us?'

To be fair to them, the owners at Birmingham didn't want me to go. They slapped a £3 million fee on me and assumed that would put a stop to interest from any other clubs. When I heard that I thought, 'Well, no one will ever pay that.' At the time I think the record fee for a manager was about £750,000, and that was for José Mourinho.

But Dave being Dave he just said to Birmingham, 'OK, £3 million it is. It will be in your bank this afternoon.'

I was blown away by that gesture. I think everyone was. I'd never cost that much as a player! But that's typical Dave. When he really believes in something, he goes for it. Nothing was going to stop him from getting the man he felt would save his club. And he didn't even try to pressure me. He just said, 'I've got some good players here. Come and have a crack and see if you can keep us up.'

I hadn't been there very long and Bolton beat us heavily, 4-1. I admit I said to the chairman, 'Dave, I don't know if we've got enough fight to stay in the division. I'll weigh things up when we get to the January transfer window but there's no point throwing good money after bad.'

And he just said, 'You're the boss. Whatever you think.'

Thankfully our next match turned things around when we beat Blackburn – Dave's old club – 5-3. It was one of those unbelievable games – Roque Santa Cruz scored a hat-trick for them and Marcus Bent did the same for us. The match had everyone on the edge of their seats and that result gave all of Wigan a lift at just the right time.

No one was happier than the man at the top and, to be fair, no one deserved it more than him. When you think of the journey Dave has taken that club on, it's incredible. He's transformed Wigan Athletic from twelve hundred people in a ramshackle old ground at Springfield Park to a 26,000, all-seat stadium, and taken them from the bottom of the old Fourth Division into the Premier League. And I know he says he's happy just to stay in the League, but for most of my last season we were in the top ten – and even in seventh place for nearly three months of that.

I doubt Dave ever thought he'd see the day where we'd be genuinely disappointed not to have beaten Manchester United but that's happened as well. Two seasons in a row United came to Wigan expecting to win emphatically and we pushed them very close. In the first match, in May 2008, we were denied a penalty when Rio Ferdinand as good as caught the ball, but the ref didn't give it. Then a year later we pushed them right to the limit and they only beat us in the last three minutes. And when we played at Old Trafford in between Fergie came out and said we were the best team that had visited that year. Taking on the best club side in the world and pushing them as far as we did gave me enormous pride so imagine how it must have felt for Dave?

The great thing about working for him is he lets you manage. In that respect he has been the best boss I've worked for. With Dave, a spade is a spade and you know exactly where you are. I think that's actually his greatest strength. He's old school, if you like. The boss is the boss and the manager is the manager.

Every manager working today dreams of a relationship with a chairman like that. Once Dave employs you he lets you get on with the job. I've worked for him twice and he never once tried to interfere. He never said, 'Why did you pick that formation?' or 'Why did you play him when I told you not to?' In that respect he's a breath of fresh air.

He also backs his manager to the hilt. When I agreed to come up from

Birmingham we didn't even talk about the money side of things. He just said, 'I am going to support you the best way I can.' And that stayed true to the day I left.

He takes a genuine interest in players but he always backed my judgement on them one hundred per cent. For example, we signed Lee Cattermole in the summer of 2008. As usual, I went to Dave to discuss it. I said, 'I've got a chance of signing a young England Under-21 player.'

'Well, tell me about him,' he said.

'He's a tough lad, a tackler, an aggressive captain-type player. He has a bit of baggage because he's got himself into trouble in the North East, but maybe it's the time to get him out of there, away from the environment he's lived in all his life.'

We spoke about Lee like that for a bit then Dave said, 'OK, it's your call. Let's see if we can do it.'

When you've got Dave's trust it's a wonderful feeling because he just lets you do your job. He's got some very good people there, like Brenda Spencer, the chief exec, and John Benson, the general manager, and they'll all say the same.

The reason the other managers like him is the same reason the Wigan players like him – because they know that for all his business success he's a football man at heart.

I'm not one for visiting boardrooms after a match so I used to wait to speak to him at the training ground a few days later. He goes down every week – especially if he needs a bit of treatment on his shoulder after a game of tennis or golf! We would always have a chat about the last match or the forthcoming one and anything else going on in the game. He wasn't there to influence me; it's just that football is in his blood. And if there had been a good performance he'd make sure he shook everyone's hand and I think the players all appreciate that. They have a huge respect for him, in fact, because he's been there and done it himself.

I think that's why he takes the view of transfers that he does. Because he's been a player he would never deny someone the opportunity to go on to a bigger club. He knows how short a career is and he knows how few and far between the big offers are. So when Emile Heskey wanted to go to Aston Villa, we had to let him. And when Wilson Palacios got the call from Spurs, we had to let that happen too – in exchange for £14 million, of course. I have to say, as much as I hated to see the lad go, it was satisfying knowing that his fee would really help the club. Dave has invested a personal fortune over the years but even he can't be a bottomless pit.

So why did I leave again? Dave's been so complimentary over the years saying that I should be the next boss of Manchester United, but do you know what? The days of a club like that plucking a manager from somewhere like Aberdeen are over. The big clubs tend to go for people who have managed other big clubs – and I honestly believe Sunderland have the potential, the backing and the resources to become a very big club indeed.

I have to say it was a complete shock when Niall Quinn came in for me. I was happy at the JJB and I certainly was not looking for a move. But a new man had taken over the Black Cats and they wanted a so-called 'big name' to take them forward. They took a look at what we'd achieved at Wigan and liked what they saw.

Going forward I know I will be very lucky to get the same level of support from a chairman again. I enjoyed my eighteen months with Wigan more than any other time of my management career. It was a delight, every minute. And that is Dave's real contribution to the club.

Steve Bruce
June 2009

Prologue

IS YOUR NAME DAVID?

'Is that a real gun, Mister?'

The soldier sitting opposite me nodded.

'Yes, it is.'

I couldn't believe my luck. I was seven years old and I'd decided to ride a bus for the very first time. Money was non-existent for a kid like me in 1944 and when I'd found a penny in the street, I knew exactly what I was going to spend it on – a trip on one of Wigan's shiny new double-deckers. I never dreamt I'd get to see a real-life soldier as well.

I'd climbed on the bus at the railway station, paid the conductor the penny fare, then waited for my journey to begin. I was so excited. Everyone in Wigan travelled by tram in those days. But red and cream buses had started arriving the year before. They were as big as houses but they moved like giant cars. It was my dream to travel on one. And now I was.

It took me a few moments to realise the bus wasn't moving.

'Why are we just sitting here?' I wondered. I had been the last person on. 'I hope there's not a problem.' Then I saw.

Walking up to the back of the bus was a soldier. He had the full kit on – the helmet, the overcoat, a large kitbag and over his shoulder a gun. A real-life gun. He had the full uniform for war. The conductor had obviously spotted him. That's why he hadn't given the driver the signal to pull away.

I watched the soldier get closer and closer. 'I wonder why he's home.'

I was three when the war started. My dad was called up straight away. I barely knew him when he left. There wasn't a day that passed when I didn't think about him. But I didn't have any memories to cling on to. I was too young. I didn't know what he looked like.

I didn't really even know if I'd ever see him again.

I watched, transfixed, as the soldier stepped on to the bus and carefully stowed his gear in the luggage area below the staircase. I couldn't take my eyes off his gun and I willed him to sit near me at the back so I could ask him all about it. I was in luck. The bench opposite me was the closest seat to him, so that's where he sat. I gave him a few seconds to get comfortable, then the questions came tumbling out.

'What kind of gun is it, Mister?'

The soldier smiled.

'It's a .303.'

That didn't really mean much to me but it seemed important to know. When I told my friends later, I had to remember the details.

'Have you got any bullets?' I asked.

'Yes, I have,' he said.

A real soldier, a real gun and real bullets. I was so caught up in the conversation I didn't even notice the bus finally pulling away. I'd been dreaming about this journey for months. Now I was as good as missing it. But that didn't matter.

'Where are you going?' I asked.

'I get off at the Honeysuckle Pub in Poolstock.'

I said, 'I'm getting off there as well!'

Now it was the soldier's turn to ask questions.

'Where do you live?'

'I live in Chadwick Street,' I replied. 'Number 70.'

He said, 'Is your name David?'

'Yes,' I said. 'It is.'

How on earth did this stranger know that?

The soldier just smiled again and I noticed how kind he looked. 'David,' he said. 'I'm your dad.'

I stared at this man's face. I wanted to recognise it but I couldn't.

'You're my dad?'

'Yes.'

There was a pause between us. Then I said, 'Can I carry your gun?'

He smiled again.

'Yes, son, you can.'

I think of that moment a lot, even now. It happened more than sixty years ago but it's as fresh in my mind as events that occurred yesterday. Lots of things have happened to me since. Some good, some bad. But I know I wouldn't have achieved anything without him. Without my dad.

While professional football clubs were pursuing my signature when I was a teenager, he was the one who turned down the big money on offer to let me follow my heart to Blackburn Rovers. He was there at every match I ever played for that club – always in the crowd, never asking for preferential treatment. I remember once travelling with him by train to a match. You did that in those days because as a player you were no richer than the supporters. The carriage was crammed with Blackburn fans. It was standing room only. Everyone was talking excitedly about the forthcoming game. The conversation near us turned to the team – and one fan asked my dad's opinion.

'What about that young right back, eh?' he said.

He was referring to me. I'd only been in the first team a few times and my face hadn't become known yet. Back then supporters had to be at the front of the terraces to get an idea what players looked like. There were no television pictures or magazine articles or advertisements.

'Oh, yes, he's quite good,' my dad replied.

'I reckon he'll play for England one day,' the man said.

'Do you think so?'

I don't know how Dad was keeping a straight face. I thought I was going to explode with laughter.

'Yeah, there's a good future for that lad,' the fan continued.

'I hope you can tell him yourself one day,' Dad said.

'When am I ever going to meet him?' the man said, and the whole carriage laughed.

I still laugh about that story myself. Thanks to the modern media, you've got reserve-team players today who are more famous than we were then. I bet some Premiership academy kids get recognised more than I was when I played in the FA Cup final.

My father could have made a lot of mileage out of that exchange on the train, but that wasn't his style. He would never steal the limelight if it wasn't earned.

'If you want to tell people who you are, that's fine,' he told me. 'But I'm not going to take any of the credit. You're the one who's done the work.'

My dad was there in the stands when I played in the 1960 FA Cup final – and he was by my side a few hours later when I woke up in hospital with a broken leg.

He was on hand when I went into business after football as well. He worked with me on the market stalls I built up into the supermarket chain that was bought by Ken Morrison in 1978.

He never saw my greatest successes, though. He never saw my JJB Sports retail business valued at nearly £1 billion on the London Stock Exchange. He wasn't alive when I bought Wigan Athletic Football Club and watched their rise from virtual extinction to a regular spot in the Premier League. He missed out on me becoming the first – and probably the last – person to play in all four English divisions and be chairman of a club in all four English divisions as well.

And he has no idea that the football and rugby stadium I built in Wigan still carries his name in its restaurants and hospitality suites.

Neither of us had any idea that all this lay ahead as we sat there in 1944 on that bus to Poolstock. I couldn't have known that my life – at the age of seven – was about to begin in earnest. It's been colourful, exciting and at times controversial – as you'll discover – and that day was the kick-off. Everything was about to turn around – but first I'd had to get through those long years without him.

And they were bleak.

One

GET WARM, STAY WARM

I had only one ambition when I was young. That was to stay warm.

People have asked me, 'Did you know you were going to be a footballer?' Some even say, 'When did you first dream of making millions?'

My answer is always the same: 'All I remember is wanting the cold to go away.' That was the fight: to get warm, and to stay warm. Only then could you be happy.

I was born in 1936 to Jimmy and Maggie Whelan, the youngest of four. There was Elsie, Jimmy, then Pauline and me. World War II began three years later and my dad was called up for military training immediately. I didn't understand what was going on but I remember him not being there one day and he still wasn't back the next. Eight weeks went by but it felt like a lifetime and then I got up one morning and he was sitting downstairs. All his regiment had been allowed home for Christmas and I can imagine families up and down the land thinking they'd got the best present they could wish for. I know I thought that. But a few days later he was dressed in his brown uniform and leaving once again. When he kissed us all goodbye who was to know it would be the last time we would see him for four and a half years?

We didn't know a thing, didn't know where he was being posted – or if he'd even survive.

We found out three weeks later that he had been sent to Iceland. British intelligence had discovered that the German navy needed to find a port in the Atlantic for refuelling their submarines. Reykjavik had been earmarked. As soon as the Allies intercepted this information they acted. Ten thousand troops were moved out to Iceland. The island would be defended. And my dad would be part of it.

As it turned out, the invasion never came. The pre-emptive move was enough and the Germans had to find their port elsewhere. My dad was safe.

But he didn't know that at the time. We didn't either. And I didn't even know where Iceland was.

'Tell me again where Dad is,' I would ask my mam.

'He's in Iceland, David.'

'Iceland. That's right. And where is it again?'

'It's a long way from home.'

That's all I needed to know.

Home for us was a two-up, two-down on Chadwick Street, about a mile from Goose Green, in the area of Poolstock. The toilet was outside, twenty yards from the back door, and we shared it with three neighbours. There were a hundred houses on our street. Rows of fifty terraces on each side of the road. Behind us was Byron Street and next to that was Pool Street. They all had a hundred houses in them too. For as far as you could see, the streets were identical, each one built for the colliers and the cotton workers. It was the same in the nearby areas of Wallgate, Scholes and Worsley Mesnes.

None of the houses had central heating and the hot water tap didn't exist in homes like ours. We didn't know anyone who had electricity. There wasn't even a fire in every room. We had a hearth in the front room – nobody called it a lounge – and a little kitchen area and that was it. Downstairs was one room, really, about eight foot by six. Everything happened in there. If Mam washed on a Monday I'd have to put the clothes through the mangle that afternoon when I came home from school. They would then go on the clothes horse and be there all day Tuesday drying out.

It was the same in every house in the area. In fact most things were the same – with one big difference. I was still very young when the amount of men in Wigan started to decrease but I couldn't help noticing as the months went by that some of my friends still had their fathers living with them at home.

'Mam, why is our dad away and Jack's dad is still here?' I asked one day.

'Jack's dad is a miner. Miners are needed here so they're not allowed to fight.'

'Don't we need our dad here?'

'More than you know.'

I didn't understand that mining was one of the occupations exempt from the call-up. My dad worked in Eckersley's Mill. He had no choice but to sign up along with all the other workers from non-essential industries.

'It's not fair.'

'No, love, it's not,' my mam said. 'But we have to make the best of it.'

That was easier said than done. It was bad enough not having our dad around but we also missed his wages. The miners still took home their normal pay. When your father was in the Army his family got 19/6, just under a pound. That's all my mam had to look after the four of us and herself. It was hard, especially in winter. If there was work to be found cleaning she would take it, but it was hard to fit in with young children. When I was at school she got a job cleaning Poolstock Labour Club. A full week's work would earn her fifteen shillings. It was nothing, but every penny counted.

We got one bag of coal a month. That was the ration. One bag – and then only if you could afford it. We had to use that for heat, for a fire, for cooking, for bath water, boiling the kettle, for everything. You'd use that in one night now. One of my uncles, Jack Waldren, was a coal man. He always delivered our coal and if he could bring half a bag extra he would do it.

Every house had a bunker out the back to store the coal but we used to keep ours under the stairs. It was in that short supply you couldn't store it outside. People were so desperate to keep warm they would even have stolen from their neighbours. By today's standards there was no real crime back then. We all felt safe. We *were* safe. But when it came to heat and food, people did what they had to do to look after their families. And nobody could blame them.

We were the same. We did everything we could to keep warm. If there was enough coal for a fire, we used to put a brick in the oven and wrap a bit of cloth around it and take it to bed like it was a hot-water bottle.

In winter I'd sleep fully clothed. If there was a spare rug on the floor I'd drag it over to cover my blanket as well. But you couldn't buy rugs in the war. You couldn't get anything like that. We had to make our own. My mam, my sisters, Jimmy and me, we'd get old clothes, cut them up into little strips, about an inch by three inches. Then we'd get some sacking, cut it open and pull the cloth through. Then we'd peg it back together and that would be our rug – and our blanket.

The only other thing that kept us warm was sharing beds. There were just two rooms for all of us so when I was small, I shared with my mam and dad, and then just my mam. Elsie, Pauline and Jimmy had the other room's two beds.

The winter of 1942 was the worst. I thought we'd all die. My sisters were worried too, although they tried not to show it at the time. It was too cold to sleep, and if you did drop off you'd worry whether you'd wake up again. That was seriously cold weather. We had snow on the ground for about six weeks. It was minus ten. I'd never known pain like it. Still haven't. It was too cold to work, too cold to think, too cold to breathe. The whole house felt freezing and damp whether it was midday or the middle of the night.

Things got so desperate I lost count of the times I had to pee on my hands just to warm them up.

I would have tried anything just to get some feeling back into my fingers. I was six years old and that was all I could think of doing.

During the war a family's best friends were its ration books. You got one for every member of the family. Adults received yellowy, buff-coloured ones. Kids' books were blue. They entitled you to sixteen units of food per week, later increased to twenty, plus a daily pint of milk, eggs and orange juice. Every person in the land was entitled to the same amounts, whether they lived in Chadwick Street or Buckingham Palace – that's what the Government said. But you still had to find the money to pay for everything. Dad's war pay of 19/6 didn't stretch very far. Not when Mam had to feed four children and herself.

Even if you could afford it, food was so scarce. I didn't taste chocolate until years after the war, didn't see a banana until I was ten – when I did see one I thought, 'What the hell do you do with that?' Unless it was home-grown, you didn't find it.

Everything that happened in our house at Chadwick Street, especially meals, took place around the small table in the front room. Everybody would squeeze round and, as the youngest, I got the most uncomfortable position – the table leg, or the corner – wherever nobody else wanted to sit. Each adult was allotted two ounces of meat a week. *Two ounces.* You eat that in one meal these days. One McDonald's Quarter Pounder has almost double that amount. Once a week my mam would cook a stew. All the family's meat ration would go in there. Then that was it, gone. For the rest of the week I'd get by on either chips and gravy or jam butties. That was my main diet.

We all heard stories about people pretending to lose their ration books so they could get a replacement and have double portions. We never tried that. But everyone was doing something. You had to. It was part of life.

About fifty yards from our house was a little piece of land where a few families had knocked some wooden buildings together and built an animal pen to house pigs. The plan was to rear them, breed them and eat them as quickly as possible. But even that was restricted. Anyone with livestock had to register their new arrivals and the Government would confiscate some of every new litter.

One sow was capable of having as many as seven piglets. If she did, you'd call up the local butcher and say, 'We've got four little pigs here. What do you want to do about collecting them?'

Really, though, there would be another three that we hadn't declared, just waiting to be divided among the families.

It was my job to run down to the pens every day with food for the pigs.

We used to keep animals in our own backyard as well, mainly pigeons and rabbits. They were too small to declare to the authorities, but you could still have a good meal from their meat. First, though, you had to kill them.

This always fascinated me. I remember, aged five or six, watching my mam or Jimmy go into the yard and open the wire cages, knowing what they were going to do. You couldn't get squeamish about it. You just had to catch the animals and kill them. Quickly. There was no room for sentiment. They weren't pets to us. They were food. They were the difference between us starving or living.

I remember the day I stopped being an observer. I was eight years old. My mam said to me, 'David, I need a rabbit for the stew. You know what to do.'

It never crossed my mind to say 'no'. I can imagine her face if I'd said something like 'Oh, I don't fancy doing that, Mam.' And I can imagine the back of her hand as well. You just had to get on with things. We all mucked in.

But that first time wasn't easy. Before you can do anything, you have to catch the thing. I was young, I was quick – but this little rabbit was quicker. I was on my knees for ten minutes chasing it around the pen. When I caught it I didn't stop to think about what I was doing. I hung it up by its legs and hit it square behind the back of the neck with my hand. I'll never forget that sensation. I actually felt the life snuff out of that little creature. I couldn't afford to dwell on that, though. There was a war on. The other Whelans were depending on me.

Killing the thing was only half the job. Next I had to cut the fur off, skin it, open it up with a sharp knife and remove the guts. I can still picture it. I was covered in blood that first time. And it wasn't my bath night. There would be no hot water for me.

I'll never forget my mam's face when I handed her the chopped pieces of meat ready for stewing. She had a smile as wide as the Leeds Canal.

'You've done well, son,' she said, and patted my head.

I was proud as punch. I felt like I was contributing to the family at last. Like a man.

I'd already been doing my best to get a few extra treats on the table. If the local farmers had a crop of vegetables on the way, my friends and I would sneak into their fields. If you could get half a dozen potatoes, or a couple of turnips, that would make all the difference at teatime. But if the farmer spotted you, you had to run. The situation – the hunger – turned us all into petty thieves.

Not that everyone had to go to such lengths. I began to notice that the families with their men around led much better lives than we did because not only could they afford their full ration allowance, they could even run to a few treats on the black market. Shop prices were all fixed – but the extra bag of sugar, the new coat or a bit more coal for the fire were all within reach if you had the money. And we didn't.

It was one thing being restricted by the ration books – but some weeks we even struggled to afford our allowance.

The financial hardship was felt everywhere. Because my brother Jimmy was six years older than me, our mam didn't have any of his things left to pass down to me. So I only had the clothes I walked to school in and that was that. They had to last. If there was a hole in my jumper it had to be darned. There was no replacement. That did me for home and for school. We had no school uniforms as such at the Poolstock Church of England School. I owned one pair of socks, one pair of trousers and a woollen jersey. That was it. That's all I had. No underpants, no vest, nothing like that. For shoes we all wore what we called clogs – these were lace-up boots with irons or 'clogs' on the bottom so the soles never wore away. They were heavy old things – and dangerous. Footballs were hard to get hold of in those days but if you did have one you wouldn't let anyone kick it if they were wearing clogs. You only needed one tiny piece of iron to be a bit rough or poking out the side of your shoe and *bang* – the ball'd burst and you'd got a dozen lads out for your blood.

Most of the time I wore my clogs they didn't fit me – they were either too big or too small. But at least they were something. There were about three families who were really, really poor and their kids used to walk about in bare feet. You think that only happens in the 1800s but it was going on during the war. Whatever the weather, those poor boys and girls trudged to and from school with nothing on their feet at all. It put your own suffering into perspective. My family didn't have anything – but we still had more than them and if we could help out, with an old shoe or a jumper that didn't fit any more, then we'd pass it on. Everyone did the same. You had to pull together where you could. Nobody threw anything away. There was always someone who could use it.

At school I mixed well enough with the other kids. I was good at sport and that always helps you fit in. The moment we started physical education and they gave us a rugby ball or a football, that's when I really came into my own. You'll never be short of friends if you can play sport well and I was soon captain of the rugby and football teams and dreaming of playing both professionally. But that's all it was for me then. A dream.

I wasn't particularly gifted academically but I don't think I got the best chances. There were forty or so pupils per class and you were taught with a rod of iron – or at least a stick of wood. Discipline was the overriding success story at Poolstock C of E. Every youngster used to get the cane then. It was only a matter of time before you were told, 'Hold your hand out.' There was none of this 'You can't touch them.' It was 'Hand' – *whack* – or 'Bend over' – *whack*. Two, three or sometimes six strikes. I would get it for talking in class or making paper darts and letting fly. Copying was another big misdemeanour then. If a teacher saw you looking over and reading someone else's paper, he'd be standing next to you with his cane before you'd even registered the answer. It used to hurt but you knew you were going to get it.

Some kids would rush out and complain to their parents if they had six of the best. I never did that. It was hard but the rules were there. If I was naughty in class, I knew I was going to get the cane. And if my mam found out, I knew I'd get a smack from her as well.

With my dad away, I think our mam tried harder than other mums to make sure we were all brought up right. We all knew what was acceptable and what was not. She was a very impressive woman, hard-working, never wanting for free what she didn't deserve. And that's how she wanted all her children to be. Occasionally, though, her strictness backfired. I had only been at school a few months when I complained my throat was sore.

'I don't think I can go to school today. I don't feel well.'

How many times had my mam heard that from Jimmy and my sisters?

'You're going,' she said. 'No arguments.'

But I *was* ill. My throat got tighter throughout the day and I started to sweat. I couldn't concentrate on my lessons. I never found it too easy to follow what the teachers were saying, but that afternoon it was like they were talking another language. Mam could tell something was wrong the second I walked through the door at home.

'Don't take your coat off,' she said. 'We're going to Wigan Infirmary.'

It was lucky we did because I was diagnosed with diphtheria. With vaccination it's virtually non-existent in the developed world these days. Back then it was quite common – and untreated it could be deadly. One of Queen Victoria's daughters died of it, and there were thousands of deaths a year in the UK alone. And I had it.

I still remember lying in a hospital bed, trying to focus on the wall in front of me, and I couldn't. The nurses, the doctors, everything was spinning. The more I concentrated, the faster the spinning got. I was feeling sicker by the minute. And I was so hot. I'd spent so much of my life trying to keep warm. Now I thought I was going to catch fire.

I didn't know this, but if the medics couldn't cool my fever then I would very likely slip into sleep and not wake up. It was that serious. I was in hospital for three weeks. For the first fortnight it was touch-and-go whether I'd pull through.

And every day my mam was there with me.

For most of my time in there I wasn't even aware she was in the ward. I didn't know where or who I was or the time of day. If she'd gone home I would never have known. But she stayed – even though it's such a contagious disease.

Our friends and neighbours all rallied round when I was in there. Our mam couldn't be expected to look after the house as well as be at my bedside. My sister Elsie did what she could, but various aunts and uncles and people we barely knew stepped up and helped out with cooking and babysitting for Pauline. That was the upside of the war. People were there for you. If someone was in trouble, everyone else pulled together. It was amazing really. I never learnt the extent of it until years later, but I'm so grateful now.

I don't remember owning any toys when I was young. Unless I made it or found it, I didn't play with it. We never celebrated Christmas with the sort of presents you get today and I don't remember anyone having a birthday party while the war was on. Most of my friends had as little as me, anyway, so I rarely felt left out. About the only thing that ever made me jealous was if I saw someone with a *Rupert the Bear* annual. As soon as I could read I used to crave my own copy of one of those books. If I found anybody with one, I'd beg them to let me have a read. But I never had any books of my own at that age.

Later, when my dad came back, that changed. I started to buy the *Beano* comic and then moved on to the *Adventure, Hotspur* and all those other action titles. The thing I liked most about them was they all had football stories in. I'd read about these fictional players scoring goals and making great tackles and getting to Wembley and then my daydreams would begin. Every time I read a new story I thought exactly the same thing.

'I wish that was me.'

During the war, though, nobody really dared to dream about anything – other than it all being over. Your entire life was shaped by what was going on. During the day you were ruled by the ration books – how much you could eat, how much you could drink. But at night there was something even worse. The air-raid sirens.

Wigan wasn't one of the Germans' primary targets but that didn't stop us being bombed during the Battle of Britain. Hitler had two aims. He wanted to prepare the UK for invasion and he wanted to bring us to our knees as a military power. London was obviously the main target, but ports like Southampton, Bristol and Portsmouth all suffered serious bombardment to put the Navy's bases out of action. And in the Midlands and the North of England, it was cities like Liverpool, Manchester and Coventry, where so much of the machinery of the war effort was manufactured, that the Nazis wanted destroyed.

It started in 1940 and continued for a year. Night after night we'd hear the sirens, about eight or nine o'clock in summer, earlier in winter. Then we'd hear the planes. That buzzing noise, so distant at first, but then you knew they were on top of you. Everyone held their breath. It was just one of those things you did instinctively.

When the siren went off at the start of the night, we were normally all right. It was later, when the missions were completed, that we had to worry. No one really understood it at the time – we only learnt much later – but sometimes the planes attacking Liverpool or Manchester would run out of time before they'd released all their bombs. Or sometimes a few would get stuck and the squadron would start its retreat. On those nights Wigan suffered.

We were directly beneath the Luftwaffe's flight path to their North West targets. They'd fly in over Wigan and they'd fly back out over Wigan. You could set your clock by them. We weren't a target as such. But rather than take any bombs home, they'd dump them on us.

I was so young I didn't really know what was going on. I didn't know my life was in danger. But when your mam's scared, so are you. Until I was about four I didn't think my mother was afraid of anything. But then the sirens started and I knew she was.

From three years old to five, all I knew at night was bombing – or the threat of it. I remember the sounds of the planes and the tension in the room. All the adults were quiet. No one knew if we'd be hit that night. Then you'd hear the thump. The explosion. I learnt everything from the expressions of the grown-ups. If the bang was quiet, they looked sad. But if it was louder, they looked terrified.

I didn't realise then that the louder the explosion, the closer the threat.

Some of the bombs were too close for comfort. The next morning us lads would hunt out the scenes of destruction. One night we went to bed and everything was all right. The next morning an entire row of terrace houses, about 800 yards away in Goose Green and identical to ours, was missing. Just like that. The whole area was devastated. It looked like a missing tooth in a beautiful smile.

When the sirens went off, everyone had to evacuate to a bomb shelter. You were expecting it but it still seemed to catch everyone out, night after night. Even though I knew the siren was coming, the sound of that high-pitched wailing cut right through me. It was a sinister, scary noise. And what happened next made the experience worse. All lights had to be switched off. Men went around manually extinguishing the gas street lamps. Windows were boarded up. People fell into a routine. They could be out of their home and down in the shelter within a few minutes. But no one forgot why they were doing it.

There was a shelter near us and more in the town centre. They were so cold and also so crowded. However many people were hiding out, no one would ever be told, 'I'm sorry, you can't come in. We're full.' They'd always make room.

Mam hated putting me and Pauline through that and luckily we had somewhere else to go. An auntie on my mother's side, Mrs Unsworth, ran an off-licence. I didn't know her family very well, but she made us very welcome in the large cellar below her shop where the draught beer was stored in its barrels. 'You can always come here,' she told us. 'Whenever you like, you just come.' So as soon as we heard the siren, that's where we would head. We had blankets, pillows, even a little lamp. I lost count of the nights I spent there or the mornings when I would emerge into the sunlight still smelling of ale or wine. Months on end for more than a year. Night after night spent cuddling our mam or one of my sisters, shivering with fear and cold, listening out for the waspish sounds of the Luftwaffe engines, and terrified that everything would be gone in the morning. If I was lucky I'd fall asleep before the attacks started. That way I wouldn't see how scared everyone else was.

Sometimes if it was early we'd sing. My mam and my sisters had wonderful voices. We'd all join in and try to forget what was going on above our heads, but that always reminded us of the one person who was missing because everyone said the same thing about him.

'Ah, David, you've got to hear your dad sing.'

My mam would say it from time to time. So would my brother and sisters. Even friends and neighbours if the subject of music came up or they had a tune in their head.

There wasn't enough laughter during the war and I loved seeing how remembering my dad made everyone smile. I felt a tingle of pride every time it happened. If I'm honest, though, I also felt something else. Jealousy. I'd never heard my father sing. Or if I had, I couldn't remember. And that just made me envious of everyone who told me they had.

'It's not fair,' I thought, 'when am I going to get to hear him sing?'

But I knew, with every day the war continued, that my chances of even seeing him again were getting slimmer and slimmer.

Two

IT'S BLOODY JIMMY WHELAN!

For the first few years of the war everyone in Wigan was talking about being invaded. I didn't know what that meant but I knew from the way it affected the grown-ups that it was bad. After 1942 when things changed out in Africa, the whole tone in the town became more upbeat. When Montgomery got his first victory, things brightened up everywhere. I even heard people saying 'We're going to win the war,' although I couldn't imagine what that meant. The war was all I knew. I couldn't remember a life without it.

It was always a surprise when a soldier appeared in town because you never knew they were coming. They weren't allowed to even tell their wives that they had leave in case the information about troop movements fell into the wrong hands. No one was allowed to know anything. Once a month my mam used to write to my dad at the address she had for his regiment's base in Iceland but she was as shocked as anyone that day I burst through the front door and yelled, 'Mam! It's Dad – he's come home!'

I don't know if she believed me but she came running to the front door and just stopped dead. I remember to this day her face as he said, 'Madge, it's me.'

She was so excited it was a few minutes before she spotted what I was carrying.

'Jimmy – have you let David carry your gun?' Then turning to me she said, 'Put that thing down before you get us all killed!'

As soon as word got round that Dad was home the house filled up with neighbours, friends and family who wanted to know how he was. Lots of them asked him for news of the war effort from abroad and a few enquired after their own relatives. I couldn't take my eyes off my dad as he chatted, surrounded by so many people. I knew I would have to wait my turn for some time with him but I was ready to sit there all night.

'Are you home for good now, Dad?' I asked the first moment I got.

He shook his head and I saw my mum look sad. 'No, I've just got fourteen days' leave.' He must have seen my face fall and explained he wasn't being sent back to Iceland but to somewhere in England. 'Don't you worry about me,' he said. 'I'll be back before you know it.'

Even though he was in such demand from the rest of the family I spent every moment I could at my dad's side. I didn't want to miss a single word he had to say about what he'd been up to.

Dad wanted us to know that he had never been in danger – although nobody could have been sure at the time. When his battalion of troops had been shipped over to Iceland there had been a very real threat of German invasion and the island remained on twenty-four-hour alert for the next few years.

In fact, the closest my dad had come to death was on the trip out. He left England on HMS *Daring* in January 1940. It was an impressive boat, a destroyer of 1,375 tons, just eight years old. During what Churchill called the Battle of the Atlantic, she was used to ferry troops. My father joined another 2,000 men at Liverpool Docks and waited. He'd never been on a boat before, let alone a ship like this. He didn't have a clue what he was letting himself in for.

'I just knew I had to make the most of it,' he told me. 'Life is for living.'

Even a ship like the *Daring* gets thrown about in the Denmark Straits in winter. By the time her passengers disembarked, they all looked the worse for wear. After she left Iceland the *Daring* moved on to Norway to help evacuate troops escaping from the German occupation of the country. She was on her way back to Liverpool, within sight of the British coast, when a German U-boat, *U-23*, fired two torpedoes. The *Daring* sank thirty nautical miles east of Duncansby Head on the northern tip of Scotland. Nine officers and 148 ratings – lower-ranked men – went down with the ship. I still remember how cold in my bones I felt when Dad told me about it.

The day before and that could have been him.

In all honesty, he admitted, the weather felt like their biggest enemy. If we thought it was freezing in Wigan, the temperatures over in Iceland must have been extreme. 'But at least we had food,' he said. There was no shortage of fish and seafood and the Army never went without. My father even found something to fight the cold.

'They have this spirit called the Black Death,' he said, laughing. It was a kind of schnapps made from potatoes and flavoured with caraway. 'Now *that* is a drink. One glass warms you up so you can feel your toes again. Two glasses and you can't feel anything at all!'

I loved hearing Dad's stories but there was one thing I wanted to hear even more – the one thing so many members of my family had promised would be worth the wait.

'Dad,' I asked. 'People say you can sing. Can you?'

I didn't know what to expect but to my surprise he stood up and gave me a song, right there and then. I couldn't believe the sound that came out of his mouth. It was like we had a professional opera singer in the room.

I realised then why all those people who'd said 'You've got to hear your father sing' had smiled when they recalled him. But as I listened that day, no one was smiling as much as me.

Before the war, I learn, Dad had spent his nights as a singer in the clubs of Wigan and surrounding Lancashire. By day he had worked in Eckersley's Mill – and now I knew why.

'Your father used to work in the colliery,' one uncle told me while we watched him sing in our front room. 'But the mines were bad for his voice so he stopped that and went to work in the cotton mill.'

'But if he'd stayed in the mines he wouldn't have been sent away,' I said.

My uncle nodded. 'But I think he would still have preferred it that way. Singing is his life.'

I quickly learnt that singing had been Dad's life in the Army as well. It didn't take long for the rest of his battalion to realise they had a natural entertainer in their midst and he was encouraged to sing at every opportunity. The top brass soon found out and he was recommended for official functions. But it went further than that. The British Army had a radio network which was used to boost morale for their troops posted all over the world. It was called ENSA – the Entertainments National Service Association – and it featured a lot of the household names of the day. Gracie Fields and Wigan lad George Formby were regular performers. Laurence Olivier and Ralph Richardson became honorary Army lieutenants for their tours around the battlegrounds of Europe. The biggest stars in the country were desperate to do their bit – but my dad was the only star I was interested in.

Every day he would sing on the radio, knowing his voice would reach the outposts of Africa, Norway and all points in between. He may never have fired a bullet in anger, but in his own way he did as much to keep the Army running as any three-star general.

It was a few days after he told me about this that a thought came to me. 'If we'd had a radio, would we have been able to hear you?'

'I don't see why not,' Dad said.

He could see what I was thinking.

'When I get demobbed, the first thing I'm going to do is buy us one. I promise.'

I hadn't known him long but I could tell my father meant every word.

A few days later, as we watched him pack his rucksack and leave the house in his brown Army suit, it was the thought that I finally knew him that stopped me crying.

The war ended in May 1945. A few weeks later my father was finally demobbed. I think I missed him more during those six months he was away than in the whole five years before that, because I didn't know what I was going without the first time. But during that Christmas period in 1944 I had got to know him and a day didn't go by after that without me wishing he'd come home and sing for us again. In June my wishes came true. When the whole of Wigan turned out for a street party to celebrate the end of the war no one was happier than me because my dad had come home.

A lot of families weren't so lucky.

Everything changed the moment Dad returned. On a practical level I had to move from my mam's bed into my brother's. But more importantly, Dad walked straight back into work at the mill. Our house was literally in the shadow of Eckersley's Mill, so at five to seven in the morning he would leave the house and join the thousands of men and women walking past to work. There were so many employees arriving by tram and foot that the roads around us were actually shut in the morning and again in the afternoon when the mill emptied. By the end of the week we had our first wage in the house. But that wasn't all. On pay day Dad also had a surprise for the family.

'What's in that box, Dad?' I asked him as we gathered in the front room.

'Just you wait and see.'

A few minutes later we all sat around the table staring at this five-valve Alba radio. It was huge and it had large brown dials. It was the most beautiful thing I had ever seen but the sound it made was even better. Word soon got around and before the evening was out the house was filled with neighbours and friends.

'I hear you've got a radio, Jimmy.'

'I have and it's a beauty. Come on in.'

My father never turned away a visitor. Everyone was welcome at Chadwick Street.

That little Alba battery radio opened a new world to me. My mam liked to listen to music but every Saturday afternoon I'd beg her to put on *Sports Special* so we could hear the football scores. Even though Wigan is such a strong rugby town and I was captain of the school team, it was football that I found myself becoming obsessed with. All the names that poured out of the radio sounded so romantic: Manchester United, Arsenal, Blackpool, Wolverhampton Wanderers – I would listen to how they all got on and imagine myself one day playing for them or against them. One name above all acquired a mystical quality. Everyone said that Wembley Stadium was the place you had to play. It was the home of legends and the home of the FA Cup final. I knew immediately that that was where I wanted to play. I had no idea how I would get there, but I could dream.

My dad hadn't been home a fortnight when he said, 'Can you swim, David?'

'No, Dad.'

'We can't have that. A man needs to be able to swim. This weekend I'll give you your first lesson.'

And he did. That Sunday morning we walked down to the Leeds–Liverpool Canal that runs through Wigan. He jumped in first then helped me in. I could just about touch the bottom at the sides. He took me through all the strokes and showed me how to tread water. We did that every weekend until he was satisfied I could do it. Sometimes Jimmy and my sisters came along as well and I can't remember any happier times.

It didn't take long before Dad started to get bookings for his singing again. He would finish at the mill, be home by five then an hour later be back out the door on his way to a working man's club. I used to wish he would stay at home longer but he always said there was money to be made in the clubs. It didn't take us long to see the benefits.

Within four weeks of being demobbed Dad had electricity installed in the house. A van from the electricity board pulled up outside one morning and two men in brown overalls came and had a look round. By the time I got back from school that afternoon it was done. There was a thick black cable running up the wall and along the ceiling of the front room. See it today and you'd be horrified, but back then I'd never seen anything like it. Where the cable stopped there was a single light bulb dangling. It was amazing and so bright. When there was no one else around I would stand there flicking the switch on and off.

I wasn't the only one who was impressed. If I thought the battery radio had been a popular acquisition, this was better. People came from streets around just to look at our bulb. It's incredible to think about now. And we didn't even have a lampshade.

When Dad bought a television a few months later, the buzz in Poolstock was even greater. I can still remember the old Alexandra Palace aerial mast that would start the BBC's programmes in the 1950s.

Suddenly we'd gone from being one of the poorest houses in the area to one of the better off. The days of scratching around for food were over. Whatever the black market had to offer, we could buy. And all for one reason – my dad's singing.

He worked every night apart from Monday, for £2 a booking. On Sundays he would do a lunchtime show in one venue and be somewhere else for the evening. He was incredibly popular. Strangers would say hello and tell him they'd seen him at the local Labour Club. If people spotted me they'd say, 'That's Jimmy Whelan's lad.' I had gone for years without knowing my father – and now everyone knew him!

It didn't take long for Dad's success to regain its pre-war levels, and soon he was travelling further afield to fulfil his bookings. And that reminds me of something. Today everyone thinks of me as 'Mr Wigan' and I am Wigan through and through. I've done what I can to put the town on the map and it has given me an awful lot in return. But I have a confession to make – I wasn't actually born there. In fact I wasn't born in Lancashire at all.

The truth came out by accident one day when I was telling a friend about being from Wigan and my mother overheard.

'You don't know where you were born, do you?' she said.

'I was born in Wigan, Mam. Like you and Dad, and Jimmy and Elsie and Pauline.'

Mam shook her head and explained. My father was a singer of awesome standing not only in Lancashire but also Yorkshire, she said. Back in 1936, when she was expecting me, he had week-long bookings in places like Doncaster and Bradford. Normally my mam stayed at home but because Dad's parents lived in Bradford she went to stay with them for a few nights to be with her husband. She had only been there two days when – *bang* – I decided I was arriving a fortnight early. So that was it – I actually came into the world in Otley Road, Bradford.

Even though it was unexpected, my mam was pleased I was early.

'Premature babies are meant to be tiny,' she said. 'You were 13 lb 4 oz. I was glad when you came out!'

So that's my guilty secret, but of course Dad had one of his own then. The tax man only knew about the wages Dad took home from Eckersley's

Mill – the cash he picked up out of hours went straight into his pocket – although not for long.

For every two pounds that he earned, my mother demanded half for the family. Every night when he came home, Dad would put a pound note down on the kitchen table and Mam would squirrel it away to look after the household. More often than not there was a two-shilling piece for me as well – that's ten pence today, but a lot of money to me then. The rest of the money, though, would usually find its way back to the club that had paid him because my father liked a drink. On a performance night he would quite easily put away seven or eight pints of bitter. Then he'd come home, go to work the next day at the mill, sing again in the evening and do it all over again. He never touched a drop of alcohol at home but when he was working in the clubs he got through it like water.

He was also a terrifically generous character, so even when he wasn't drinking himself he would buy a round for all his friends or members of his audience. He was just as entertaining when he wasn't on stage and he soon got through his allowance. But as long as he had that pound note on the kitchen table in the evening my mother was happy.

Jimmy and Elsie were old enough to see Dad perform but Pauline and I weren't allowed. But when Dad asked our mam to join him on a few numbers, our luck changed.

'You've got a lovely soprano voice, Maggie,' he said.

'You know I don't have the time with the children.'

'Well, bring them along.'

And so she did. I was so excited. As we trudged towards Scholes Labour Club that Saturday evening – me and Pauline running to keep up – I couldn't stop thinking about all the times people had told me 'You've got to hear your father sing'. Well, tonight I was going to hear him properly – and my mam as well. I couldn't wait.

A dozen pairs of hands clapped Dad on the shoulders the moment he stepped through the door and when he introduced the rest of us we felt like stars as well. I'd got used to Dad's popularity but this was something else. He was like a king in that place – and all this before he'd sung a note.

Word had got round about what was happening and there were a few posters up in the club that said 'Saturday Night Special: Jimmy Whelan & Madge'. Pauline and I sat with some family friends at a round table and then a hush went round as a voice on the microphone made the introductions.

'Ladies and gentlemen, give a warm Scholes welcome to tonight's special guests – Jimmy Whelan and Madge!'

The whole room erupted and they were still clapping when I saw a beautiful woman walk out on to the small stage. I couldn't believe what I was seeing. This was my mam – and here she was singing to a room full of people.

Her voice was the most wonderful thing I had ever heard. So perfect and clean and high, a proper soprano. I couldn't take my eyes off her. She sang a whole song on her own and I still remember some of the lines.

'I have swum to thee deep in the quiet waters.'

Suddenly there was a boom from the back of the hall and my dad's unmistakable tenor joined her. Everyone spun round in their seats and there he was walking from the darkness with his arms out, singing to my mother on the stage. There was a big round of applause as he passed through and climbed on to the stage, never missing a note. It was an amazing finish to the song and nobody wanted it to end. They did another number together and then my mam walked off stage. She'd done her couple of songs, that was enough for her. I'd never felt so proud.

Left on his own Dad really got into his stride. He wasn't a big man – only about 5'7" – but on that stage he was a giant. He had everyone eating out of the palm of his hand. He wasn't particularly handsome but he looked like a movie star to me.

Over the next few years I saw him hundreds of times and I was never disappointed. Sometimes he would sing the classics, from Verdi or Puccini. His performance of Leoncavallo's 'On with the Motley' was always a big hit. That had been Caruso's first million-selling song, but when my dad sang it, you couldn't imagine any other version. He'd mix those with songs from the shows that everyone could join in with.

Before he'd sung a note my dad would often spin a little tale to set the scene. There was a song called 'Shake Hands with a Millionaire' that was very popular at the time, so Dad would introduce it by saying:

'It was there on the corner that I first saw him, his clothes all battered, a tattered hat on his head. When I asked him if I could do something for him, he smiled his thanks and then he said . . .'

And then he would launch straight into the song: 'Walking down the streets in ragged clothes is not a joke . . .'

When she was old enough, my sister Pauline started to replace Mam on the duets, which was better because she could appear in the weekdays as well as weekends. Like our dad and Elsie, she worked in the mill by day. Pauline was another one with a lovely soprano voice and demand for the act just boomed. At one point Dad was booked for two years solid. Unfortunately one or two of these bookings were made towards the end of the night when he had sunk the thick end of eight pints and he didn't always remember to write them in the diary.

That led to the odd engagement being missed due to him being double-booked. In those days there was an entertainment federation that oversaw the talent hired by Labour and Conservative Clubs and if you failed to turn up for a booking you would be blacklisted for ten weeks. This happened to Dad more than once, but he had a way round it.

Audiences would turn up at the working men's clubs as usual and the ale would be flowing and then the compère would announce the night's entertainment.

'Tonight, ladies and gentlemen, we have a treat for you. It's a singer all the way from Rome. He doesn't speak any English and he only arrived in the country a week ago. I want you to please give a very, very warm Wigan welcome to Mr Tony Rigaletto!'

The whole room would be silent in expectation because international singers very rarely made their way to Wigan at the time. Then the music would start, the singer would come out on to the stage and everyone would say, 'That's not Tony Rigaletto – it's bloody Jimmy Whelan!'

Tony Rigaletto! I laugh every time I remember the audiences' faces. In fact it was such a good trick that I knew I had to do something to keep the name alive and so when I built the JJB Stadium for Wigan Athletic I installed an Italian restaurant in the main complex. People come from all over Wigan to eat there and it's open every day and evening, not just on match days. The food is marvellous and no one leaves hungry. And what's it called? Rigaletto's, of course.

But a lot of diners say to me, 'I've never heard of this Italian chain – do they have restaurants anywhere else?'

No one knows it's named after my dad.

It wasn't just Dad's singing that took us to the local Labour Club. A year after the war ended my sister Elsie married Bill Dean and we had a little party there to celebrate. They couldn't afford to go on a honeymoon and they didn't have a house of their own – they had put their names down for one of the new 'prefabs' going up in Wigan – so they came back to ours with a lot of their friends. We all sat around drinking beer or tea and continuing the celebrations, but I remember Elsie coming over to talk to me.

'Aren't you going to bed?' she asked.

'I'm not tired.'

Ten minutes later she was back again.

'Aren't you going up yet?'

In the end I asked my mam, 'Why does she keep trying to get me to go to bed? You said I could stay up late tonight.'

My mam just smiled.

Eventually I had to give in and went upstairs to sleep. When I woke up the next morning I was snuggled up with my sister Elsie on one side – and her new husband on the other!

Imagine having your baby brother sharing your bed on your honeymoon night! No wonder the newlyweds wanted me asleep before they came up!

Having our father home meant financially we never looked back, but that didn't stop us working hard. Everyone wanted to pull their weight. Jimmy began an apprenticeship and like the girls and my dad, when he came home he put his money on the kitchen table for my mam to have for the household.

As a youngster there wasn't much I could do to contribute, but the less I cost my parents the better. I hatched various ways of making money, some more legal than others. One scheme involved stealing empty pop bottles from the grocer's yard – then handing them back in to claim the penny deposit. Another idea took a lot more trouble.

In 1944 the old Poolstock greyhound track reopened and suddenly our town was flooded with American servicemen from the US aerodrome about seven miles away in Burtonwood. Even after the war ended the troops stayed stationed in the area and the dog track thrived.

My mam took a job working for the Tote, taking bets from the customers and paying out any winnings. It was a lot more fun for her than cleaning, and better paid. Best of all, she could get us into the track to watch the races. They ran every Saturday and Wednesday night so I got a job putting out the seats. I say seats – they were old tubs made from balsa wood that we tipped upside down – and people usually just stood on them.

The American servicemen weren't the only people who enjoyed the races but they definitely had more money than the locals. They also had better access to cigarettes, which used to make our men and women green with envy. Cigarettes, like everything else, were very hard to get hold of during rationing, but the US planes used to smuggle crates of them over and their boys and girls were never without. Because they had no shortage of them, the Yanks weren't as careful with their smokes as the Brits. Our people used to smoke them to the death but the Americans would stub them out with an inch to go, then light up another one a minute later.

I realised there was a bit of business to be done here. While everyone was watching the racing I walked through the aisles, eyes glued to the floor. Every butt I saw I picked up and dropped in a bag. The first time I did it was even more successful than I hoped. From a hundred or so chaps down from Burtonwood, I found about five hundred butt ends.

I couldn't get home fast enough for the second part of my plan. I sat in our backyard and went through the bag, stripping the paper off each butt. My dad had his own little Rizla rolling machine so I got hold of some cigarette paper and packed it with tobacco from my bag. It was a bit trial-and-error to start with and I had to throw a few attempts away. But I knew there was profit to be had so I persevered. The result was fifty brand-new cigarettes.

There was no shortage of customers willing to buy them from me. Every Englishman was a potential customer and nobody questioned why a ten-year-old was selling a bundle of five for tuppence.

One day I decided to sample my own product. I thought, 'Everyone else is smoking, why shouldn't I?' I held the cigarette over the gas ring and lit it, then quickly went into the yard. I didn't have a chance to even take one puff because the back door flew open and my dad was standing there.

I threw the smouldering cigarette on to the ground and waited for him to tell me off but it didn't come. He just smiled.

'Ah,' he said, 'you fancy smoking? Wait there.'

He went back indoors and returned with a cigar, about five inches long and to my eyes nearly as thick.

'If you want to smoke like a man, smoke something proper.'

My hand was shaking as I took the cigar from him. I didn't have a clue what to do but I put it between my lips.

'Go on,' he said as he lit it, 'take a deep breath and puff away.'

I did as I was told and inhaled. A second later I was coughing my lungs up. It was disgusting. I spluttered and I puked and I've never been able to face a cigarette again. Not from that day. Even the smell of one makes me feel ill.

When I'd finished choking I looked at my dad, who just smiled.

Aged ten or eleven I had energy to burn. I was in the school rugby team and I played with a couple of lads who went on to play for Wigan at rugby league, which was the town's main sport at the time – if I'm honest, it probably still is. I lined up alongside Keith Holden for the Poolstock School under-11s and he went on to play for Great Britain. He was a great centre.

My position was stand-off. That suited my personality, because I was the general of the team, I directed play. You need a bit of everything to do that role well – as well as good vision for what's going on in front of you, you've got to be able to kick, throw with your left and right, and you need speed.

When I was ten I saw my first Wigan rugby league match – they weren't called Warriors then. Some of our dads would take it in turns to escort three or four lads to Central Park, one of the most famous grounds in the sport. We'd all hand over our thruppence and pile into the 'hen pen' – the kids' enclosure. Over the years I saw some of the greatest-ever players at that stadium – and most of them wore the cherry and white of Wigan. Billy Boston, Eric Ashton, Jim Sullivan, Joe Egan, Tommy Bradshaw – they were legends of the game and still are.

But it was football I was really interested in so I turned out for that school team as well.

Despite so much going on outside school hours, I still had plenty of appetite for mischief – and with the adults of the town busy working every hour they could, there wasn't much to stop us.

Because all the streets in our area were the same, the kids knew their way around them. At the back of our yard was a wall which ran the entire length of the street. You could walk from number 1 to number 101 and see into the houses on both sides. Our neighbours didn't like you doing this, but there was one night when it was always worth the risk of getting caught: Friday night.

Bath night.

Every single household in the neighbourhood seemed to follow the same pattern as they all got ready for the weekend. The big old tin bath would be dragged in from the yard and placed in front of the fire. The iron kettle and whatever pots and pans were free would be filled with water and put on to boil.

And then the daughters or mothers of the house would come into the kitchen, take all their clothes off and hop into the bath – all within perfect view from the wall at the end of their yard!

One freezing January night, three of us heard the bath from number 31's yard being dragged inside. The young lady of that house was particularly attractive and so we all agreed it would be worth putting up with the cold to catch a glimpse. As we scrambled along the wall we were so busy listening to our teeth chattering we didn't notice that the yard's lavatory had someone in it. Suddenly the door flew open and the girl's dad was standing below us with his belt in his hand. He'd heard every word of our plan – and he was not happy.

'Come here, you filthy peeping toms!'

You've never seen boys move so fast. One of my friends fell off the wall in shock and had to scramble out through someone else's yard. We just legged it along the wall as fast as we could even though it was slippery with ice. I didn't dare look back – I didn't need to. I could hear the man climbing up the wall behind us.

When we got to the end of the row we jumped down and started sprinting towards Goose Green. I thought that would be the end of it but a few seconds later there was a crash, some swearing, and the man came thundering after us again.

We must have run a mile that night before we shook him off. All that weekend I waited for the knock on the front door but he obviously hadn't got a clear look at our faces in the dark.

There were dozens of scrapes like that, but one close call in particular eventually changed my whole life. It started out as a bit of innocent fun as usual but it nearly turned very nasty. Four of us were in a farmer's field stuffing our jackets with turnips. We'd done it loads of times in the war out of necessity. Nowadays it was just something to do and our mams were always grateful for the extra veg. I'd always say I found it by the roadside or it had fallen out of someone's bag. That way my mam didn't worry about disciplining me because obviously she was pleased that I'd brought some food into the house.

On this night we were clearly having too much fun because we were heard. All of us dropped what we were holding and froze. By the sound of his voice, the farmer was very close – and he was out for our blood.

'Oi, you little thieves. Come here!'

Suddenly I could see him rushing towards us. The wall to the field was just a dozen or so yards away and so we made a dash for it. With every stride I took I expected to feel a hand on my collar, but it never came.

The last thing I heard was the farmer yelling, 'I know who you are!'

As we scrambled away into the distance I laughed. Whenever the fella chasing gave up running he would always yell out that same threat just to put the wind up you. He knew we'd spend the whole night at home on our toes, waiting for that knock on the door.

Two hours later I was playing a game of cards with Jimmy when there was a knock on the front door. My blood froze as my dad went to see who it was.

As soon as I saw the policeman in the doorway I knew I was in trouble. The farmer had identified me.

'He'd seen you with your family at the Labour Club,' the policeman told my dad. 'So he put two and two together and called me.'

That was the first and last time I regretted being 'Jimmy Whelan's lad'.

Three

THIS PLACE WILL SORT YOU OUT

My father and I had missed out on a lot of years together because of the war, but since he'd been home he'd done his best to make up for lost time. At the very least, he saw to it that I knew right from wrong. Or so he thought. When a policeman appeared in our doorway asking if I was home, Dad had every right to be disappointed.

'What's the problem, officer?' he asked.

'Your lad's been spotted stealing turnips from the farm at Goose Green.'

'Oh, I see.' Dad looked at me. 'Is this true, David?'

I nodded meekly. There was no point lying.

I stared at the floor but I heard Dad inhaling loudly. I didn't want to see his face.

'What do you want to do about it, officer?'

'If you tell me you'll handle it, Jimmy, I'm happy to leave it there. Can I ask you to do that?'

My dad nodded. 'Trust me, officer. He won't be stealing again.'

It was a funny position to be in. I was only stealing for the family. But by being identified I'd brought shame on the Whelan name. No one wanted a reputation as a thief or a troublemaker. Times were too hard and you needed to trust your neighbours. Even though every family was doing the same thing, we weren't proud of it and the wrong word whispered about you could make life very difficult.

My dad had a big belt, but to that day he had never, ever used it on me. He'd wrapped his hand around it plenty of times and waved it at me as a deterrent and it had always worked. I was frightened to death of it. Once the police officer had left the house, though, I thought I might actually get a taste of leather for the first time.

I didn't dare look at my dad, I was so frightened. But he didn't go near the strap. He put his hands on his hips and said, 'It seems to me you've got energy to burn, David.'

I said, 'Yes, Dad.'

'You need discipline and I've got just the thing for you.'

I didn't have a clue what he meant but the next day everything became clear. As soon as he came out of work Dad marched me over to the Wallgate part of Wigan. I didn't go over that way very often. It was so rough the police patrols wouldn't walk around in pairs – they'd only go out in threes!

As we were walking my dad said, 'I was the same as you at twelve. A lad's got to have something to put his energy into or the only way is down.'

We arrived at Clayton Street and stopped outside a scruffy-looking building.

'Here we are,' my dad said. 'This place will sort you out.'

The sign on the front door said 'Wigan Boys Club'. I knew of it by reputation because the older boys at school used to talk about it, especially the ones who'd got into a bit of trouble. We didn't have community service in those days so the police and parents were just happy to get kids off the streets but there wasn't anything to do. Then one day a chap called Mr South, who was the manager of the William Deacon Bank – old Willie Deaks as we called it – had bought this old building and turned it into a place where lads could come and do all sorts of sports. It started out being the kind of club where troublemakers would be sent so their parents knew where they were, but everyone soon knuckled down and enjoyed the activities on offer.

That was exactly what my father was hoping would happen to me.

We were met by a Liverpudlian man called James Gibson who ran the club. He told my dad how much success he was having working with the police and the local families to keep some of the wilder lads out of mischief.

'Anyone can join but we get a lot of boys who are told to come here by the police,' he laughed. 'If they get picked up for some silly crime the bobbies give them a choice – get sent to prison the next time they're in trouble or come to Wigan Boys Club and get some sort of order in their lives. So that's what we do here,' he said proudly.

'That sounds perfect for my boy here,' Dad said. 'When can he start?'

Mr Gibson looked at me.

'He can join as soon as he reaches thirteen years of age.'

Without missing a beat my dad said, 'Well, that's all right then – he had his birthday last week. Didn't you, son?'

'Er, yes, Dad.'

I could barely get the words out. It *had* been my birthday but it was my twelfth, not thirteenth.

There was a fee of four pence to cover a month's enrolment – a penny a week. This went some way to paying for the hot chocolate that you could get there at the end of the evening, but I soon found out that if you didn't have the money Mr Gibson still let you in. He didn't want gangs of lads roaming the streets just for the sake of a penny.

Wigan Boys Club changed my life. There is no shadow of doubt about that. I was in danger of going off the straight and narrow before I walked through those doors in Clayton Street. I wasn't the worst kid by any means, but I didn't care about anything. Looking back, not having a dad around all those years must have had an effect. I had so much energy and absolutely no direction. At Wigan Boys Club all that changed.

I went there seven days a week and I loved every minute. On weekdays it opened at six and shut at half past nine. I was always there the moment Mr Gibson threw the doors open and I wasn't the only one. We'd be queueing to get hold of the footballs or rugby balls or bicycles first. At weekends we would spend all day there playing matches against other clubs in all sorts of sports. That place was a complete life-saver for me – we were all too busy and too tired to get into any trouble – and to think I only found it thanks to that farmer recognising me and my dad lying about my age.

I tried my hand at everything. I was a kid in a sweetshop because I hadn't played half the sports before. I'd never held a table tennis bat, never pulled on a boxing glove, never picked up a cricket ball. We even went rowing on the canal – that had always been a sport for toffs to my mind, but I enjoyed that as well.

The first thing I got into was football, of course. We had four teams – two under-16s and two under-18s – and they'd all play on a Saturday and then take part in the Sunday Schools League. We didn't have a proper pitch, as such, just this patch of land, all dust and cinders. It was owned by a local firm called TE Gallaghers, but the governor of the factory loaned it to the Boys Club.

Considering most of us at the club had been sent there as a sort of punishment, or at least to keep us out of trouble, we were just grateful for somewhere to play. Looking back, though, it was absolutely diabolical that kids were expected to play on that surface. But it taught you to be a better player, actually, and you quickly learnt to stay on your feet. One sliding tackle too many and you'd end up with half a dozen splinters sticking out of your leg – if you were lucky. One lad wasn't so fortunate. He took a fall one week, gashed the side of his leg, but got up and carried on playing. I didn't see him for a few days, then Mr Gibson told us he had septicaemia.

The ground was about a mile from Clayton Street so once we'd got changed at the club, we then had to walk or run there. Running in boots isn't easy. No one had screw-in studs in those days. You used to knock them in with a hammer and if you walked on hard surfaces too much they'd push through and gash your foot. We could lose a couple of players to foot injuries even before we got to the pitch.

Rugby was still a big sport for me as well. The PE teacher at Highfield Secondary Modern made me captain and later I achieved the same honour at the Boys Club. Saturdays were for football – that was a given – but the next day I'd be leading a team of thirteen out on to the pitch. In a town that was crazy for rugby league that was a proud achievement. That was the sport that people would turn out in their thousands to support – a record 47,747 packed Central Park to watch Wigan play St Helens in 1959. Wigan Athletic Football Club, on the other hand, picked up only a few hundred faces at its Springfield Park ground. In the 1940s they were playing in the Lancashire Combination – not even in the Football League. Even so, if I'd had to choose which I preferred to play I would have gone with the round-ball game. There was something about it that excited me more. That was the sport I dreamt of playing professionally like the players I heard about on *Sports Special*.

Of course, I didn't have a clue how anyone became a sportsman for a living. I was just a schoolboy having fun. I was just happy to be playing at all.

Another sport that really excited me at Wigan Boys Club was table tennis. I'd never even heard of it before I stepped in there but I watched a couple of lads smacking a ping-pong ball across the bumpy table and I couldn't wait to have a go. I took to it instantly. The little bat had seen better days but one of the boys showed me a few serve techniques, and how to slice and put topspin on the ball, and I was away. I went weeks without losing a game there and word got round that I was looking pretty handy. One day Mr Gibson came over while I was playing.

'How do you feel about competing for us?'

There was a table tennis league in Wigan and the winners of that went on to play against the other towns' champions. Normally it was the older boys who represented the club because the bigger you are the longer your reach around the table. I wasn't tall by any means – I never went past 5'10" as an adult – but I was lightning around that table. I had reflexes like a cat on a stove and Mr Gibson knew that.

There were five of us in the table tennis team and we used to travel to all our matches together. We'd meet at Wallgate, pick up our bats and balls, then we'd jump on a bus or borrow bikes or run. The adults in the other teams hated playing against us because they got so much stick from their friends if they lost. We turned up at a pub's back room for one match and I heard this fella say, 'They've just run here, they must be knackered – we'll wipe the floor with them.'

As I walked up to the table another chap said, 'Go easy on him, Sid, he'll be puffed out. You don't want to embarrass the lad.'

These days you'd call it mind games, but we were young and fit as butcher's dogs. Those men didn't take a game off us all night.

*

I didn't think I could ever be interested in anything unless it involved some sort of moving ball – but then Mr Gibson got us all around him one evening and called over someone we'd never seen before.

'Lads, this is Mr William Haydock. He's going to be the conductor of the Boys Club Brass Band – now who wants to sign up?'

Bill Haydock was quite a name in the music industry because he'd conducted Bickershaw Colliery Band in the 1930s when they'd won every competition going. Now he wanted to do something for the youth so he'd been persuaded by Mr Gibson to start up and run a band for us.

There was only one problem.

'Mr Gibson,' I said. 'We haven't got any instruments.'

That's when Mr Haydock stepped in.

'Now, lads, first things first. If you show me you want to play, we'll sort out the instruments soon enough.'

When you've had nothing all your life, you need to grasp new experiences with both hands. If you don't like it, fine, move on. But you owe it to yourself to have a go. So that's why my name was the first down on Mr Haydock's list. I regretted it almost immediately.

He was a real disciplinarian and the first night he kept going over and over and over the importance of teamwork and being part of a large brass band.

'Everyone in your band is relying on you – never forget that,' he said. 'If you don't try, then you don't just make yourself look bad – you make the rest of us look bad as well.'

It got worse after that. Because we didn't have any instruments he spent a whole hour going over musical theory and he didn't stop until we all knew the notes of a scale. If he pointed at you you had to stand up and recite the order:

'Every Good Boy Deserves Favour – E G B D F.'

It was really boring and I thought, 'What am I doing here?' But at the end of the hour he said, 'You've done well, lads. Next time we'll be putting the theory into practice so make sure you bring plenty of breath.'

Before we did anything else the next week, those of us in the music club were told to help unload a van. A few of the chaps didn't take too kindly to this.

'No wonder he told us to save our breath,' I thought.

But we got a surprise when the back door rolled up. There must have been fifty brass instruments in boxes in there. Mr Haydock had tracked them down and Mr South had put up the money, as usual. I didn't have a clue what half the instruments were but we unloaded that van in double-quick time – we couldn't wait to give them a go.

When all the instruments were in the room Mr Haydock started matching them to a player. First he wanted to see what sort of mouths we had. It was like a vet inspecting a horse.

'You need tight lips to play a cornet,' he said to one boy. 'You'll not do – why don't you try this trombone?'

And that was how it went on. He stared at your mouth then said 'euphonium' or 'trumpet' or whatever. I was one of the last to be assigned anything. I thought he might run out before he got to me.

'Right, lad, show me your lips. Good, I think you'll be able to play that' – and he handed me this giant brass tubular thing. I didn't have a clue what it was but it felt nearly as big as me. 'That's an E-flat bass,' Mr Haydock said. 'It's a very important instrument so you look after it.'

The rest of the evening was one of the funniest and noisiest I've ever had. Fifty boys going red in the face trying to get a squeak out of their instruments was an incredible sight. I was no better. Mr Haydock walked around everyone and showed them the right technique. At the end he said, 'Now, I want you to take your instruments home and practise, practise, practise. Just keep blowing until you can get a noise, then you'll get the tone. And then you'll be able to play those scales we learnt last week.'

We had such a laugh that night but as I watched my friends pack their tiny cornets into small cases, I thought, 'How am I going to get this thing home?'

Normally I ran straight home from the club but not that night. Just walking was ambitious but somehow I struggled with it out the door. It felt like I was wrestling a robot octopus.

My mam was still up when I got home, worried that I was so late. When I lumbered through the door she said, 'What on earth have you got there?'

Proud as punch, I told her. 'I've got to learn how to play it,' I said, 'then they'll let me be in the band.'

'They won't let you be in anything if you don't look after it,' she said. 'Look how stained it is already. Come here.'

Mam was brilliant that night. She gave me a rag and some Duraglit polish and showed me how to buff the thing until I could see my face in it. It came up beautifully but I was ready for bed at the end of it – and the polish was gone.

'That thing's more expensive to keep than you are!' Mam said.

One day Mr Haydock said they were short of trombone players.

'It's a whole different style of playing – do you think you're up to it?'

'I'll give it a go,' I said.

He was right about it being different. Where the bass and euphonium had valves, the trombone works on a slide. It was a whole new concept and really I was starting from scratch just trying to get a note out. My poor family had another few weeks of me getting to grips with a new instrument, but at least it was smaller and cheaper to clean. In the end, though, I really began to enjoy it and I knew I'd found the instrument for me. In fact, even to this day I still play. Every Christmas I dust it off and six or eight of the old Boys Club band go round the town, starting at Wigan Golf Club, to play and raise money for the local hospice. It's given me an enormous amount of pleasure over the years and it all started at Wigan Boys Club.

I loved playing my trombone and the brass band got quite good. Mr Haydock eventually decided we were decent enough to be seen in public and so we began to play on Whit marches and at other festivals for the local church. Then we started entering competitions. It started with little local contests but soon we were all travelling on a bus to play further afield. We actually won all the Lancashire and North of England heats but the highlight for everyone was being invited to play on the steps of St Paul's Cathedral in London. You've never seen a prouder bunch of musicians – or a prouder bunch of parents. But proudest of all were Mr Gibson and Mr Haydock.

The band was an important part of my life but my real calling was still sport. By the time I was fourteen our Boys Club football team was playing in the Lancashire League – not against other boys but fully grown adults and some of them actually semi-professional.

Stepping out against men twice your age was one thing for a table tennis match but another on a football pitch. But I soon realised I could more than hold my own. In those days there was no 4-4-2 or 4-3-3. Teams played with the same traditional line-up: goalkeeper, right back, left back, right half, centre back, left half, then five forwards. In other words, two full backs, three middle-of-the-park players and five forwards. What I lacked in height I more than made up for in speed, so the right-half position was perfect for me. I didn't mind where I played. We began to pick up wins and before long I was made captain. I was one of the youngest in the team so it was a compliment that no one complained.

Our team started doing quite well and whispers of coaches from some of the First and Second Division clubs being spotted in the stands began to surface. One week I asked Mr Gibson who a chap was I'd seen him talking to after the match.

'That was a scout from Blackpool,' he said. 'A fella from Wolverhampton Wanderers was here as well.'

Sometimes we had scouts from Liverpool, Everton, Blackburn or Preston, who were all top teams then. The trainers from Wigan Athletic were regular visitors and even though the club was in such a low division, it still gave us a buzz knowing people from 'proper' teams were watching. All the lads would talk about it afterwards.

'Who do you think he was watching?'

'I hear they're short of keepers.'

'Centre forwards are their problem.'

It was just a bit of fun between the players and then we'd get on our bikes and go back home. But for the first time I started to believe that maybe my dream could come true.

'I'm captain of the team,' I thought. 'If these scouts are coming to watch players, perhaps they'll take a look at me.'

Meanwhile my days as captain of the Highfield Secondary Modern teams were coming to a close. I was quite good at science and maths at school but not really tuned in to English, geography and history. The only thing I excelled at was sport, but in those days you couldn't take it any further within the education system. And so, at the age of fifteen, with no academic prospects ahead of me, I left school for the last time.

The idea of anyone earning a living from kicking or hitting or throwing a ball was unheard of for a boy like me. I didn't consider it seriously as an option and neither did my parents. It was a dream and nothing else. But I needed a career so I signed up for an apprenticeship at Melling's Ironworks. Melling's constructed the winding machinery that drove cages up and down the pits and they actually employed some very skilled technicians. It was my mam's idea that I go there.

'They don't want labourers any more,' she said. 'You have to have a trade.'

That's why I was training to be an engineer – a fitter they called them, as opposed to a turner.

It was hard. I started at seven and finished at half past five, plus Saturdays from eight till twelve. It was a full week. I was apprentice to five mechanics who were meant to be showing me the ropes. Basically I was their lackey. If they wanted anything, I was the one who got it. That was fine unless they all wanted something different at once.

'Oi, Whelan – where's that washer?'

'Have you got my blow torch yet?'

'Where did you leave those spanners?'

Busy, busy times but right from the start I began to pick it up. I had to. This was going to be my trade for the rest of my life. I was determined to make a success of it. I knew I only had to get past the first twelve months and they'd bring in another apprentice, which would put me one rung up the ladder. I couldn't wait.

And the upside was that I got paid. For the first time in my life I was able to come in the front door and put my pay packet down on the table. My dad had done it, my sisters, my brother – now it was my turn. I didn't mind one bit seeing it go, even though I only got two shillings of it back as pocket money. That was the way our family worked.

The first thing I bought with my earnings was a bike. I was happy running to and from most places but now I was working it was harder to fit everything in. I got a lovely old Raleigh with three gears. I'd never ridden one with gears before – nobody told me you had to back-pedal while you changed. I got away with it once but the second time I wasn't so lucky. I flicked the gear, didn't back-pedal and the chain fell off. Immediately I was thrown forward and banged my bollocks on the crossbar.

Despite a full working week, football was taking up more and more of my time – even when I wasn't playing. My sister Elsie and her husband Bill Dean had moved into their new 'prefab' house in the Norley Hall area. It wasn't big but it was fantastic, I thought, because it was so new. The best thing about it, though, was it had a television. There were a few tellies about then, all black and white, but only twelve inches square. Elsie's was 14" and the best thing I had ever seen. It was in their front room, in May 1953, that I watched my first-ever FA Cup final, Blackpool versus Bolton. It was an awesome day. I'd never seen anything like it on television.

If it was a privilege to watch the state-of-the-art television, the football just made it all the more memorable. With Bolton 3–1 up it looked all over for Blackpool – but that was before Stan Matthews started weaving his magic. The end result was 4–3 to Blackpool and the whole match became known as 'The Matthews Final'.

I remember watching in awe. 'What I'd give to run out on that pitch.'

I had a final of my own a few days later. Mr Gibson had entered a team into the under-18s Lancashire table tennis competition and told us to enjoy ourselves. As the weeks went by and I stayed in the competition, he started to get quite excited and even travelled with me to some of the matches. His enthusiasm paid off and by Christmas I was the leading player in Wigan, which qualified me for the final.

'Now all you've got to do is win it!' he said.

The final was held in Bury and all the area champs would be there. Mr Gibson drove me down there in his car and I was happy to see a dozen or so of the lads from Wigan had made the journey as well. I was sixteen years old and I thought I could beat anyone with a table tennis bat, but the moment I arrived at the venue I was struck by the most incredible sensation of nerves. To this day I have never experienced anything like it. I'm always confident of my own ability. I never get intimidated by the surroundings or the occasion. But that day I did. For the first few games I didn't know one side of the bat from the other.

In the end it didn't matter. When Mr Gibson drove me home that night I was the under-18s table tennis champion of Lancashire. I had never felt so proud.

That trophy marked the beginning of a lucky few weeks for me. The following Saturday I went to work as usual then cycled to play for the Boys Club football team. After I'd got changed I noticed Mr Gibson waiting for me. He had another man with him.

'David, this gentleman is a scout for Preston North End. They'd like you to go for a trial.'

A trial? Me?

I don't know who was more pleased – me or Mr Gibson. A date was arranged to go to Preston and the scout disappeared. I couldn't believe my luck. Even though Les Campbell, Jimmy Shepherd and a few of the other lads from the Boys Club had already been noticed by big clubs, I never honestly thought I'd be chosen as well. I'd dreamed, of course – but nothing more.

Preston weren't the only club interested in me, though. Over the next couple of matches I got requests from Burnley, Blackburn Rovers, Wolverhampton Wanderers and Everton and my diary suddenly became very full.

I had to pinch myself. Dave Whelan – a young lad from Poolstock? I couldn't wait to get started.

Four

WHAT AM I UP AGAINST HERE?

When you're a kid you don't know how the world works. There are all sorts of jobs out there being done by hundreds of people that you don't even realise exist. Then one day you come into contact with them and your eyes get opened. The world of football is as mysterious as any other business when you're on the outside. As I turned up at Preston North End's training ground that autumn's day, I couldn't have been more nervous.

Trials in those days were very different from today. You didn't do keepy-uppies or weaving in and out of cones. You just turned up on a Saturday, gave your name to the trainer and played a game with the club's B team. All clubs had the same structure: first team, reserve team, A team and B team. That was it, you were just thrown straight into a match. No hellos, no pleasantries. You didn't even get introduced to the other players. The idea of a club taking a player on for a month's trial like you see in the Premier League was unheard of.

When I made myself known to the Preston B team trainer, he just looked at his list and said, 'Whelan – you're playing number four. Get stripped and ready.'

I couldn't have felt more alone as I looked round the changing room. At the Wigan Boys Club I was captain. I had known everyone in that team for years. But here I was surrounded by ten part-time professionals and amateurs who were all best friends. They played for the B team week in, week out. Now I was expected to slot right in.

As soon as the ref blew his whistle my apprehension disappeared. I had a good game and as I came off the pitch I hoped I'd done enough to impress. The trainer didn't give any clues. He just said, 'Thanks, lad,' and that was it.

The following Saturday I had pretty much the same experience at Blackpool. The week after that I travelled to Burnley and once again went through the same process. In between each match I had to go to work and be bombarded by questions from the other guys at the factory.

'How did it go?'

'Did you get in?'

'Are they signing you?'

I couldn't tell them anything because I didn't know. Then a few days before I was due to go to Blackburn a letter arrived. Finally! It was from the trainer at Blackpool. He'd been impressed and he wanted me to go for another trial. A letter came from Burnley saying the same thing and then Mr Gibson told me that Preston had been in touch with him and they'd like to see me again as well.

I was disappointed that no one wanted to sign me outright but at least none of the clubs had rejected me.

As I set off that Saturday to show Blackburn Rovers what I could do, I wondered if it would be a case of fourth time lucky. But the day didn't start very well. Rovers normally train at Feniscowles, just outside Blackburn, so that's the train station I got off at. I quickly discovered they were playing that day at Witton Park and I should have got off at the next stop, Cherry Tree. I looked at the clock. It was twenty minutes to kick-off and there were no trains due for half an hour. There was only one option: I'd have to run.

By the time I arrived red-faced at Witton Park the B team was already changed and ready to take to the pitch. I counted the players: there were eleven out there.

'I've blown it,' I thought as I walked up to the trainer. 'I'm too late.'

It turned out to be my lucky day. The trainer wasn't impressed with my timekeeping, but there must have been a note next to my name because he called over to the lad wearing the number four jersey and said, 'Sorry, son, you'll have to get changed again. We need to see Whelan play today.'

I couldn't look that lad in the eyes as he handed over the strip but then the match kicked off and I forgot all about it. It was only afterwards that I considered how fortunate I'd been. 'If I turn up that late at Wolves next week, they might not be so forgiving,' I thought.

Wolverhampton Wanderers were a big team at the time. Stan Cullis had taken over in 1947 and they'd gone from strength to strength. By the end of 1960 they would win the League three times and the FA Cup twice – much to my personal disappointment. I couldn't wait to get down there to show them what I could do.

Before my next trial I had another six days at Melling's. I spent a lot of the Monday, as usual, telling my friends at work about the Blackburn trip. The next night I was walking home when I saw a car parked outside number 70. We didn't have many visitors to Chadwick Street who drove so I was intrigued who it might be. When I stepped through the door I found out.

'David, this is John Carey,' my dad said and introduced me to a man in his mid-thirties. 'He wants to sign you for Blackburn Rovers.'

Even in the age before television John Carey was a big name. He'd been at Manchester United most of his career and had captained them to the title in 1952. He'd retired the following season and walked straight into his first management job at Ewood Park aged thirty-three. Barely a year later he was standing in our front room, describing what an exciting set-up he had at Blackburn, and asking if I'd come to play for him.

What do you say to that?

These days you'd get the camera out and make sure everyone knew who'd been to see you but it wasn't like that then. My dad was as chuffed as I was to see this Irish legend up close but he hid it well.

'Well,' Dad said, 'that's very kind of you but there's four or five clubs wanting him to sign. He's going to have to think about it, so can we tell you tomorrow?'

Mr Carey smiled. 'Of course you can.'

We just about managed to control ourselves long enough for him to leave the house. Then huge smiles broke out all round.

'Johnny Carey was in our house!' Dad shouted. 'Wait till the lads hear that.'

'And he was such a lovely man,' Mam said.

We were so bowled over by him actually coming to see us that we almost forgot the reason why.

'What do you think about it then, David?' Dad asked. 'Blackburn's only about fourteen miles up the road but it's Second Division football.'

He was right. Mr Carey had painted a picture of a club filled with potential, but Rovers had been relegated from the top flight five years earlier. Everton were also in the second tier, although on their way back, but Blackpool, Burnley and Preston were in the First Division and Wolves were threatening to actually win the title. I knew all this from listening to *Sports Special* on our little Alba every Saturday afternoon.

'What do you want to do, David?' Mam said.

I didn't know. The other clubs were bigger names, that was for sure, and the ones I'd seen already had expressed an interest in me. Who knows whether Wolves would say the same thing? I have to admit, though, the fact that Mr Carey had come to see me personally made me feel ten feet tall. But was that enough to base my decision on?

Before I could answer we heard another car pull up outside the house. No one ever had two visitors drive to see them so we didn't think it would be for us. The sound of the engine, though, made me pull back the curtains and take a look.

'Blimey, Dad, it's a Rolls-Royce.'

'You're right, son. Who the heck has one of those round here?'

A second later there was a knock at the door. When Dad opened it we both recognised Sid Littler – the chairman of Wigan Athletic. He was a regular face at Dad's Labour Club performances and a well known local figure.

What a night this was turning out to be!

Mam still had the kettle warm from when John Carey had been there so she quickly served up another pot of tea. We all sat around the table and Mr Littler told my dad why he was there.

'Jimmy, I've come to sign your lad.'

Wigan were in the Lancashire Combination at the time and about to win it that year. Compared to the other clubs I'd had trials for, they still had a long way to go. On the other hand, the draw of playing for your home town is what anyone dreams of and Mr Littler knew from the large grin on my face that was what I was thinking. Once again my dad played it cool.

'There's a lot of clubs after him, Mr Littler. We've just had Blackburn Rovers here not half an hour ago.'

Sid didn't say a word. He just reached into his pocket and put a stack of five-pound notes on the table.

'There's £200 there, Jimmy. That's for you if your lad signs for us.'

Two hundred pounds! That was a huge amount of money in those days – four times more than we had to live on for a year during the war. My dad stared at it and I could see he was thinking about all the things that it could buy. But he said, 'It's not up to me to make that decision.'

He looked at me.

'David, Mr Littler's offered this money to us if you sign for Wigan Athletic. Do you want to sign for them?'

I looked from the five-pound notes to my dad and back again. Then I said, 'I'm sorry, Dad, I know it's a lot of money, but I want to sign for Blackburn Rovers.'

Mr Littler was obviously used to letting his cash do the talking for him and he didn't stop smiling. But my father did. He looked seriously at our guest and said, 'Mr Littler, put your money away. Thank you very much for coming to see us but he wants to sign for Blackburn Rovers.'

After Sid had left Dad asked me if I was sure.

'OK, you don't have to sign for Wigan but what about the other clubs? What about the First Division? What about the rugby league?'

He knew that Wigan had been looking at me. A scout had told Dad that an offer was due to be made in the near future.

'I want to play football, not rugby, and Johnny Carey came to our house, Dad. The Manchester United captain came here while the other clubs just sent a letter. So I want to play for him.'

'Well, if you're sure.'

'I am.'

And I was, even though it meant turning my whole life upside down.

Football had always been my hobby, something I did for fun. Now it was to become my livelihood. A few weeks after my seventeenth birthday I signed official papers with Blackburn Rovers and two days later resigned from my job at Melling's Ironworks. I had a new life now.

And for the first time I was on my own.

I was really excited about playing football but the idea of leaving Wigan was intimidating, especially as I didn't know where Blackburn was. I'd had the chance to stay and be a local hero at Wigan Athletic and sleep in my own bed each night, but I hadn't chosen that, for footballing reasons. The prospect of going off to live without my family, even if it was only fourteen miles away, was daunting. Only the thought of coming back every week to play with the Boys Club Brass Band, which would accept me as a member until I was eighteen, cheered me up.

These days all the big clubs have people to look after a player's every requirement. They'll help you find a house, get you a car or driving lessons if necessary and make sure you know exactly where to be at every minute of the day. For the foreign players especially, this can be a life-saver, because some of them are young lads travelling abroad alone. They're strangers in a strange land and they need all the help they can get.

I wasn't travelling from abroad but it felt like it. I'd never been out of Wigan for anything more than a night before. There was nothing like the money in the game there is today, but Rovers still said they would sort me out with somewhere to live – 'digs' as they called it. Basically all the players who didn't have families would go and live in a room in somebody else's house. You'd have to pay for it, of course, but it was very cheap and you got all your meals thrown in. It was meant to make you feel like home from home – but I hated it.

I reported to the stadium on my first day and the assistant trainer said, 'Right, first things first. I want to introduce you to Mrs Brown, David. You'll be staying with her.'

That night I got the bus to her house, a nice semi-detached in a place called Intack. Mrs Brown was a lovely woman and very kind. Her sons had already left home so she had plenty of room and she was used to having people around the place. She was fantastic with me but I was homesick from the moment I arrived. For a start I could never relax in her house because I knew it wasn't mine. And I just wasn't used to having to explain the things I liked and those I didn't. When you live at home your mam knows more about you than you do. I discovered this on my first night.

'Now, David,' she said to me, 'you come from Wigan, so I've made you a special dish for your tea.'

I thought, 'Great, steak and kidney pie or something.' Maybe life there wasn't going to be so bad.

She brought a plate to the table but before she'd even put it down my face must have fallen. It was tripe and onions – a really popular meal in Wigan, but one I hated.

It was a horrible situation to be in. I had this big dish in front of me and the last thing I wanted to do was offend my new landlady, but she sensed it.

'Don't you like tripe, David?'

I shook my head. 'Sorry. I like tripe but I don't like tripe and onions.'

She looked crushed and took it away, saying she'd cook me something else. I felt terrible. You never had to worry about things like that with your mam.

My mam's influence went even further than that. Before I left home we'd argued about my future. Blackburn Rovers wanted to take me on full-time but she wouldn't hear of it.

'You've got to have a trade, son.'

'I'm going to be a footballer. That's my trade.'

'But you need something to fall back on. What if it doesn't work out?'

I knew it was going to work out but there was no arguing with your mam in those days. Your dad brought in the money but she ruled the roost. It was the same in every family I knew. So even before I'd been to Ewood Park for the first time I'd already applied to the Northop Loom Company to continue my apprenticeship from Melling's. When they agreed it meant I could only play part-time for Blackburn. Every day I worked from eight till five as a big hammer fitter at the factory, then two evenings a week I would go and train with the other part-timers from 6.30 to 8.30, with a match for the B team on Saturday. Training in those days was mostly running up and down the training ground and as there weren't proper floodlights it often ended in darkness.

I got a £10 signing-on fee, even as a part-timer, which was the limit you could get then. The memory of Sid Littler's wad of notes on our table at home was still fresh in my memory, but ten pounds for a seventeen-year-old was a fortune. On top of that they were going to pay me £5 a week during the season and £4 during the summer – my dad didn't get that much working at Eckersley's Mill – and that was before the bonuses you got from actually playing. In the A team you got ten shillings for the draw and a pound for a win. Playing in the reserves, it was a pound for the draw and two if you won. If you were lucky enough to line up for the first team then you could expect £2 from a draw and four for a win. It was a lot more lucrative than the apprenticeship.

But that didn't matter – I hadn't signed for Blackburn for the money. Johnny Carey had impressed me because he had come from Man United just as the Busby Babes were getting going and he knew the importance of the youth set-up.

'I am building Blackburn Rovers on the same lines as Manchester United. We're going to have a fantastic youth team and I want you to be part of that. The first team will come soon enough if you work hard enough.'

That's exactly what I wanted to hear. Even though I was only playing part-time, I thought, 'I'm going to fight for a place in his first eleven with every breath I've got.'

Mr Carey was as good as his word. Great players like Bryan Douglas, Ron Clayton, Peter Dobing, John Bray and Michael McGrath, like myself, all came through his youth set-up. It wasn't long before the local press started picking up on it.

'You've had the Busby Babes – these are the Carey Chicks,' one paper wrote and the name stuck. Everywhere we went, whether it was the reserve team, the A or B team or the first eleven – that's what we got called.

These days new signings go straight into the team. Usually that's because of the power of agents and the huge fees involved in the transfers. But even when Liverpool ruled Europe in the 1970s and 80s players would be groomed when they were seventeen or eighteen and only unleashed in the first team when they were nineteen or twenty. They had to pay their dues first – and that's exactly how it was in 1953.

It's funny the airs and graces players have now. Back then you couldn't afford to have anything of the sort. There was a pyramid of power and us youngsters were at the bottom. But it was fair. Even the stars of the First Division were young once and they started out doing the same chores as I did.

It was a rite of passage that you were made to earn your stripes, so to speak, with the stars of the team. After a match or a training session the reserves would be charged with cleaning the boots of the older players. I didn't have anyone in particular to look after. They would just throw their boots into the middle of the room and we would come in and pick a couple of pairs up and take them away to scrub. In fact the whole kit would get tossed into the middle of the room. I remember going in and smelling the sweat coming off this huge pile for the first time. I'd been in teams all my life but this seemed different. When you have your face in a dozen sweaty shirts while you carry it all to the laundry rooms everything seems different.

We had to clean the changing room out as well. There was one communal bath and one cold plunge – no showers and no individual baths. You had to take the scouring brush to them then mop and sweep the dressing room out.

The job I hated most though was darning. Socks seemed to last long after their sell-by date. Every day someone would have a new hole and we'd be thrown a needle and thread and told to stitch it up.

That was how it was, every afternoon. The same ritual, regardless of how well you were doing in the under-18s or the reserve team. There was no way out of it.

Can you imagine Championship squads today doing this for the first eleven? Players at Crystal Palace, Nottingham Forest, Barnsley – they wouldn't even be asked. And they wouldn't stick around long if they were.

But it wasn't as if the top lads were living in the lap of luxury. You only had one pair of boots to last the year, and one pair of rubbers – shoes without studs in. It didn't matter if you were new boy Dave Whelan or Harry Leyland, you all had the same.

If that was a bit tight, we even had to fetch the stuff ourselves. Once a year the kit man handed me a chit of paper with a note on: 'Please supply Dave Whelan with one pair of boot studs.' Then I'd take it into town to the sports shop and they'd redeem it. What no one told you was that the sports shop was owned by Mr Forbes – the chairman of Blackburn Rovers! Can you imagine if I ever told Emile Heskey or Arjan de Zeeuw to get themselves down to their nearest JJB shop to get kitted out?

I trained with all the other youngsters but only half the week. I was at Northop during the days then down to the park with the other lads on Tuesday and Thursday night, six till half eight. I might start flagging during work but as soon as I had my kit on I was bursting with energy. I was so fit then I thought I could dodge raindrops.

Whatever they had me doing, I went at full pelt. I was young and I was eager and I was doing the thing I dreamed about. Blackburn didn't have their own training centre like clubs do today so we used to train on school fields about a mile and a half away. You'd meet at Ewood, get changed, then run to the pitch. It was just like being at Wigan Boys Club again. Some of the lads hated doing anything that didn't have a ball but I loved running and I'd race them all there and back and win every time.

In fact I wouldn't meet my match until I moved up to training with the first team.

Training standards have changed out of sight since then. There were no gyms, no special diets or other modern aids. We spent a bit of time doing ball control, then either had a practice match or did even more running. I didn't care what we did – it certainly beat being in an engineering factory – but I liked the way they worked. Johnny Carey would take some of the sessions but mainly it was down to the reserve-team coach to put us through our paces. I'd always played half back for Wigan Boys and they kept me in the same position. It was amazing to get some real coaching after so long just surviving on natural talent and instinct, and even if I disagreed with what was being said I just smiled. I felt so lucky even doing it.

When you're good at sport you tend to mix well with other people – I've met a few odd exceptions, and I really do mean odd, but generally you blend in. I'd always got on with everyone at school and Wigan Boys Club and I slotted in nicely to life in Blackburn. I was beginning to get games with the A team, which is the junior level, and I'd even had one or two chances with the reserves. That was an important step for a part-timer because the manager himself used to watch the reserve-team matches. In those days if the reserve trainer gave you a good report you might get a run-out in the first eleven, but nothing beat being seen by Mr Carey personally.

It was a tremendous time and I couldn't actually believe I was being paid for doing it. There was only one problem. I was still homesick. Travelling back once a week to play in the band just rammed it home. I hated getting that train back to Intack knowing I'd be sleeping in a stranger's house again. I came to a decision: I was moving back home.

It was so nice to be back in my own bed – and the best thing was I had a room to myself because Jimmy and Pauline had both left home. I slipped back into family life so easily it was like I hadn't been away. Every week I put my earnings on the table and my mam gave me an amount back. That was how it should be, in my book, and I was happy.

I still had my apprenticeship in Blackburn though and I worked out that if I got up at half past six I could get to Northop by train for about quarter past eight, which was fifteen minutes late but they allowed me to do that because I was a Blackburn Rovers player. On the midweek training session nights I would get home at half past ten. They were full days but I didn't mind. I was just happy to be home.

My mam was over the moon as well. She disapproved of my football career to a certain extent but she wanted me to make the best of it. On my first morning back I was haring around the house getting ready when she said, 'I've prepared something for you.'

She was holding a glass of something so I said, 'What's that?'

'Never you mind, just get it down you and you'll be fit to face the day.'

I took it off her and peered nervously in. It looked a bit like milk but obviously wasn't. I took a deep breath and knocked it back in one. It tasted foul – and there was a definite acidy aftertaste.

'What was that, Mam?'

She told me it was two eggs whisked with sherry. Her dad had always drunk it for energy and what was good enough for him was good enough for me. Every day she made me drink it and eventually I actually quite liked its taste. But as a non-drinker it was an odd way to start the day.

It was also great being back among my friends. Some of them I'd known all my life and there was a real closeness among us. They didn't treat me any different just because I was a football player half the week. In fact most of them took the mickey out of me for turning down the chance to play rugby league.

Round about that time I discovered a new interest. One by one my friends started going around with girlfriends. The opposite sex hadn't really been on my radar till then. When you're in the band and sports teams you don't have much time to meet anyone because you're always surrounded by boys. But at seventeen we could go to a dance, and the Empress in Wigan was the number one spot in the area for young people to enjoy themselves and maybe meet someone. For the first time in my life I suddenly took an interest in my appearance. My mam was always impressed by how tidy I looked on a dance night.

'You're so smart I didn't recognise you, David.'

Footballwise my move back home had no effect. I didn't mind travelling to Blackburn every day for that, especially as I could kip on the train, but I was starting to resent the amount of time being an apprentice at Northop took up. I'd look at other young lads like Ron Clayton, who was only a year or two older than me, or Bryan Douglas or Peter Dobing being able to concentrate only on their football. They were all in the first team.

'How am I going to get my chance if I'm only there half the week?' I thought.

But I wasn't doing too badly. I became a regular in the A team and in my first year we got to the final of the Youth Cup. The following year we won it. Pulling on the blue and white jersey to play for Blackburn sent a shiver down my spine every time. I just wished I was playing for the first team – but as a half back my options were limited. Ron Clayton was tearing the place up in the same position. I couldn't see a way in with him in such fantastic form.

Then I had a bit of luck. I'd just turned eighteen and was coming home from a shift at work. I was filthy, covered in soot and oil. I saw a car parked outside number 70 and I realised immediately whose it was – it was the same vehicle John Carey had driven when he'd signed me.

It was a complete surprise. What on earth could be wrong that he would come this far?

I ran in the house and the manager said, 'There you are, David. You're playing in the first team tonight.'

The first team!

'How do you mean, boss?'

'Ron Clayton's injured his ankle. You're next in line.'

I had no idea I was so close to starting. Mr Carey must have been impressed with what he saw in my reserve-team appearances.

'Can I get a quick wash?'

'I think you'd better.'

I ran over to the sink and started throwing water at my face. Five minutes later I was changed and ready to leave.

Then my mam said, 'How are you going to get home, love?' I hadn't thought about that and right then I wasn't bothered.

My dad had been quiet throughout all this. I think he was so proud he was nearly speechless. But he piped up then.

'Can I jump in the car with you, Mr Carey?' he asked.

'Of course you can.'

'There's a ten o'clock bus back from Blackburn. I'll see that he gets on it.'

Later that night I couldn't remember a moment of the journey to Ewood. I was so excited there was only one thought in my mind: 'I'm actually going to play for the first team!'

In her whole life my mam never saw me play football. 'I don't want to see you get hurt,' she always said. But my dad never missed a match. Even if I was playing in the B team in Bury, Rochdale, you name it, he'd be there. How he used to get there I don't know. He had no car and no licence, although he taught me to drive using a friend's motor. But everywhere we went he would be there. I'd step off the bus and he'd be at the stadium gates waiting for a ticket.

He wasn't one of these fathers who shout. I'd never know he was there if I didn't see him beforehand. He never tried to tell me what to do or shut other people up if they were having a go at the team. He just watched his lad. To be honest, he'd always been more of a rugby man. I don't think he'd seen more than a dozen football matches in his life before I started playing.

Considering the trouble he went to to follow my youth matches, there was no way he was going to miss my debut for the Blackburn Rovers first team.

It was a seven-thirty start and we made it in good time. John Carey gave Dad a ticket and he disappeared through the turnstiles. I was taken inside the players' entrance and for the first time I was allowed to change in the main dressing room. Looking around all those established faces was awe-inspiring. The left back for England, Bill Eckersley was there, Eddie Quigley and Bobby Langton – all household names in Blackburn. And there was me alongside them.

I was so nervous I remember saying to Jack Weddle, our trainer, 'I can't find my shin pads.'

He took one look at me then slapped me on the back.

'You're wearing them, you daft bugger!'

As I walked down the tunnel I experienced the Ewood roar for the first time as 40,000 voices boomed out around the packed ground. I'd heard the cheering before – I'd been part of it for a year now – but I'd never felt it. You have to be a player stepping over that white line to feel it like I did that night.

All my nerves had gone now. I was excited. More excited than I'd ever been before. And I couldn't wait for the referee to blow his whistle.

West Ham United had been relegated to the old Second Division in 1932 and would stay there until the late 1950s. When we met them they were a decent team with players like Malcolm Allison, Jimmy Andrews, Ken Brown, Noel Cantwell, Albert Foan, Gerry Gazzard, Harry Hooper on the wing, Andy Malcolm, Frank O'Farrell, Derek Parker, Dave Sexton, George Wright – all of them big lumps. Their manager, Ted Fenton, had got them playing nicely – and I was going to line up against them.

As a half back, my job was to stop John Dick. He was a large fella from Glasgow, about 6'2", and the first Hammer to play for Scotland. I took one look at him and thought what I always thought when I saw someone much bigger than me:

'I'll soon show him who's boss.'

It didn't matter how big other players were. I was 5'10" but I was fast and I wasn't afraid to let them know I was there. At Wigan Boys Club they called me 'Crunch' Whelan because of my tackles and the name had followed me to Blackburn. I was determined to make a good impression on the manager and the quickest way to do that was to kill the threat from this bloke.

The first chance I got I took the ball but I made sure I smacked right through Dick as well. A huge roar went up from the crowd near me. They could see what I was up to and they liked it.

There was only one problem. John Dick didn't seem to even feel it.

When you go on a football field and you let someone know you're there the way I'd just done, you expect a reaction. Most players would have gone down like a sack of spuds after a crunch like that. These days they'd be stretchered off. John Dick didn't say 'ouch', he didn't swear, he never even blinked.

That threw me. I thought, 'Christ! What am I up against here? I just kicked the hell out of him and he's not moved.'

I'd never seen anything like it, but that was the difference between the youth teams and the first eleven. I was up against real men. He must have known what I was up to – older heads than mine would have tried to stop him the same way, to keep him quiet with an early knock. I knew then that I'd have to up my game.

West Ham weren't the only decent side out there, though. We had some handy players in our team that day and in the end the match finished 2–2. To me, though, it felt like a win. I'd just had the best ninety minutes of my life.

Hearing that Rovers crowd cheering every time you get the ball – or the man – is an unbelievable experience. It made me feel like I was capable of anything. I knew at the end of the match that I'd got a taste for the big time.

'I want to do this again,' I thought.

Playing again was all I could think about. I didn't care about the £8 appearance fee or the extra £2 for getting a draw. I just wanted to get out there again in the blue and white. Unfortunately for me, Ron Clayton recovered in time for the next game. There were no substitutes in those days so I didn't even get a place on the bench. But I'd had a taste of the high life and I wanted more.

I knuckled down in training and kept my head down. I was too old for Wigan Boys Club by then so I didn't have that distraction. About three months later I got another chance. This was a Saturday match, my first for the club, and as I travelled over to Blackburn with my dad I couldn't wait for the match to start. I wasn't the only one. On a match day the train stopped at all the little areas like Chorley and Cherry Tree and the carriages got packed more and more with Rovers fans. Dad and I were hanging off a strap from the ceiling trying not to fall over when we overheard the conversation about me.

'That young lad from Wigan's playing today. He's only eighteen but he doesn't half bloody clog them.'

I thought I was going to burn up and it wasn't just because I was so squashed. I felt so embarrassed but my dad just gave me a nudge and joined in.

'Aye, I've seen him, not a bad player, is he?'

I was staring at the floor praying he wouldn't drop me in it, but that wasn't his style. I could have introduced myself to the fans but I didn't want the attention, and neither did my father. When we fell off that train we both burst out laughing.

Blackburn is a onc-club town but in the 1950s even its biggest fans couldn't always put a face to their players. You had to be around for quite a while before you were recognised. As I ran out that second time I thought, 'Will this be it for another six months?'

I was in luck. I started six games in a row at the end of that season and the following year I would play even more, either deputising for Ron when he was injured, or just behind him if that spot was free. It was everything I ever wanted.

Life was almost perfect – but I was still working at Northop Loom Company and I blamed that for my slow progress.

'I would have been in the team much earlier if I'd put in as much training as the rest of the lads,' I thought. 'If I'm not careful it could cost me my place again.'

I knew what I had to do.

Telling my mam was the hardest part.

'I'm leaving Northop. I'm going to go full-time as a footballer.'

'But what if it doesn't work?'

'It is working, Mam, I just need to give it a chance. Trust me – I can do this.'

She wasn't happy, but I was determined. I resigned as a big hammer fitter and told Mr Carey I'd be available full-time for the next few months.

'You know what this means, don't you?' the gaffer said.

'I do, boss, yes.'

Even though the war had been over nearly ten years, we still had National Service in the country. Every boy had to serve from the ages of eighteen to twenty. The only way around that was by doing an apprenticeship but as soon as that was over you had to sign up. By quitting my job I was immediately eligible, as a nineteen-year-old, for the call-up. It was a huge risk to my professional football career.

'But,' I thought, 'I've got to take it. I have to give myself the best chance to make it as a pro.'

I just had two years' Army service to get through first.

I prayed my place in the team would be there when I got out.

Five

YOU'RE IN THE ARMY NOW

It seemed to take ages for the Government to process my National Service forms so I had a few weeks of playing for Blackburn and loving every minute of it. I also took the chance to socialise a bit more with my Wigan friends before I was sent away for two years.

The Court Hall was still the place to go for youngsters and I went there one Saturday night after a match. Dances were all very formal, organised affairs back then. There were ways to do things – and ways not to do them. Rule number one was that a lady waited to be asked to dance. As much as a lad might have wanted it the other way round, it wasn't the done thing.

There was only one time when it was acceptable – and that was during the Ladies' Choice quickstep as it was called. For this one dance, girls could pick their own partners. It was a nerve-racking time for us lads. We'd all be standing there with our mates, trying not to look too bothered if we didn't get picked, but really having our fingers tightly crossed.

I thought my chance had gone when suddenly I felt a tap on my shoulder. I turned around.

'Hello again.'

It was a beautiful young girl called Pat. I'd met her a year or two earlier, just before I'd moved to Intack, and we'd had a date. It had gone well and we agreed to meet again. The next Saturday, however, I waited for her at the bus stop but she didn't arrive. That was that – I went home, signed for Blackburn shortly afterwards and never saw her again.

Until now.

'You're a bit late for our second date, aren't you?' I laughed.

She looked embarrassed. 'Do you remember the fog that night? They cancelled all the buses into town.'

'It doesn't matter now,' I said, but she was determined I believe her.

'Did you wait for me at the bus stop?' she said.

'Yes, I did. And you didn't show up.'

'Well, if you remember, the bus didn't show up either, did it?'

I shook my head and we both laughed. I'd been pretty cut up at the time but it all made sense now. Then we did the quickstep together and I was still smiling at the end of it. There was something about this Pat, I realised, that got to me. She wasn't just good-looking, she was clever and funny as well. I found myself thinking about her a lot over the next few days and I couldn't wait for our next date.

'If she doesn't turn up this time that's it,' I told myself. But she did, and we saw each other as often as we could over the next two years.

Making any sorts of plans is difficult when you're in the Army. My papers finally arrived and on Tuesday 7 February 1956 I caught the train to Oswestry in Shropshire to join the Royal Artillery in 64 Regiment. On the way I couldn't help thinking, 'I don't know when I'll be allowed to play for Rovers again. I could have given up football for two years just to play it full-time.' It was a harrowing thought but I knew it was a gamble I had to take.

Oswestry in winter is cold and there were a lot of lads joining that day who weren't the best equipped to deal with it. These were fellas who had desk jobs or they were academics or they worked in factories. There weren't many like me who spent their lives running around in the snow and the rain. I'd been in the Boys Club – that place toughens anyone up.

At Oswestry we had to fill in a lot of forms telling them who we were and what we did. One question said: 'profession'. I couldn't help smiling. A few weeks ago I would have been tempted to put 'engineer', but I'd put that life behind me. So I wrote 'Professional Footballer' and proudly handed the form over.

We were given our uniforms and shown our billets. These were huge wooden halls with twenty beds. That first night was awful. Every other bed had the sounds of snivelling or crying coming from it. These were men who didn't want to be there and had never spent a night away from home before. Even though I hadn't enjoyed lodging for those five months in Intack, at least I had experience of being alone. I knew I could handle it. Most of the young lads I was with, unfortunately, could not – and it was only going to get worse.

The next morning, at six o'clock on the nose, our door burst open. The first thing most of us knew was the sound of an angry man shouting:

'Hands off cocks

Grab your socks

And get on parade, boys –

You're in the Army now!'

The sergeant in charge of our group was marching around the room banging a stick on the end of every bed. You've never seen twenty men move so fast. We were up and dressed like lightning.

I could tell from their faces that most of my new colleagues had never had a man shouting orders at them like this before. When you've worked in sports you get used to that. A football team runs a bit like a military unit – there's training, there's a plan and then there's action. This was the easy bit for me and in fact I was quite looking forward to signing up for the regiment band as soon as I could, but I could see a lot of the others were in shock.

Everyone was soon suffering a few minutes later. There was a queue fifty yards long just to get into the mess for breakfast. I was standing there with two small metal tins in my hand, freezing my bollocks off and wishing I was anywhere but there.

Then I remembered Northop Loom Company and I changed my mind. If anyone saw me smile at that point that's the reason.

'I don't care what they throw at me,' I thought. 'It's worth it not to be an apprentice any more.'

As it turned out, I wasn't the only one who was pleased with my career choice.

That first morning we were given a lesson in marching. It was a joke, a complete shambles. I'd been able to walk with a trombone on marches through Wigan but this was something else. When we stopped for a break I was given a message.

'Captain Harrington wants to see you.'

I didn't know this chap from Adam but I quickly learnt that Peter Harrington is one of life's good guys. He still comes to see matches at Wigan as my guest, half a century later, and in fact he recently went with me to visit the Somme. My grandfather fought there and I had never been, so Peter gave my grandchildren and me a tour of Flanders Fields. It was incredibly moving and emotional for me. He's a fantastic man – and I knew that the first time I met him.

'Whelan.'

'Yes, sir.'

'You've written here that you are a professional footballer.'

'That's right, sir.'

'Who do you play for?'

'Blackburn Rovers, sir.'

'Which team do you play in?'

'The first eleven, sir.'

He was impressed by that.

'The first team? When was your last match?'

'It was last weekend.'

'Who are you playing next?'

'We're playing Doncaster Rovers away, sir, this Saturday.'

'Do you think you'll be selected?'

'I would have thought so, if I were available, sir.'

I didn't know where this was going but I was happy to talk about football and be in out of the cold. As it turned out, things got even better.

'I'll tell you what I'm going to do, Whelan,' the Captain said. 'I'm going to give your manager a call and if he says he wants you in the team this weekend then I'll let you go.'

Imagine hearing this! My father went in the Army and we didn't see him for nearly five years. His entire life ground to a halt. I'd only been there for a few hours and already this fella was trying to help me out.

I just had to pray Mr Carey wanted to select me!

As I stood there, Captain Harrington got his sergeant to make the phone calls. The next thing I knew, he was speaking directly to John Carey. But I could only hear half the conversation – what on earth was being said?

'I see. I see. OK, very good.'

I didn't dare breathe in case I missed something.

'Right, Whelan,' he said, hanging up. 'It's your lucky day. Your manager would like you in Doncaster and I'm going to give you a forty-eight-hour pass.' I wanted to pinch myself. 'You can go Friday at four o'clock and I want you back on Sunday at ten o'clock at night. If you're a minute late you never play again, is that understood?'

'Perfectly, sir. Thank you very much, sir.'

I had a spring in my step for the rest of the day. The marching drills flew by and even the weather seemed warmer. There were still tears that night from a lot of the new recruits but not from me.

That Friday I appeared at the gate, presented my pass and set off for the station. Halfway there I decided to see if I could save the fare. I'd heard that when you're wearing khaki everyone will give you a lift so I thought I'd put it to the test.

It worked. An old Leyland truck pulled over for me and I was home in about two and a half hours. My mam's face was a picture when I walked through the door but that was nothing compared to Pat's when I saw her at the Empress that night.

The next day I got myself to Blackburn in good time to leave on the coach with the rest of the team. It was bad enough being a part-time player and an apprentice – being a soldier at the same time seemed ridiculous once I stepped on to that bus and the rest of the lads ripped me to shreds. I didn't mind. I was privileged to even be there.

We drew that match 2–2 and afterwards I made my way back to Wigan. Then on Sunday it was time to return to Oswestry. With Captain Harrington's threat about being late still in my ears I didn't risk hitching – I'd been lucky on the way down but it was sod's law there would be no bugger stopping now I was in a hurry. So I caught a train instead – a decision I regretted the instant I stepped off to change at Crewe.

'Hold it, soldier!'

The voice was loud and authoritative and about a dozen people near me froze. But I was the only one in uniform. It took a second for the penny to drop:

'He's talking to me!'

I spun round and saw two MPs – military policemen – hurrying down the platform. They looked poised for a scrap. Why? Who were they chasing?

It turned out it was me. I don't know who these boys were used to dealing with but they were rough as hell with me – and I hadn't done anything wrong. Or so I thought.

'What's going on?' I asked, anxious.

'We have reason to believe you're going AWOL.'

Absence without leave from the Army was the worst offence during the war. They clamped down on it big-style to make an example to the other soldiers.

'What makes you think that?'

'For a start you're not wearing your beret.'

Damn! I'd forgotten to put it back on when I'd left the train.

'Show us your papers, son.'

I did as I was told and said, 'I've got permission. I'm on a weekend pass.'

They could tell I was wet behind the ears.

'When did you enlist?'

'Last Tuesday?'

'Tuesday – and you want us to believe you're on leave already?'

'It's the truth.'

I showed them my pass and they studied it.

'How the hell have you got off already?'

'I play football.'

'Who for?'

'Blackburn Rovers.'

'Oh, hell. That explains it. OK then, clear off – but if I catch you without your uniform again you're for the high jump.'

That little episode sent a jolt up me. Passes were obviously like gold dust. I made a promise to myself to do everything Captain Harrington asked in order not to jeopardise any future privileges.

I honestly didn't know whether it would be a one-off or not, but the next day I saw the Captain again. He told me he was happy for me to play as many matches as I could get to on that length pass. In the meantime he was going to pull a few strings to make sure nothing else got in the way.

It was like I had my own guardian angel there. He didn't know me at all but he wanted to support sport. From that day on he looked after me while I was on National Service. I had to do my training like everybody else but Captain Harrington kept me away from Korea. Men I had shared a dorm with on my first night were being shipped out all over the world. I thanked my lucky stars I could stay in Oswestry.

Training was compulsory, however – and it was hard. I had one eight-week course of intense education and endurance. It was part survival exercise, part torture experiment. We had to walk on the hills, yomp over marshland, in all weather, trying to do our orienteering and carry our own weight in equipment. The conditions were horrible and I only got off about three or four times during that whole period. But I still managed it.

It all seemed a little too good to be true and I kept waiting for the pay-off. Then one day it came. When I heard what it was, though, I couldn't help laughing.

I was sent for by the Brigadier. His house was at the edge of the camp so he could monitor everything. Captain Harrington said, 'I'll take you up there,' so we marched in together. The Brigadier came straight to the point.

'Captain Harrington here says you're a decent footballer,' he said.

'Thank you, sir.'

'Well you'd better be because you've had enough time off at our expense and now I want you to earn it. 64 Regiment has never won the Royal Artillery Football Cup in my thirty years here and I want that to change.'

The Artillery Cup was a big tournament featuring all the different Army teams from around the country. Because of National Service there was a chance that a few sportsmen would be on the books of any given unit. Apart from me, Oswestry had two other professionals, while just up the road Bobby Charlton had been seconded at Shrewsbury.

'Will you make sure we win it?' the Brigadier asked.

'I'll certainly make sure we try, sir.'

'That's all we can ask,' he said, but by the way he smiled I knew he was expecting more than trying. He wanted this trophy – at any cost.

'You're the captain, Whelan. As far as your players are concerned, you can do what you want, keep the hours you want, and even eat what you want. You're in charge: I want your boys doing whatever they have to to win.'

When we were outside Captain Harrington gave a whistle.

'You've got carte blanche there, Dave' – he was one of the first people to call me that. 'You have to train this team like they're professionals. And if that means missing all your Army duties, so be it. If that means eating with the officers in the NAAFI, so be it. But you have to get this team ready and bring that cup back.'

Things started well. The first few rounds were a bit rusty but we grew together as a team. The quarter-final came and went and suddenly we were one match away from an appearance in the final. I'd had my share of cup success with youth teams and so I took this in my stride. The Brigadier and the Captain, on the other hand, were cats on hot tin. They must have asked me about preparations a dozen times a day.

'Everything's in hand,' I assured them. And it was – up to a point. But when the draw for the semi-final was made, we were given Saturday, which clashed with Blackburn versus Arsenal at Ewood Park. Fortunately Captain Harrington had a plan.

'It's our home match,' he said, 'so I've scheduled it for the morning. If we kick off at 10.30 it should be over by twelve o'clock. Ten past twelve, out of here. I could get you to Blackburn by half past one.'

I didn't see that coming but I was grateful. 'But what if traffic's bad, sir?'

He thought about that.

'OK, if you go three goals up I'll let you come off and we'll get on the road early.' There were no subs in those days so this would be a massive gamble. First, though, we had to get those goals.

The two other professionals in our side were both from Scotland. Jock Buchanan played centre forward for Hibernian while the other lad had played a few games for Falkirk. They were both very good so I called them together.

'Look, lads, the Captain will let me go if we get three in front. I need some goals from you, Jock.'

'I'll do my best.'

Kick-off came and we got off to a flyer. With twenty minutes gone Jock had scored twice. I just needed a third before half-time and I could be off in Captain Harrington's car.

'Come on, Jock, one more and I'm out of here.'

The last few minutes of the half were nail-biting but moments before the whistle we had a corner from the right and who was there to nod it home but Jock.

'Fantastic,' I thought. 'I won't even need to come out for the second half.'

But Captain Harrington had other ideas. 'Look, Dave, heads will roll if we lose this now. Give me ten minutes in the second half and if we're still winning I'll hook you off.'

With no substitutes it took a brave man to haul a player off, especially your captain, knowing you'd be down to ten men.

Minutes later it all went wrong. The lad from Falkirk got on the ball and – *snap!* – broke his leg. It was a freak accident. Nobody clogged him, no one was even near him. He just got on the ball, turned his body and his ankle didn't move. It was a nasty one and they took a while to get him off the pitch. I didn't fancy his chances of even walking for a while, let alone playing again.

Things didn't look very good for me, either. We were a man down with half an hour to go. I looked over at the touchline and Captain Harrington shook his head. 'I'm sorry, Dave, I can't do it,' he shouted over.

'What if we get four?'

'Get four and I'll think about it.'

Right, it was sleeves rolled up and even harder into the tackles. I wanted that ball in the other half for as long as possible.

'Jock,' I yelled. 'He wants four! Pull your finger out, will you!'

With seventy minutes on the clock I got my wish. The place erupted. Everyone at the little ground in Oswestry was cheering – apart from the Captain. I could see he was wrestling with a big decision.

'Sod it – come on, Dave, we're off!'

I ran over and jumped straight in his car in my kit, boots and all. I had my civvies with me – my trousers and Blackburn first-team blazer – so I threw them on while we drove. All the way Captain Harrington was sweating on the result. 'How long can nine men hold out for?' he asked me.

'The lads will be all right,' I said, but I knew if anything had gone wrong that would be the end of my professional career for a while.

We got to Ewood about ten minutes to two and an hour later I was playing my second match of the day. I could run for ever back then so I didn't mind that, although I didn't want Mr Carey finding out I'd already done seventy minutes. He must have had his suspicions when he saw I was already muddy before a ball had been kicked. Ron Clayton went to say something but I said, 'Don't ask' and out we went. It finished 2–2 and by the end I was ready for a bath. When I came out Captain Harrington was waiting by the car.

'Fantastic result!' he said, beaming.

'A draw's not bad against Arsenal,' I said.

'Not that score,' he said. 'I've been on the phone to Oswestry. We won 4–0. We're in the final!'

What a great journey back that was. The transformation of the man from the anxious fella who'd driven me to Blackburn was incredible. That's what sport can do to you – you're down one minute and up the next. It works both ways, though, and over the years I've seen it first-hand.

When we got back the news about the chap from Falkirk didn't look good. His bone was smashed and it would be a while before he was mobile again. That was the end of his Army days – and maybe even his football career as well. It was a sombre mood that night, even though we'd won, and we all thought, 'There but for the grace of God go I'.

I'd always had my health and like most young lads I took it for granted. 'If an injury ever took me like that I don't know what I'd do,' I thought. Perhaps my mam had been right all along. I really did need to think about a back-up career after football.

The final was in Chester and the pressure was really on but we strolled home winners that day without any problems. The Brigadier could not have been happier. He marched into our little dressing room, picked up the trophy and said, 'I think I'll be looking after this – after all, you lot won't want to be carrying it around on your week's leave, will you?'

Incredible – he gave us seven-day passes just for bringing home the cup. When I thought of all the lads from the barracks who'd been posted to Korea and other hot spots I thanked my lucky stars for football – and for my dad dragging me to Wigan Boys Club all those years ago.

When I got picked for the British Army team, things got even better. Not only were the top brass at Oswestry proud as punch but I could forget all about pretending to be a soldier and just concentrate on playing. Our sergeant major was a real soldier who'd fought from Normandy to Berlin, but after I was picked for that team he suddenly didn't want to know me. The first time he said anything about my absence I showed him my pass from the War Office and that was it.

'Look, do me a favour, Whelan,' he said quietly. 'Just clear off, will you? Don't bother me. Don't even come back here after training if you don't want to because if I tell you to do something the Brigadier or the War Office will just tell you to do something different. Just let me know where you are and that's all I need.'

The British Army team was based at Aldershot because it had the best facilities but the players were scattered all over the country. I was in Oswestry, Bobby Charlton was in Shrewsbury, and then you had Duncan Edwards, Dave Mackay, Gerry Hitchens, who was soon on his way to play for Inter Milan in Italy, Eddie Colman from Man United, and the flying machine from Spurs, Cliff Jones. It was a cracking team and we could have given anyone a match. We used to play Second Division teams and beat them – and I think we'd give any Premier League team today a bit of a lesson.

I liked all the lads on the team, but when you talk about gentlemen you're talking about Bob Charlton. He was the most honest, up front person you could ever meet – and he was exactly the same as a player. Bob and I used to travel back to our bases together after weekends with our clubs. He'd come from Manchester and I'd go from Wigan and we'd meet at Crewe station for the 1.30 a.m. train. I'd get off at Oswestry and he'd carry on through to Shrewsbury. We spent hours together chatting on those journeys and I guarantee he's the same man today as he was then.

Even at eighteen I could see that Bob had immense ability. He didn't strike the ball like everybody else. He seemed to caress it with no effort. He'd barely move but would that ball fly. That's what you remember about Bob. If you played with Dave Mackay, what struck you was the colossal work-rate he had. Up and down the pitch – a truly dynamic figure. Then there was Duncan Edwards. I only played with him once or twice but what a magnificent player. He was eighteen but he had the physique of a real man. Big, powerful legs, an awesome player. Everything you would want to see in a midfield player, he had. The moment I saw him play I thought, 'That lad's an England captain'. And like Bob he had that aura of invincibility that Manchester United seem to breed into all their players. Eddie Colman was exactly the same. I don't know how they do it but Matt Busby's players had it and Fergie's players have it today.

Before I joined the Army, the furthest I'd travelled was the Isle of Man. Now thanks to football I was told I'd be playing all over Europe. I couldn't wait to get on an aeroplane for the first time and I didn't really know what to expect when we landed in Portugal. Obviously the heat was a major difference, but the thing I remember most about arriving in Lisbon was how beautiful it was. What really catches your eye is the different colour of the brickwork. You're right on the coast and you're looking at all these breathtaking buildings and the difference really hits home.

It wasn't just the colour of the buildings that impressed me. I couldn't believe it when I saw they had coloured wine glasses over there as well. I'd never seen anything so exotic. They were expensive – about twelve shillings a set in escudos – but I couldn't resist buying half a dozen as a present for Pat. I can't believe I wasted that money. Fifty years later we've still got two left as a reminder!

On the way to Portugal we all laughed about how we were about to have a nice easy holiday.

'The Portuguese army team will be a soft touch,' I thought, and everyone else agreed.

We couldn't have been more wrong. The players were all conscripts like us and they were excellent footballers. I learnt later that most of them played in the national team – in fact we were lucky to finish with a 2–2 draw.

In fact, every country we visited in Europe gave us really good games. We arrived in France to have a match with Lille and expected to roll them over. We won in the end but it was hard fought. It was the same in Italy and Holland. Everywhere we went we put on a show – it was like having the national team come to your town, because we were all decent players and everyone in Europe had heard of the clubs we played for. The only one of us who wasn't a professional was the manager. The War Office appointed this fella to be in charge of us. He was a big Arsenal fan – but he'd no experience. His great skill was working out who knew best and listening to them, so if one of us suggested something for training or a way to play in a match, he'd take it all on board and usually tell us to try it. He was a really decent chap and he put himself out a lot to help us. Anything we wanted, he would try to get. He didn't mind one bit that he was an officer who was told to babysit these sportsmen. He loved the game and he loved winning respect for the British Army all around the world.

My week was just football, football, football. I had to get to Aldershot on a Monday – but there was no rush because we didn't train till Tuesday – then play on Wednesday, back to Oswestry on Thursday, then I'd be off on Friday to play for Blackburn on Saturday. Up the road Bobby and Duncan would be doing the same, playing for the Army on a Wednesday then disappearing at weekends to turn out for United. It was fantastic. All the other lads at Oswestry called me a 'jammy bugger' and worse, but I didn't blame them. We were all meant to be doing our National Service but while they were doing square-bashing with rifles I was either playing trombone in the Army band or swanning around the world playing football.

Even I had to do a bit of training, though. Over a period of two years there were about twenty-four weeks that were compulsory for everyone. If I could get away I would, but if we were stuck out on the moors with a compass and a penknife and no way home, then that was tough. I couldn't complain, though. The Carey Chicks were doing well in the League, I had a wonderful girlfriend at home and I was seeing the world. Life was good.

'But,' I thought, 'it could be better.' And I knew exactly what to do.

I was home on leave for a few days over summer and because there was no Blackburn match that Saturday I had a bit more time on my hands than usual. The first chance I got I popped into town and found the shop I wanted then got ready to go dancing at the Empress that night. As usual Pat looked sensational and I couldn't wait to get her away from her friends. It was actually as we were dancing that I said, 'Pat, I've got something to ask you'.

'What's that?' she said, but we continued our waltz.

I suddenly realised how loud the band was playing. I was nervous enough and having to shout made it worse. But there was no turning back now. I pulled my mouth close to her ear and said, 'Pat, will you do me the honour of marrying me?'

At the same time I pulled a little box from my pocket. It was the ring I'd bought earlier.

I realised we had stopped dancing and that Pat had the biggest grin on her face.

'Of course I will,' she said.

I was the happiest man in the world that night.

As a Blackburn regular I was earning around £15 a week – £20 if we won. The average fella would be pulling in around £4 or £5 a week then. On top of that I got a little salary from the Army. Every week when I went to play a match I would stop off at 70 Chadwick Street and drop my pay packet off. I wouldn't say anything and my mam didn't either. I just put it on the table, wrapped in Cellophane with a little piece of paper saying what the bonus was, depending on the game's result. Before I left she would give me £5 back. I kept on handing over everything I earned until the day I came in with some important news.

'I've got something to tell you, Mam,' I said. 'I'm getting married.'

'David, keep your money now,' Mam said that day. 'You'll need that.'

I said, 'Mam, I've got to pay you something.'

'OK, you can give me ten shillings a week. From now on though you're earning for your wife. You'll have to start putting her first.'

It was harsh hearing her say those words but she was right. Once Pat and I tied the knot I knew I'd have to concentrate on supporting her, but I didn't expect my mam to say I should start saving immediately.

Giving up my contribution was a big sacrifice for my parents. I had been handing over my earnings to them since I was fifteen and it would have been a big drop. Mum wasn't somebody who craved money. All she wanted was for us to be happy. As long as she could put a square meal on the table, she was content. That was why it was so hard for her during the war when she struggled to feed us.

Dad was pulling in his pound or two a night but he still came home with only half of it. That was their arrangement. I don't think he ever saved a penny in his life. That was all down to my mother.

It wasn't just his own money that Dad liked to spend either. I saw him after a match once and he said, 'David, I've bought you a car.'

You don't expect your dad to come out with something like that, not when you know money is tight. There was a twist, though.

'Come on,' he said. 'Let's go and pay for it.'

We went round to a house not 200 yards from where the JJB Stadium sits now and met this fella who was selling his old Citroën DS – one of those long ones with the funny suspension that rose when you started the engine. It was quite a beautiful thing and the guy only wanted £10 for it.

But it was £10 of my money.

I could never get upset with my dad, especially not over money. He was right when he said a man doing the miles that I was travelling needed a set of wheels. I'd been able to drive since I was a young teen and my Army licence had come through so that weekend I drove back to Oswestry feeling like I was king of the road. And instead of it costing me money to get there I actually made a small profit. There were five other lads in Wigan who were on leave. I gave them all a lift in exchange for £1 each. With petrol at ten pence a gallon I thought it wouldn't be long before the car paid for itself.

I got quite used to bombing around the country in that Citroën, but as I pulled into Poolstock one day, I saw some smoke coming from the engine. The next thing I knew there were flames licking out from under the bonnet. The car was still moving when I leapt out!

My dad said he would sort it out so I got off to Blackburn. By the time I came back the next weekend he'd had it towed round the back of Chadwick Street, stripped the engine – and turned it into a hen house!

The next car I bought was as a married man because a week after my twenty-first birthday Pat and I tied the knot. I got a fortnight's leave as a wedding present and we made the most of it. It was a lovely ceremony at

Poolstock C of E church in Wigan and Pat looked a million dollars in a traditional white gown as her father walked her down the aisle. My best man was Tony Ledwith, one of my pals from Wigan Boys Club. Like most of us from my school, Tony had failed his 11-plus exam, but he hadn't given up on his education. He managed to get a place at the local technical college and now he's Professor Ledwith. There was no talk of education that November night, however, and Tony made sure we all had a good celebration. Then Pat and I said goodbye to everyone and it was off to London for five days for our honeymoon.

It was a great start to married life but by the end of the week we were back living at my parents' house and getting ready for my return to Oswestry. I fully expected Pat to move back in with her family just outside Wigan until my service ended in three months' time, but she refused.

'I'm your wife now,' she said. 'This is our home until we get our own place.'

It was true. Her parents' place was a palace compared with the ramshackle little two-up, two-down we had. Her father was a pitman so he used to earn quite a good bit of money and whereas my dad liked a drink, Pat's dad put it all into the house. That place was immaculate. They had a garden, not a yard, electricity throughout and carpets. Who would choose Chadwick Street over that? But Pat wouldn't budge.

'It won't look right if I up sticks the second you leave. The neighbours will think I'm leaving you.'

I thought she was barmy but she stayed there with her new family until we moved out together five months later.

I came out of the Army in February 1958 and immediately we made plans to move to Blackburn. Because I was such a regular in the team now the club bought a house for me to live in. They weren't known for their generosity so this was a surprise. You had to rent it back off them at a pound a week but as you were going to be living there they even let you choose it.

'You can buy anywhere you like up to the value of £1,000,' the manager told me.

Pat and I had a good look round and chose a lovely little place in Brantwood Avenue. There was only one hitch – the price.

I went back to Mr Carey and said, 'We've found a house – the only problem is it's £1,200. Can you run to that?'

He pulled a face and didn't look happy. 'I don't know about that. I'll have to ask the board.'

So he did. They had a meeting and then he pulled me aside one morning in training.

'You're in luck – I had to twist their arms but you can have the extra money. Go and do the deal.'

You always remember your first house. It wasn't a big place but we had our own indoor toilet, our own bathroom and carpet on the stairs, which I'd never even seen before. There's no point having a nice house and not taking care of it, though, and we'd only been there five minutes before Pat started knocking me into shape.

We thought we'd won the pools with our little house but I was put in my place when John Carey signed Ally MacLeod from St Mirren. They found him this lovely big house a short walk from the ground so he didn't even have to travel far.

'How come you get this mansion and I had to fight for twelve hundred quid?' I asked him.

He smiled.

'Don't forget, Dave – I'm a star.'

'In Scotland,' I said. 'But this is England.'

He was a cheeky so-and-so but what a wonderful footballer. In fact we had a team full of them by then. Peter Dobing and Roy Vernon were banging in the goals and then you had Ron Clayton, Bryan Douglas, Bill Eckersley, Harry Leyland, Mick McGrath, Tommy Johnston, Matt Woods – and we were on fire. We were tearing through the opposition in the FA Cup – Everton and Liverpool were two memorable scalps considering we were just a Second Division team – and then it was a semi-final against deadly neighbours Bolton.

I didn't play in that match at Maine Road but when Peter Dobing put us ahead at half-time I joined in with the rest of the lads, daring to think of reaching a final. Two goals from Bolton's Ralph Gubbins put an end to that dream, though.

For a small club like ours to get so close and fall at the last hurdle was a sickening feeling.

'That could be it for me,' I thought. 'I'll never get a better chance to play at Wembley.'

Two days before I was decommissioned from the Army I heard some news that put my own disappointment into perspective. An aeroplane had crashed at Munich Airport on its third attempt at taking off in bad weather. Twenty-one of the forty-four passengers had died instantly. I felt terribly sorry for all the friends and families of those people but I had my own reasons to be horrified. Matt Busby's Manchester United team were on that plane. My friends Bobby Charlton, Eddie Colman and Duncan Edwards were involved – and I had no idea if they'd survived.

I remember exactly where I was at the time. My 64 Regiment team had just trained that morning for what would be my last time with them and we were sitting in the NAAFI having a bite to eat. Then one of the cooks came running out of the kitchen carrying a radio.

'United's plane has crashed!' he shouted. 'They've all been killed.'

I've never felt so sick in my life. I don't think any of us had. Bobby hadn't caught the Crewe train with me last weekend because he was flying from Manchester to Belgrade with his team. Had I really seen him for the last time?

The news service in those days was nothing like today and details were slow to come out. Then I heard. Eddie Colman, Geoff Bent, Roger Byrne, Mark Jones, David Pegg, Tommy Taylor and Liam Whelan were among the fatalities. Matt Busby, Bobby and Duncan were seriously injured and in hospital.

You feel so hopeless in these situations and I was distraught. Everyone in my regiment knew how close I was to Bob and Eddie and they'd all heard me rave about the young sensation Duncan Edwards. Every man on that base was grieving for the Munich lads. In fact, the whole country was shaken up. The Busby Babes were world famous. You didn't have to be a football fan to have heard of them. It affected us all.

Obviously it was a lot worse for the team's loved ones – and I saw that first-hand. Matt Busby's son, Sandy, was in the Rovers reserve team at the time. He was actually celebrating his birthday when he heard about the accident. Watching him struggle to come to terms with the news about his dad was shocking.

Bobby was let out of hospital a few days later while Matt Busby had the last rites read to him twice before he pulled through. But Duncan Edwards wasn't so lucky. On 21 February 1958 he died.

It was a tragic day for football. He was such a young lad and one of the best players I had ever seen. He would have been a world-beater. More than fifty years later it's only right that that terrible accident is still commemorated at Old Trafford.

You don't get over something like Munich. Not as a person and not as a footballer. I'd flown with the British Army team dozens of times. That could have been any one of us on that plane. If I'm honest, I was glad those days were coming to an end for me. I can't tell you how happy I was to learn that Bob had survived – but I was not looking forward to the next time I met him. What do you say to a person who has been through something like that?

I didn't actually see Bob again until almost a year later when we lined up against each other at Old Trafford. It was good to catch up with him, of course, and we reminisced about a lot of the good times abroad with the Army team. The one topic we did not discuss was Munich. A football team is as close to a family as you'll get, and I know to this day he remains devastated by what happened to his friends. But it's not my place, or anyone's, to intrude on his grief and ask him about those events. If Bob wants to talk about it then he has to initiate it. Half a century of close friendship later, I still haven't had that conversation.

There was serious talk after Munich that Manchester United might fold as a club. How could it go on after that? But I think it was the right decision to try to continue. Those boys would have wanted it and it's fitting the club continues to be such a success today.

But it was hard. Matt Busby didn't recover in time to manage another game that season and with youth team and reserve players stepping up, United only won one League game. They did, however, manage to limp through to the FA Cup final. Unfortunately Bolton, their opponents on the day, had not read the script and United lost.

Watching Man U pull themselves together was an incredible spark for the rest of us. If they could overcome this disaster then we all had to as well. At Blackburn, once Bolton had put us out of the Cup, we were able to concentrate on the League. Two top-four finishes in a row had really got the lads' tails up and we dared to think that this could be our promotion year. But we didn't dare count our chickens.

Peter Dobing really had his eye in. He was electric and got four in our 5–0 win over Bristol City. When he wasn't scoring then Roy Vernon was banging them in. 'Taffy' was a tremendous target man and we strung five victories together: Donnie Rovers home and away, Rotherham at home 5–0, Boro 3–2 away and Leyton Orient 4–1 at Ewood. Now there were four clubs chasing the two promotion places – us, West Ham, Fulham and Charlton were all in the frame – and two games to go.

You don't want to be travelling for tight games but our penultimate match was in London at Craven Cottage on a Wednesday night followed by Charlton at the Valley three days later. Not a nice prospect at all. It was two points for a win then and we needed three to go up. If Fulham beat us they would only need a draw on the Saturday to go up.

It was a horrible wet night and all Fulham's star players were up for it. I was up against their outside left, Trevor Chamberlain – he was a tough bastard. Jimmy Hill was at right half, but the man most Cottagers paid to see was 'The Maestro', Johnny Haynes. He was one of the most famous footballers in the land because he was the Brylcreem man – you couldn't walk down a street without seeing a poster with his face on it and his hair all immaculately slicked back with Brylcreem. He was the David Beckham of the day and people loved him.

When we went 1–0 down things got heated and Johnny Haynes and Taffy Vernon clashed in the middle of the field. They were both on the floor, kicking out at each other in the rain.

As he got up, Johnny shouted, 'You want to learn how to tackle' into Taffy's face, and threw a few choice words in for good measure. That was absolutely the wrong thing to do to Taffy. He scooped up a handful of mud and smacked it down right on Johnny Haynes's head.

'Get back on your bloody Brylcreem poster, you tart!'

The sight of their star man with a clod of turf on his head was irresistible and even though there was so much pressure, we all cracked up at that. You get those moments in a game and sometimes it's hard to concentrate afterwards. Fortunately for us Ally MacLeod was wide awake and he grabbed a very late equaliser. That put Fulham out of the race but we still had to go to the Valley and win.

It was simple: if Charlton beat us, they went up. Luck was with us that day. Bryan Douglas scored one, Roy Vernon got another then Peter Dobing bagged a third. With twenty minutes to go we were three up. Then they scored.

'That's all right, we can hang on for ten minutes,' I thought.

Then they got another.

All hell broke loose. It was a fight to the finish and absolute mayhem for ten minutes. In the end we won 3–2. We'd done it.

Blackburn Rovers were into the First Division.

Six

I'M NOT WEARING THOSE

Winning promotion, even as runners-up to West Ham, was an incredible feeling. The old cliché about the League being a marathon not a sprint is absolutely true – and when you've been in a marathon you really know it. As a treat the Rovers directors lined us up with an end-of-season tour to Holland. Clubs do their travelling during pre-season these days but it was quite common then to have a little junket somewhere in Europe before summer.

We had to play two exhibition games, one of them against Werder Bremen, but generally we just relaxed. It was an all-expenses-paid trip but being Blackburn the hotel wasn't exactly five-star and the travel was cattle class as usual. Then there was our spending money. Each player had an allowance of 3/6 per day for out-of-pocket expenses. That's about twenty pence – they didn't exactly push the boat out. I remembered that penny-pinching years later and swore I'd never inflict it on my players. When Wigan got promoted to the Premier League in 2005 I took the entire squad on a trip to Barbados – and that cost more than twenty pence a player.

The 1958/9 season was a landmark for me. It had been a long time coming but I was finally a full-time first-team player. I really believed I deserved my place alongside Ron Clayton, who was captain of England,

Bryan Douglas, Roy Vernon, Peter Dobing, Mick McGrath, Bill Eckersley, Harry Leyland and Ally MacLeod. But I wouldn't be playing as a half-back. If I wanted that permanent spot, I needed to change.

With Ron Clayton playing in the same position as me my opportunities were obviously limited. So when Mr Carey said, 'Can you play as a full back today?' I grabbed the chance. I slipped in just behind Ron on the right flank and the chemistry worked straight away. From that day on, that was my new position.

In the first team.

It meant so much to be able to concentrate on playing football without the distractions of a job or the Army. I don't think I'd have minded if we'd been in the Lancashire Combination. But we weren't in the Combination, we were in the First Division, which meant a whole new array of challenges. The first of those was Newcastle United at St James' Park.

The Magpies weren't in the best of shape then and had narrowly avoided relegation in nineteenth spot – there were twenty-two in the league back then. So even though we were the new boys we fancied our chances.

They hadn't built the big stand on the side back then so the place was open to the River Tyne and the wind howled down, but it was still an impressive stadium. Luckily we were playing them in August and it was fine, a lovely day. Jackie Milburn had just left and their top scorer, Len White, wasn't playing that day but they had Bill Curry, another big centre forward. I was up against their outside left, 'Twinkle Toes' Bobby Mitchell, a big, solid lad who played for Scotland.

It was their manager Charlie Mitten's first game in charge and so we didn't really know what to expect. Nobody, though, imagined we'd be winning 4–0 with ten minutes to go. We absolutely battered them. Then somebody sent over a cross and I leapt to head it away. The wind took hold of the ball and it skimmed off the top of my head and straight into the back of the net. Clean sheets are like goals to keepers and I got a right going-over from Harry Leyland.

'What are you playing at? I had that covered!'

The heck he did, but we were still arguing about it on the coach home. We beat Newcastle 5–1 in the end and then it was Leicester followed by Spurs back at our place. We put five past them – each of them – conceding none.

'This First Division lark is a piece of cake,' I thought.

Our fourth match was away to Leicester this time – the matches weren't spread either side of Christmas then – and that was 1–1. Our fifth match in the First Division, though, would be the hardest test yet but the gaffer wasn't letting us worry.

'Lads, you've scored sixteen and conceded two in four – we've nothing to be afraid of at Old Trafford.'

We went up there with our heads high. As we stepped off the bus, though, something very odd happened. There was a man personally greeting every one of us.

It was Matt Busby himself.

As I approached he held out his hand and said, 'Hello, David. Welcome to Old Trafford.'

I thought, 'Wow, Matt Busby knows my name.' For a twenty-one-year-old that's major stuff. 'Why has he done that?'

Afterwards I knew why. It was mind games. You're so honoured that he knows your name and had bothered to shake your hand that you dwell on that. It puts you in your place a little bit and reminds you that you're in the presence of the mighty Man United.

Do you know what? It bloody worked. They stuffed us 6–1.

I'd played at Old Trafford before but only in the reserves. There was a decent turn-out that night and they made a lot of noise, but nothing compared with the gladiatorial roar that thundered out for this League match. The sheer volume of 70,000 voices singing, shouting and swearing at you affected every player. I had never, ever experienced a sound like it and it dulled my brain. I was playing against a lad called Albert Scanlon who was quite quick and direct and he ran me ragged. We all had a really tough day.

'Welcome to the First Division,' I thought.

Years later I discovered that Matt Busby actually wanted to sign me for United. His son, Sandy, was on Blackburn's books and he'd obviously given Matt some good reports. The bosses at Ewood turned him down flat and that was the end of the matter. Can you imagine a player not being told today?

We had some decent results over the remainder of the season, beating Arsenal, Man City and Everton, and eventually finished tenth. It was a very creditable performance – but I think we could have gone further if a few things hadn't happened.

Everton had been managerless since the last few games of the previous season and in October 1958 they came in for Johnny Carey. He agreed to go (and would later infamously be sacked in the back of a taxi).

'I'm sorry, boys,' he told us, 'but they're such a big club. I think I've got a real chance of success there.'

He obviously didn't rate our chances, then. By sod's law, though, we were due to meet at Goodison Park a fortnight later. Every single player wanted to show the gaffer what he'd given up and we earned a good draw. Back at our place we beat them 2–1. It's a wonderful feeling when there's something personal riding on a game and you win – although it's terrible if things don't go your way.

Rovers moved very quickly to replace Carey and were soon introducing us to Dally Duncan, the old outside left for Luton Town. He had a reputation for being a bit of a hard man – and didn't he want to prove it the moment he stepped through the door! But he had no respect for the lads and we had none whatsoever for him.

All the players were summoned to the dressing room. It was freezing in there as usual so we were all huddled round the single gas fire in the middle of the room. His first words were, 'Right, I want everybody to roll their sleeves up.'

Roll our sleeves up? You could see everybody in the room thinking, 'What the hell for?' But we did it.

Then he said, 'Right, your sleeves are rolled up – and that's how we play. If any of you are not prepared to roll your sleeves up on the field, you may as well leave now.'

I reckon he'd been preparing that little speech in his car because he looked very pleased with himself at the end. Unfortunately it didn't quite go to plan. One person in the room hadn't rolled his sleeves up. Roy Vernon just sat there motionless throughout the manager's performance. And when Duncan said, 'You may as well leave now,' Roy just stood up and walked out.

So much for the new manager's opening move – he'd just hacked off the leading scorer in the Football League. Suddenly it got very interesting for the rest of us and we couldn't wait to see how Dally handled it.

Not well, as it turned out.

'What's his problem?' Dally asked us.

'I don't know,' Ron Clayton said. 'You'd better ask him.'

So Duncan marched outside and found Taffy kicking a ball around.

'What do you think you're doing walking out?' he demanded.

'I didn't like the way you were speaking. I play football. I can't be doing with these silly games.'

Taffy was not an easy one to handle but that definitely wasn't the way to get the best out of him and their relationship never recovered from that. They barely spoke to each other and it was no surprise when Duncan eventually sold him – to Everton. John Carey couldn't believe his luck. Taffy was a 20+-goals-a-season man. He never let you down on that score.

What a striker he was! But he wouldn't kill himself on the field. You've got lads who will run and fight and run and fight and then you've got lads who will do the business, and put the ball in the back of the net. Gary Lineker was one of them. And so was Taffy.

The really memorable thing about him was his penalties. He was renowned for them and I'll never forget the first time I saw him take one.

He came for a trial at Blackburn when I was seventeen. I'd only been there three or four months but I was captain of the A team and we were having a game. This lad turned up to play with us, thin as a rake, and small. He was always slim but he was like a blade of grass when I first saw him. A penalty came our way and the trainer called out to me, 'David, give it to the trialist.'

We were on ten shillings per win then and I didn't want to gamble on this unknown quantity costing me that bonus.

I yelled, 'There's only ten minutes to go. I don't want to risk it.'

The trainer said, 'I've got orders, son. The boss told me if we get a penalty, he has to take it.'

All the while Taffy just watched. Then he put the ball down slowly, looked at the keeper and said, 'It's going in that corner,' and pointed to the left.

'Oh great,' I thought. 'This is all we need. A kid with attitude.'

He walked away, casual as you like, then strolled up to the ball and – *whack*! It went straight into the bottom-left corner. It was brilliant. Then he looked at the keeper and said, 'Where were you? I told you where it was going.'

Barely seventeen and arrogant to the nth degree. But I thought, 'Lad, you can play.' He got into the team a year later and he was scoring goals immediately. Everton paid about £27,000 for him but that was cheap. He was their leading goalscorer every year.

We had a load of characters in that team. Bryan Douglas and Ally MacLeod were big personalities. When we travelled away there was none of this 'have your own room' business. It was two single beds in a room, three if they could fit them in. Ally always made sure he shared a room with me.

'What's so special about sharing with Crunch?' Dougie asked him.

Ally just laughed.

'He never eats breakfast, does he? So every morning I order two and scoff the pair of them!'

After every training session I used to race Ron Clayton, who was a total fitness fanatic, back to the dressing room. We were all supposed to jog back as part of the training, but Ally and Bryan were two of those who would always try to hitch a lift with a passing car if they could. Taffy was another one, of course. The only time they were interested in exercise was when a ball was involved. We used to play five- or six-a-side matches on the old cinder park we trained on and we would place some serious money on it. There'd be half a crown per man and for that kind of money you would kill them.

Camaraderie was fantastic then and money was often at the heart of it, but only to make things interesting. One day a friend of Ally's said he had a couple of greyhounds for sale. They came from a reliable source in Ireland – did we want to buy them? I used to enjoy my days at Wigan's track as a youngster so I said, 'I'd be interested in having a piece of a dog.'

'Me too,' Roy Vernon said.

'Count me in,' said Ally.

'And me.' That was Bryan Douglas.

The dog we chose cost £100 and was called Black Beauty. It was a tiny little thing, all light on its feet, but you could see it was fit. We decided to get it registered to race that week. All dogs have to do a time trial first to qualify, and so the bookmakers know how to rate them on the odds. Ally MacLeod took charge of this but before he went down to the track he put a large bowl of tripe in front of Black Beauty and said, 'Tuck in, my girl.'

I couldn't believe he'd get away with this so I went down with him. The dog was put in a cage then timed doing a lap behind the hare. The fella with the stopwatch said, 'That dog looks a bit heavy to me. Have you fed it recently, lads?'

I immediately started looking at my shoes but Ally was cool as you like.

'That dog hasn't touched a thing for six hours.'

'Is that right?' The trainer looked at his stopwatch, said, '1.40, not bad,' and told us to come back Friday night. I don't know if he was being kind to us or what – but he put Black Beauty in trap five and we knew she could run.

Come race night the four of us were standing up on the banked spectator area waiting to get a bet on. 'Trap five? She'll walk it,' I thought. The plan was to each put a little amount with a different bookie so they wouldn't get suspicious and slash the odds. They all watch each other and as soon as one gets wind there's something special about a runner their odds will tumble and the others will follow. Black Beauty was 4–1 as I queued to place my bet.

But before I could get to the front, the bookie licked his finger and wiped the odds off. Then he wrote next to Trap 5 '7–4'. I couldn't believe it. What had gone wrong?

Then I found out.

Matt Woods, our 6'3" centre back, was with us. He wasn't part of our syndicate but we'd told him this dog was going to win and of course he wanted to lump on as well. But he hadn't been too clever about it and had put so much down that the bookie smelt a rat and the word went round.

We weren't too happy about that. I still put my fiver down and we waited for the start.

Sport for me is all about adrenalin and I got quite a buzz knowing my dog was about to be in action. I couldn't take my eyes off the hare as it came round the track and then, whoosh, the traps opened and the dogs were out.

What a start Black Beauty had! By the first corner she must have been twelve yards in front.

'Yes!' I shouted and the rest of the lads were going mad as well.

Our dog was nearly on the hare as it approached the first bend and I was already thinking of collecting my pound notes at the end of the race. But it didn't work out like that. The dog was going so fast she couldn't take the curve. She just kept running straight and jumped over the fence at the far end of the ground! It was two days before we found her.

That was the end of racing for us. We packed it in there and then.

I never got into horses. That's often the next step up, but it wasn't for me. We weren't really gamblers, although we used to play poker on the coach going away – lads still do it. I never bet silly money but you see players who do. Every team has them. I've seen footballers lose their wages on a turn of a card, and that's upsetting. The fever for gambling gets into people's bones but it's something I can't figure out because if I go to the races now I think, 'I'll wager fifty quid – bet £10 a race. If I win, fine, if I lose, fine.' How they gamble thousands and thousands of pounds beats me. It must be a drug.

We had so many characters in our team but our captain, Ron Clayton, was an absolutely fantastic footballer. He was Steven Gerrard to a tee. They are exactly the same type of brilliant attacking players. Get the ball and surge forward. Always. Ron never defended and very rarely does Gerrard tackle. He just bombs forward exactly like Ron did.

Ron was so good he was made England captain. But he was a nightmare to play behind – which was my job. He used to forage upfield and I'd be on my own down the right. In those days playing five across the front – two wingers, a centre forward, and two inside forwards – it only worked if the inside forwards came back into midfield. If you had somebody going missing, like Ron, it used to create some nasty gaps.

I wasn't allowed in the other half. Full backs weren't wanted that far forward and if I did stray over the halfway line I'd get a rollocking.

Johnny Carey told me when I started, 'I don't want you in their half. Get rid of the ball. If you get to their half – trouble.'

It was his big fear that someone would get in behind the full back and he wouldn't have that. He wasn't the only one. Only when Jimmy Armfield started to forage forward did managers begin to allow full backs into the opponent's half of the field. José Mourinho is the same sort of manager. He's defence-minded and he plays a tight system. But you can't argue that it doesn't work.

We didn't have substitutes in those days so the first eleven would pretty much stay the same each week and that was the group that used to socialise together. It helped that everyone was British, I think, because the language was all the same. We could even just about make out Mick McGrath's Irish and Ally MacLeod's Scottish accents.

Something else that really made the camaraderie so unbelievable was the fact the wives got on as well. Pat used to come and watch all my home matches and she still goes along to Wigan games every week. She is football-mad. Ronnie Clayton's wife was the same, and Bryan Douglas's wife and Roy Vernon's – if they could get to a match they would, and of course they travelled together. It made sense and so they became very close as well.

They were the early WAGs, those women. They used to sit together, stay at the same hotels, eat together – and stick up for one another. Football is a team game and you get criticism and you get praise. The girls were very, very protective of their husbands. As players you can ignore it but it's hard for the wives to sit there and listen to it.

In March 1959 we were introduced to one of the biggest characters yet. We were on our way to play Arsenal at Highbury when Dally Duncan told us he'd made a new signing for £15,000 from Portsmouth – and the fella would be meeting us there. He was actually going to play in the match that day. When Derek Dougan strolled into the dressing room I thought, 'Bloody hell, it's Humphrey Bogart.'

He was wearing a huge Crombie overcoat, immaculately polished shoes, with matching scarf and leather gloves. He looked every inch the film star.

We all just sat there with our mouths hanging open as he carefully took the Crombie off and hung it up on the centre forward's number-nine peg. Every single item of clothing that came off was folded neatly.

Finally he was ready to put his new strip on.

When I say 'new', I mean new to him.

There were eleven players and eleven pairs of socks, which were kept in a skip in the middle of the room. These days socks get thrown away after a match but Rovers used to darn holes until there was more new cotton than old on them. And darned socks are really uncomfortable to wear. The kit man also used to boil them, which just made them shrink. Not only were they all knotty and bumpy from repairs but instead of a sock pulled up to your knee it would be flapping down by your shin. The rest of us knew all this so we would grab a pair as soon as we could to try to get something decent.

By the time Derek Dougan had finished folding his clothes there was one pair left. He picked up the socks and looked at them. I could see the darning on the heel from where I was sitting so it must have been really obvious to him. And they weren't very long, either.

'Am I supposed to wear these?' he said in his thick Belfast accent to the trainer, Jack Weddle, who was an old Portsmouth man as well.

'Well, they're the only pair we have, lad.'

Dougan looked at the socks again then chucked them back in the bin.

'I'm not wearing these. Get me some more.'

We were all watching and thinking, 'Wow, no one has ever dared say that before. What's going to happen now?'

'Only the manager can approve new socks,' Jack said.

'Well get him to approve it then. I'm not playing in those.'

So Jack sent the twelfth man off to get Dally Duncan. When he came in the trainer said, 'Boss, he won't wear these socks.' Duncan looked at Dougie, then at the socks, then back at Jack.

'Have we got any new socks?' he asked.

Jack scratched his head. 'Yeah, I've got one spare pair.'

'Well let him wear those then,' the boss said.

Dougan smiled. A brand-new pair of socks, just like that – and he'd only been in the room ten minutes. The rest of us were in shock. We would never have dared say that but he'd come from a different club, had a different attitude, and had been used to being treated differently. Blackburn Rovers, one of the founding members of the Football League, one of the oldest clubs in the land, wouldn't even give you a decent pair of socks – how ridiculous was that?

Dougan scored on his debut and we left Highbury with a 1–1 draw. More importantly, we also took away a new sense of freedom thanks to him. I think he revolutionised the club with his action. After that the rest of us then started to object if we didn't fancy something. He put into our minds the idea that we had power and that we could get what we wanted. You only had one pair of boots for the year, and one pair of rubbers, and mine were threadbare already. I'd put up with them for too long but then I remembered Dougan's cheek. I thought, 'I'll have a go at that.'

I found the trainer and said, 'I want a new pair of boots.'

'You want what?'

'I want a new pair of boots. I'm not wearing these any more.'

And I got them – and it was all thanks to Derek Dougan. I went right off him a while later but at that moment he was a pretty special character. He was a maverick with everything – with women especially. He would have one or two in a night. He would bring one lass to a party, take her home and come back with another one. And the girls would know it. But he was 6'2", good-looking and a complete charmer and they could not resist him.

You get all sorts of people in football but the really good guys are few and far between. Without question Stan Matthews was one such person, and I couldn't wait to play Blackpool that season because he was on fire for them.

We got two draws against the Seasiders but personally I had a torrid time. I went out on to that pitch, like all young bucks do, thinking, 'I'm up against my great hero – I'll show him what I can do.' I was twenty-two and he was forty-three. 'I'll have him in my pocket,' I thought.

How wrong can you be?

Stan played outside right but he used to drift right across the pitch and he came up against me several times. I really did think, 'Come on, old man.' We all did, but that's what youngsters are like. But I couldn't even get near him. He was such a magical player – and he made me look a fool.

He got the ball and that was it – it was stuck to him, glued to his boots, and he would virtually walk it past player after player. You knew he was going to move his body and you were ready for it, but he would still send you the wrong way. Don't ask me how. The top half of his body went one way and the bottom half seemed to go the other. You had to watch the ball, not the man, but as soon as you saw his body go you couldn't help but react. The instant your weight shifted he was off the other way and you're chasing thin air. Once he did it to me, then again, then again. I thought, 'You're not making me look a mug four times in a row.' But he did.

He was a fantastic, truly awesome player but he demanded the ball at his feet. The rest of the team knew this. If they put a ball over and there was an opponent near by, he'd leave it. He wasn't interested in fifty-fifty balls. He probably didn't even go after sixty-forties. He wanted the ball to his feet, with no pressure, because he was totally aware that lads like me were going on to the pitch thinking he was a famous scalp they could claim. How many of us wanted to say, 'I put Stanley Matthews in his place'? And none of us got close, even when he was in his fifties.

The more the game went on the more my blood began to boil. In my head I thought the crowd would be laughing at me if I didn't do something.

'Crunch him, Whelan!' one fella yelled out.

But how do you 'crunch' someone if you can't touch them?

I began to get a little bit desperate. I watched the ball and before Stan dummied me I just kicked him. That surprised him. A few minutes later I did it again.

Did it work?

Not at all. He just started going past me even quicker. If it was a race to the ball I would win it, and he knew it. So he didn't try. But now he knew I was getting desperate he just turned it on even more.

He knew everybody wanted to have a go at him and he could have stayed on the other wing, but he kept coming over to let me have another chance – and beat me every time.

After the match I did something I'd never done before. I thought, 'I've just had a masterclass in football. I'm going to get his autograph.'

Stan Matthews was a very individual person. He would train on his own on Blackpool beach, he never got involved in training matches in case he took a knock, and he had his own dressing room at Blackpool. When I went to look for him he was wearing a white dressing gown with his initials on – I'd never seen anything like it before. At Blackburn you couldn't even get new boots without a fight.

I went up to him and said, 'Mr Matthews, could I have your autograph please?'

It was quite unusual for a player from the same division to do this to another player but I think he was used to it.

He looked at me and he said, 'You tried to kick me, David.'

Guilty as charged.

'Yes I did,' I said.

'That's not right. That's not the way to play football.'

'I'm sorry, but it was the only way I could think of trying to stop you.'

He laughed but he still told me not to do it again.

I walked out of that dressing room with my programme inscribed: 'Best wishes to Dave Whelan – Stanley Matthews'.

I told the others what he'd said and they had a good laugh at that.

'Crunch Whelan's been told off by Stanley Matthews!'

'What will you do next time we play against him?' Bryan Douglas asked me.

I thought about the great man's words.

'What kind of a person do you think I am?' I said. 'I'll kick him of course!'

Being in the First Division meant we came up against all the best players. Blackpool also had Stan Mortensen, but then there was Nat Lofthouse at Bolton and Tom Finney at Preston – and we were playing against them all.

To my mind Tom Finney is probably the greatest player there has ever been. He could play at right wing, left wing, centre forward, inside forward and probably in goal if he put his mind to it. He was more direct than Stan – he would just tear you to shreds.

Young players love to stamp their mark on a game and the quickest way to do that is by taking on a superstar – and leaving him on his backside. That was my plan the first time I came up against Tom. I watched him out on the other wing for most of the first half, then he came drifting over to collect the ball. I saw the move happening and I knew it was my chance.

I was lightning-fast from a standing start and I knew I had that pass.

'I'll show Tom Finney,' I was thinking as I stuck out a leg and slid in to hook the ball.

It all happened so quickly I didn't even realise at first that I'd missed. The next thing I knew, Tom was running full pelt towards my goal – and I was kicking air. I wasn't the first defender to make himself look like a fool going up against Tom Finney and I knew I wouldn't be the last. He moved like quicksilver and the ball stuck to him. You had to be playing at your best and hope he was having an off day just to stand a chance.

Nat Lofthouse, like Mortensen, was an awesome centre forward. He was another one who used to do the same trick over and over – but there was nothing you could do to stop him. When there was a corner Lofty used to stand on the corner of the penalty area, maybe even wider than that. That was the worst place a defender could want him. You want to be up tight to the man you're marking because if you're close there's a good chance of getting the ball. But Lofty didn't stay still and a player with momentum is impossible to touch.

As soon as the corner was taken he would start to run along the line. I'd watch him go and follow but he had the initiative. When he was moving he could get higher, he was tougher, he was bigger, and he used to put the frighteners on all of us. When he ran across that line you knew he would hit that ball somewhere. And if he didn't hit the ball he would hit you. And at the pace he was moving, that would hurt.

Every time we came up against Nat I'd think, 'OK, I know what you're up to. You're not doing it again.' But he would. These days I don't know why managers don't get their strikers doing the same thing. I've said it to Paul Jewell and I've said it to Steve Bruce. 'Why doesn't somebody look how Lofty did corners?' But new managers have their own ways of doing things. One day someone will try it and it will work and they'll all do it.

Lofthouse, Finney and Matthews were all such tremendous players and a real privilege to play against. Tom Finney in particular would do something for me a couple of years later that would prove him to be a superb gentleman as well, but as a young professional I couldn't help admire them all because they were stars.

There was something else they had in common, though – *they were all FA Cup winners*.

We'd got close the year before, losing our semi-final to Bolton. But the day I got Stan Matthews's autograph I remembered watching the match they called 'The Matthews Final' with my sister Elsie five years earlier and I thought, 'I want to get to Wembley more than anything.'

I thought if I ever played on that famous pitch it would be the happiest day of my life.

I had no idea how wrong I could be.

I really enjoyed our first season in the top flight, but come the summer I started thinking about the words my mam used to drill into me: 'You've got to have a trade'. When I was seventeen I hadn't thought much about that at all. But as a twenty-two-year-old I knew I only had ten years maximum left in the game. 'What am I going to do then?' I thought. 'I'll still be a young man.'

Our next-door neighbour worked in retail, he was general manager at the Co-operative Store and I would chat to him over the fence whenever we were both in our gardens. He always wanted to know about Rovers, of course, but I liked hearing stories about his job. He couldn't understand that, but one day I was firing so many questions at him that he offered to let me have a look round his shop.

'I'll show you the ropes if you like,' he said. 'Although God knows why you'd be interested.'

I went along and immediately I could see myself in that sort of business. There were people queueing up to buy things in there, just handing over money. No one was getting covered in coal dust, no one stank of machinery oil – they were just taking cash and handing over a few goods.

I could see that as a way of life when my playing days were over but I'm an impetuous sort and I knew I couldn't wait that long. I started to have a look at shops that were on the market near us and began to do a few sums. One day I found a little property not far from Ewood. It was a grocery shop and the owner wanted about £950 to buy it, plus stock – altogether it came to £1,100.

I only had a few quid savings but I knew I was in line for a handout from Blackburn. Because club contracts were so powerful in those days, and because you couldn't change teams even if you wanted to without your chairman's say-so, they rewarded long service. Any player who had been there for five years was entitled to a one-off lump sum of £750. I thought, 'With that amount I'll only need a little bank loan to buy the shop.'

I went straight to see Dally Duncan to chase my payment and he said he'd sort it for me. He came back the next day and said, 'Sorry, Dave, they're only giving you £500.'

I said, 'I thought it was 750?'

'Normally, yes. But you've been in the Army so you weren't here all that time.'

I said, 'But I've played most weekends. I've been in the first team for three years.'

'Dave, I'm only telling you what the chairman told me. I'm sorry.'

I knew he could do nothing about it. After tax I only got £420 and I thought, 'There's no way I'll get a loan for the rest of it now.' But the next morning I woke up and saw a poster advertising the Midland Bank. They were calling themselves 'The Listening Bank' so I thought, 'I wonder if they'll listen to me?'

I got hold of the shop's accounts and went in to see the bank manager. There were three clerks in the branch and one of them recognised me immediately. 'Hi Dave, how are you?' he said. 'How can I help you?'

I said, 'I'm fine, thanks. Can I see the manager?'

'Of course you can. I'm sure he's got time for you.' He came round the front and stuck his head round the boss's door. 'Have you got a few minutes to see Dave Whelan, sir?'

'I've got the whole day if he wants it,' he said. 'Send him in.'

The manager was a real Rovers fan and I could tell the moment I walked in that I'd made his day just by being there. He got me a cup of tea and we chatted about the season and the team. I thought, 'I can't go wrong here. The loan's as good as mine.'

Eventually we got down to business and I said, 'I want to buy a little shop and I need to borrow about £600.'

He took the accounts and, still smiling, he began to go through them. Then he looked up and said, 'I'm sorry, Dave. Based on these figures I don't think it's a goer for us. I can't lend you the money.'

I said, 'You're meant to be the listening bank.'

'Well you can't say I haven't listened, Dave, but I still can't lend you the 600.'

I thought, 'Oh damn. The first time I've asked for anything and I can't have it.'

I was so depressed as I walked out. It didn't matter that I was a successful sportsman, or that my name was known all over this city and to anyone who read the back pages of the national papers. I'd really fancied getting into retail and the chance had gone. If I'd been a drinker, I reckon I would have started drowning my sorrows big-style and maybe I would have done later. But as I started walking back home I passed a branch of Barclays and I thought, 'I've got the accounts with me – it can't hurt to ask in there, can it?'

Once again I got an immediate audience with the manager, a chap called Mr Bardsley. I handed over the accounts and told him how much I wanted. He gave them a thorough going-over then he said, 'I'm not going to lend you £600, David.'

I thought, 'Not you as well.'

But he went on. 'I'm going to lend you £700.'

I said, 'But I only want six.'

He shook his head. 'No you don't. You'll be short of money very quickly and you'll be knocking on my door again within the month and I don't want that.'

He warned me about cash flow being tight for new businesses and I drank in everything he said. I left that office a changed man – and to this day I've banked with Barclays because of Mr Bardsley. He had a bit of faith in me, showed me a bit of respect, and I like to think he's more than earned a few quid out of my investments over the years.

The shop was in Mill Hill, near the station, and because it had a little cottage attached to the back it meant a lot of upheaval for Pat. She'd always worked in Wigan but there hadn't been the need for her to get a job in Blackburn and even though we didn't particularly need the money at the time, she was looking forward to keeping herself busy behind the counter. We had everything you'd expect in a grocery store, from a big old cash register to scales for weighing sweets, and even a little bacon slicer, and Pat couldn't wait to get started.

We opened a week after taking over and even the night before I wondered if I'd done the right thing. But the next morning when I turned the sign in the door window to 'Open' for the first time I felt a thrill running through me. A few hours later I knew I was right. I was born to sell.

I was also born to buy. I loved going to the cash and carry and sorting out the bargains. I'd do that once a week and help out in the shop when I could, but Pat was the main person people saw. In pre-season Rovers trained a lot in the afternoon, but once the new term started I would be round the corner training from ten till one, so then I'd be straight back to get my apron on and serve the customers. I think it really helped business having me there because suddenly a lot of husbands who didn't normally do the shopping would come in just to have a chat with me about the team – and nobody ever left without buying something.

I learnt a lot about business very early on in that shop. The balance sheet is the most important thing but cash flow was crucial as well, and we didn't have a very good supply. Because we were a local shop, a lot of our regular customers would put their shopping 'on the book'. Most people got paid on a Friday, and if they came in on a Wednesday or Thursday for something, they might not have the cash so they'd get it on account. Come Saturday, we'd have dozens of people settling up. It helped out dozens of families doing things that way but it meant that money was tight for us until they'd all settled. We were pulling in around £400 gross a week but I knew that the key to being successful was to change things around. Loads of other shops did the same as us but I instinctively knew it wasn't right.

'I can't have people owing me money if it means I have to go short,' I thought. 'I need to find a business that puts me in charge and not the customers.'

But those worries were for another day, when I wasn't a professional footballer. Right then, in 1959, I had my second season in the First Division to look forward to and another crack at the FA Cup.

Seven

HE WON'T BOTHER ME NOW

They say that getting into the top flight is the easy part – it's staying there that counts. Since the Premier League came into existence, almost half the promoted teams have gone straight back down again, including big names like Derby, Manchester City, Wolves and Bolton. These days there is a ton of money riding on it which wasn't the case in the 1950s and 60s – we just played for football's sake. And that was reason enough to stay up.

Our second season in the First Division started well. We won 4–0 at home to Fulham on the opening weekend, then 3–0 away at local rivals Bolton. It's funny to think that fifty years later I'm still battling the same opposition in the Premier League. A draw at Nottingham Forest followed, then wins in the home fixture against Bolton and Sheffield Wednesday before Wolves stopped us in our tracks. We definitely won more than we lost that season, though, and by Christmas we were in the top three and in with a fighting chance of the League title. Then the FA Cup started – and that's where it started to go wrong.

Top-flight teams joined the Cup in the third round – and they still do. Our first match was against Sunderland at the old Roker Park. They were in the Second Division at the time, under Alan Brown, and, if I'm honest, struggling. Brian Clough hadn't joined yet from Middlesbrough and they weren't enjoying the lower league at all.

Sometimes it's the teams you're supposed to beat that give you the biggest headaches, because they've got something to prove. We came away from Roker Park with a 1–1 draw and on the following Wednesday had them at our place. Fifty thousand home fans turned up that January night to cheer us on and it worked. In the first match Roy Vernon had been the villain, getting a silly sending off, but he more than made amends at Ewood with two cracking goals. We ended the night 4–1 winners and I couldn't wait for the following Monday to see who we would draw in the next round. All the lads huddled round a small transistor radio in the changing room at Ewood and waited for our name to be called out. Finally we heard what we wanted: 'Blackburn will play Blackpool'.

Another clash with the great Stanley Matthews.

More importantly, it was a home match. We'd played them on Christmas Day at home and won 1–0, losing the reverse fixture the next day by the same scoreline, so the teams were evenly matched.

'The home advantage,' Dally Duncan said, 'is everything.'

For once he was right.

Trouble was brewing, though. The fallout between Taffy Vernon and the manager had never really been resolved and matters got worse when he asked to play in a Welsh testimonial for one of his mates and was given permission by one member of the staff – then stopped by another one. Eventually he played but it left an unpleasant taste in the mouth and from that moment we kept seeing newspaper headlines saying 'Hands Off Vernon' where the manager kept being asked about his availability.

For all Dally Duncan's words, once Taffy had put in a transfer request all the other clubs went on red alert. There was no shortage of offers but as soon as Johnny Carey picked up the phone there was only going to be one winner. Taffy signed for Everton in February 1960 and was an immediate success. Even with Eddie Thomas coming to us as part of the deal, and Louis Bimpson joining from Liverpool, the departure of the League's sharpest goalscorer left a huge hole in our team and the Blackpool game suddenly looked a lot more daunting.

Stan Matthews was still the main man there, although Stan Mortensen had retired. We scraped a 1–1 at Ewood and based on our recent League results didn't fancy the replay. In the event, we surprised ourselves and won 3–0 at Bloomfield Road. It was another gripping wait by the radio the following Monday.

'Tottenham Hotspur will play Blackburn Rovers . . .'

Now this was serious. Spurs were the favourites for the Double that year and were on fire in the League and Cup. They were the team to beat and they had big, quality players, including Dave Mackay, who I'd played behind in the British Army team.

It was 20 February 1960 when we went down to White Hart Lane. As usual, I met my dad outside the ground and gave him a ticket. Then it was in to prepare with the lads. It was cold as you'd expect and we didn't have tracksuits or anything like that then, so everyone just jogged on the spot in the changing room until it was time to run out for a warm-up. We didn't have any of the rituals you get today with the whole squad out there for half an hour before the match, cones and all that training paraphernalia. We literally had five minutes to run out, get our legs warmed up and our muscles going, then back inside until the ref knocked on the door. It's ridiculous when you think about it. Eleven players dancing in the shower area because that had the biggest open space, all of us doing star jumps and sprinting on the spot just to keep everything ticking over.

It's fair to say we weren't expected to win this one, but we'd beaten City the week before and, whatever Dally Duncan said, we all felt on top of our game. In the end it went our way. Whatever Spurs threw at us, we gave them back with knobs on. There's something about cup competitions that gets the blood rushing. In the League there's always the next week to try to put things right. In the FA Cup it's instant death – and that day we avoided it. It finished 3–1 and it was like we'd won the Cup.

Even the Blackburn directors were celebrating that little victory. As we came off the pitch I could see old Forbes, our chairman, with a face like the Cheshire Cat. He was pumping every lad's hand as they walked by. Then I realised – he wasn't just shaking their hands – he was putting something in them!

The rules on bungs and other financial misdeeds were very tight back then and you weren't allowed to offer any incentive other than contracted wages. But we'd all heard from friends in other teams that if they'd won a particularly important match, one of their governors would slip them a few bob as a 'thank you'. I'd never had anything like that, not since the Brigadier had given me a holiday for winning the Artillery Cup. Blackburn Rovers were too tight to buy new socks – there was no way they were wasting money on handouts for the players. I'd been there five years and I'd never got a sausage.

But as I got closer to Mr Forbes I could see he was definitely palming something into everyone's hand. Harry Leyland was walking next to me.

'Hey, Harry,' I said, 'I think we're on a little earner here.'

'I reckon you're right,' he said. 'What do you think it will be? A tanner?'

'I'd be happy with a pound note,' Matt Woods said.

'I'll let you know in a second,' I said, and I stuck out my hand to Mr Forbes.

'Well done, Whelan,' he said. Then, with a wink, he added, 'A little something to show my appreciation.'

I felt his hand close over mine like he was going to shake it, and sure enough, something was definitely pushed into my palm. I couldn't wait to get out of sight of the crowd to see what I'd got. When I opened my hand I couldn't believe my eyes.

Right behind me Harry and Matt were just as shocked. It wasn't a tanner or a fiver or a pound note.

We'd all been given a Mint Imperial.

'Tight bastard!' Harry said. 'He could at least have given us a packet each.'

Back in the changing room you have never heard language like it! When the chairman dared to stick his head round the door a few minutes later, the air was suddenly filled with flying Mint Imperials.

I think he got the point.

Whatever era you play in, the fixture list is always capable of throwing up a few coincidences. The week after we put Spurs out of the FA Cup we had them back at our place – and lost. But it got worse than that – for the following two weeks we were scheduled to play Burnley in the League and then in the quarter-finals. As it turned out, that wasn't the whole story.

There's no love lost between Blackburn Rovers fans and their local rivals Burnley and some of the chants you hear these days are pretty strong.

The language wasn't as ripe fifty years ago but the sentiment was the same. This was a derby no one wanted to lose.

The League match at Turf Moor was a pretty ugly affair and we lost 1–0. Seven days later we were back again and determined to get even.

Over the last few seasons Burnley had finished sixth and seventh and that year they would actually win the division, so they were a decent side. In the first half, we kept them quiet, hoping to hit them on the break after half-time. Unfortunately it didn't quite go to plan. We'd only just restarted when the ball fell to their winger, Brian Pilkington, and he put it past Harry Leyland.

'We can do it, lads, keep pushing,' I yelled.

Famous last words!

A few minutes later, Ray Pointer, the 'Blond Bombshell' as he was known, had made it two and then the youngster John Connelly hit another. There were twenty minutes to go and we were all but out of the Cup – and didn't the crowd let us know it.

There's nothing like 51,000 Burnley fans reminding teams how crap they are to sting you into action. I don't know if the home side started coasting or whether we just went up a gear. What I do know, though, is that things started to click for us.

We had a bit of luck to start us off. Ally MacLeod punted a ball into the penalty area, more in hope than expectation, and it ricocheted off the left back Alex Elder's boot and on to his arm.

The whistle went and the ref said, 'Penalty!'

I couldn't believe it – and neither could the home fans. The ref's name was Mr Hunt – and you can imagine some of the things he was being called. All the Burnley players were in a bit of shock at the decision, and they started moping around the pitch. Bryan Douglas didn't care how it had come though. He snatched the ball off the ref and planted it on the spot.

'Come on, Dougie,' I thought. 'We're not going down to this lot without a fight.'

A quick run-up then – *bang* – straight in the net. Their keeper Adam Blacklaw looked as hacked off as the rest of the team and he barely moved. He was just as stationary a few minutes later when Peter Dobing lobbed a beauty of a shot over his head.

A hungry cat was among the pigeons and the Burnley players didn't know which way to turn. They'd been twenty minutes away from the semi-final and now they were desperate just to cling on. All they had to do was stop us scoring again.

But in the last minutes we got a free kick and Matt Woods put the ball down. With so little time on the clock I was praying he'd smack it straight at goal – and he did. But as soon as it left his foot I could see the goalie had it covered. As Blacklaw came for it, Mick McGrath dived in and stuck out his boot. The ball flicked off him, against the post and in.

We'd done it! From three down to 3–3 – and now they were coming back to our place.

For our third match against the Clarets in a fortnight we had our tails up. Footballers are a superstitious bunch and the way we'd pulled back that draw meant a lot. To a few of us it said the Burnley match was ours. They had other ideas, though, and despite our best efforts the ninety minutes ended goalless. It was extra time now, and our last chance to assert ourselves. Eventually Peter Dobing got the break and slid the ball home. As Burnley pushed for the equaliser a few minutes later, Ally MacLeod banged in number two. When Mr Hunt, the same referee, blew to end the match we all fell to the floor exhausted.

After all the drama of the derby I was relieved to get Sheffield Wednesday next. There's no home advantage when you get to the last four, so we met the Owls at Maine Road, home of Man City. As we went out on to the pitch you could feel the weight of expectation physically making running harder. Every tackle that went in wasn't just to win that match – it was to get us into the final.

It was to get us to Wembley.

Wednesday were another quality team then. Don Megson – Gary's father – played right back for them and he was a decent pro, old Meggy. But we had something special that day. Derek Dougan had a reputation for being a bit of a 'homer' – he preferred to turn it on when he had 50,000 supporters behind him. But that day he was on fire. He scored the first goal, a brilliant solo effort, and we were away. They never really recovered and we won 2–1. We'd done it. We'd reached the final.

When Spurs beat Arsenal 5–1 to get to Wembley for the Carling Cup final in 2008, they celebrated like they'd already won the thing. It's such a big deal for players knowing that you're going to play at the home of football, and we were no different. Rovers being Rovers, we had to find our own celebration, but a local company called Duttons said they would do something after the match. If we won there'd be a party – if we didn't they'd still put on a meal for us and our wives. That night we all went down to a pub right on the river in Great Harwood, just outside Blackburn, and had a right old knees-up.

It wasn't a party like you'd see footballers having these days. There was no drinking culture then at Blackburn. Only some of the older pros who had signed from Everton used to have a beer because they were twenty-eight, twenty-nine. Apart from my mam's egg-and-sherry cocktail I never touched alcohol. I didn't take my first proper drink until I was twenty-seven and I still don't enjoy spirits now.

A lot of people say football has changed a lot, and in many ways it has. But in plenty of others it's exactly the same, and the one thing that hasn't changed in half a century is the way footballers think. If there's a World Cup or another big tournament coming up, all the international players take their foot off the pedal in the League. They don't mean to but subconsciously they've got their minds elsewhere. They don't run for fifty-fifty balls any more in case they pick up a knock, they pull out of challenges they would go for any other week. It's exactly the same when there's a cup final on the horizon. No one wants to get injured and miss the big day.

That's exactly what happened to us. Between playing Wednesday in March and the final in May, we barely won a ball, let alone a match. West Brom, Leicester, Man U, Birmingham and even Luton all turned us over. We were in freefall in the League and what made it worse was the steady progress of our neighbours at Turf Moor. If they weren't careful they were in real danger of winning the division – they only had the small matter of Wolverhampton Wanderers to beat.

That's where the manager should have stepped in and earned his money.

'Hey, MacLeod, you're not pulling your weight – you're out.'

'Whelan, you're not giving me one hundred per cent – I'm resting you next match.'

But Dally Duncan never said any of these things. Maybe he was as excited about Wembley as we were or maybe he was scared to say anything out of turn in case we told him where to shove it. But he was too weak and we knew it. He might have come to us with a reputation of being a hard man, but when we needed a leader with a bit of spine he wasn't that man.

At home Pat and I talked about the final non-stop. She and the rest of the girls had got their tickets and transport sorted by the club. The plan was that whatever the outcome of the match, we would all go out for a banquet the Blackburn directors had arranged for us afterwards.

It's incredible the effect a cup final has on a town. I was used to being able to go anywhere in Blackburn without being bothered. Yes, people recognised me and I was always addressed by my name in shops and restaurants, but it was respectful and generally folk were just interested in whether I was fit to play or not. Now everywhere I turned I had a stranger asking me for a ticket for Wembley!

These days players aren't allowed to sell their ticket allocation but back then the black market was an accepted part of a footballer's income. It helped to look after your family, put food on the table. If you were lucky enough to get to a cup final, you were handed a hundred tickets for friends and family – and if you chose to sell them, that was your business. I had a queue of people willing to pay £3.10 for a 3/6 ticket and everyone in the club was doing the same. And who could blame us? The players were the last ones to benefit financially from the occasion.

Our FA Cup match was the first time the final had been broadcast throughout Europe by television. They said an estimated 100 million people watched it, and that's on top of the 100,000 people in Wembley Stadium. And what did I get paid? £28.10 before tax – and three quid of that came from the Milk Marketing Board because we had done adverts for them saying that after every training session we all drank a glass of milk! There were photos plastered all over town showing us standing there with white moustaches from the milk. That was my first taste of marketing and I was amazed at the power it had over people.

The dearest seat at Wembley was about £2 and the cheapest was three and six – so if you say the average is a pound, 100,000 of those is a lot – and that's before you get your slice of television money. Even if it's split three ways between the two finalists and the Football Association, Rovers still got a third of it – but the players didn't get a look-in.

I look back now and I think, how could they rob footballers like that? And where did all that money go?

It was the principle of knowing that the directors were enjoying a handsome pay-day on the back of our hard work that bothered us. Honestly, though, we would all have played that game for nothing.

Although our League form was going from bad to worse, we all knew the reason – we were saving ourselves for 7 May. On the other hand, Wolves were still going hammer and tongs in the Championship so they couldn't rest for a minute.

'That's got to count in our favour,' Ally said. 'They'll be knackered when they get to us.'

It's fair to say we were all quietly confident – but then disaster struck. In our last match before the final, Derek Dougan started limping. After the game the manager was straight over to him.

'Have you got a problem, Derek?'

'No, boss. Just saving myself, you know?'

'I'll be the one to decide that, you lazy beggar,' Dally said, but that was it – his interrogation was over and Dougan got changed and left the ground.

I heard this little exchange between them and I didn't like it. I'd seen the way Dougan was walking on the pitch. I'd seen the way he'd tried not to limp as he came off and I knew full well what he was up to.

He'd pulled a muscle and he didn't want the boss to find out because he knew he'd miss the final.

I didn't know what an injury was until we got promoted to the First Division. I was Crunch Whelan and I could bounce back from anything. That first season in the big time, though, soon opened my eyes.

We were playing Preston North End at home and as I ran for a ball something went in the back of my leg. This pain shot right up my back and I just fell flat on my face. Our trainer was only a few yards away so I yelled, 'What's up with my leg, Jack? I can't run! I can't run!'

He said, 'You've pulled a muscle, you daft bugger! Get off that pitch now.'

So off I went. These days that would have been the end of it but there weren't any substitutes back then – you only left the pitch if you were unconscious. I made my way down the tunnel, wincing with every step, and Jack was waiting for me. He took a giant roll of Elastoplast bandage and wrapped it around my thigh again and again. He'd looped it about seven times, top to bottom, then he said, 'You'll live, soldier – now get back on that pitch – you're playing centre forward!'

It's criminal to keep on playing when you're injured because you just tear the muscle further, but we didn't know that then. What we did know was that defenders have to be super-mobile, but an injured centre forward can just hang about and get in the way – and if he's lucky set a goal up or score one himself.

So one of the other lads dropped back into defence and up I went – and within ten minutes I'd scored!

The record books show that D Whelan got the first goal of the match – but they don't say how I scored it. Ally MacLeod whipped in a corner and all I wanted to do was get in a few defenders' way. I saw the ball coming my way so I jumped as high as I could. The pain in my thigh was unbearable, and perhaps that's why I completely missed the ball with my head. But it smacked against my shoulder and flew past the goalie, an old Wigan lad called Fred Else.

'You jammy git,' he shouted.

'They all count, Fred!' I laughed, and jogged slowly back for the restart.

I spent the next ten minutes trying not to do anything other than loiter around Fred's goal because the pain was becoming unbearable and I couldn't move. Suddenly a ball was knocked up the middle of the park and all thoughts of pain left my mind.

'I'm having that,' I thought, and I leapt in the air again, intending to flick the ball on for Dougie.

Fred Else knew full well my last attempt at a header had been a fluke so he didn't expect me to get this one either. He came charging out of his goal, but as I flicked the ball it looped straight over Dougie – and straight over Fred into the empty net.

Two lucky goals – and all because I'd pulled a muscle.

Believe it or not, they weren't my only goals – I scored another one against Sheffield Wednesday in a similar situation when I had been injured and told to go up front and make a nuisance of myself. After that you could see the manager thinking, 'I've got a secret weapon here.'

A bit later during a match against West Brom, one of the strikers had to go off with a serious knock so Dally Duncan said, 'Whelan, get yourself up the front.' It was a gamble, but I'd be alongside Mike England, who had come up through the youth system two years behind me. I went as centre forward and Michael moved to inside forward and it worked a treat – at least I thought it did. I set up two goals for Mike and he took them beautifully – but the manager didn't notice my part at all. He was disappointed his master stroke hadn't resulted in me scoring – and he never played me up front again.

I was back training within ten days of the Preston match and on the Friday before Saturday's game I was put through my paces.

'I want you to do four laps of the track,' Jack Weddle said. 'Proper pace – no slacking. Then ten sprints – fifty yards full whack.'

It was standard procedure to really put the pulled muscle through its paces. There was no point sending someone on to the pitch if their leg was going to collapse again – before substitutions you were as good as throwing the game away.

I plodded around the track as fast as I could and Jack seemed happy. Then I started the sprints. I was nervous on the first couple but my leg seemed to be holding. Then on the tenth sprint it went – *boomf* – just like that and I was straight back where I'd started.

This is the injury Michael Owen has been plagued with so much, though at least these days they can give you a scan and see if there's any scar tissue in the muscle. But then, all you could do was wait and see. The physio would say, 'You're out for a fortnight. Rest it for a week then you can start to jog,' which is so wrong. You need ten days minimum, depending on how bad it is. So on that occasion I was out another couple of weeks, five weeks in all, just because they were bringing me back too soon.

Our physio was an old fella named Joe and then there was a doctor called Dr Burke. Joe was as qualified as any physio – it came entirely down to how many different injuries you'd experienced. He always wanted to give players a rest but the manager put him under pressure to get us back on that field as quickly as possible.

I hadn't been back playing long when my leg just locked in a game against Man City. I couldn't believe it – I'd never even bruised my ankle before the First Division and now I was limping off again.

This time it was different – my leg just locked while I was running. It wouldn't straighten and I fell straight over again. Dr Burke had travelled with us and he immediately knew what was up. 'You've torn your cartilage – it's an operation for you next week.'

I was sent to Manchester with the fella who used to operate on the United team. He put me through an X-ray machine but on X-rays you can't see cartilage, only bone. These days they can go in and trim the cartilage in the knee with keyhole surgery. It's totally non-intrusive and they just shave off the bits that are causing the problem. There were no such techniques when I went under a general anaesthetic. When I woke up the doctor had just whipped the whole lot out! To this day I have no cartilage in that knee and I suffer all sorts of other complaints now because of it.

I was in bed for a week and then on crutches for another three weeks. It was a serious operation to recover from because you're talking about eight or ten stitches across the knee. When I came round from the operation I found myself lying in a bed with my leg completely suspended in the air. Half an hour later the doctor explained all.

'I want you to keep it like that,' he said. 'I need to keep the stitches in the knee protected and we're going to let gravity bend the leg for us.'

It was so uncomfortable having my legs several feet above my body but the three days eventually passed and the doctor returned. He gave my leg a thorough going-over and pronounced himself satisfied.

'Right, we're going to let nature take its course,' he said. 'I'm going to lift your leg out of the sling and let gravity go to work. You shouldn't feel a thing.'

I watched nervously as he got hold of my leg. It had been suspended for so long that I'd lost half my sensation in it and it didn't even feel like me.

But I had to admire the man because as he lifted it, the leg below the knee started to fall. Ever so slightly at first, then lower and lower.

'There you are!' the doctor beamed. 'It's bending.'

It was bending all right – too well. Suddenly there was a tearing sound and a column of blood shot straight out of my wound and into the air like a hot-water geyser.

'Christ! I'm exploding!'

I went white – then green – then red as the blood splattered down all over the bed. I was covered, the doctor was covered and the floor was a mess.

I thought I was dying, but even though he was caked in my blood the doctor hadn't moved. He was still holding my leg and completely unfazed.

'Don't worry about that,' he said cheerily.

'Don't worry? My knee's just burst open!'

'We'll get you stitched up again in no time – but at least you've bent your leg!'

As our date at Wembley drew closer, the subject of injuries was on everyone's minds. We were all aware that Derek Dougan was not fully fit – all, that is, except for Dally Duncan.

As the days passed and the manager still hadn't picked him up on it I began to panic. We had to hope that even if Dougan made it to London he'd be caught out there. 'The sprint test will catch him out. He'll never pass that.'

We all caught the Preston train on Wednesday morning and checked into a lovely hotel just outside London, where we could train and play a few rounds of golf. It was a very nice place – not what we normally got with Blackburn. As each day went by I could feel the nerves tightening among a lot of the players, although I was more interested in monitoring Dougan's fitness.

'They've got to notice soon!' But so far he was getting away with it.

On the Friday afternoon we all got on the bus to have a look at Wembley and acclimatise ourselves for the following day. For me it was just like any other journey to an away ground. I tried to imagine how it would look the next day when there were crowds along the streets.

'I wonder if they'll turn out for us?' I thought. I needn't have worried.

We weren't permitted to train on the fabled Wembley pitch but we were allowed to have a walk on it. As soon as I stepped foot on that lush, green grass I felt like I was walking on a carpet.

'Oi, Dougie,' I said, 'where's all the mud?'

'You'll find it!'

Wembley Stadium back then wasn't this big commercial machine that hosted pop concerts and American football games. As for the idea of tarmacking it for a motor festival like they do now, forget it. Only international matches were played there, plus cup finals. It was only used about six times a year maximum and it felt like it.

Compared with the pitches we were playing on it was completely alien. We had no irrigation then, no under-soil heating – and you certainly couldn't lay a new pitch during an international break like they do today. The grass you kicked off on in August was the same as the grass you finished on in May – if there was any left. Normally by April we were playing on mud. There were huge areas, especially around the goals, where there hadn't been a blade of grass for weeks, and because by then the weather had warmed up it was solid, like playing on concrete. But that was the way we knew.

At Wembley it was like walking on a trampoline.

'This will take a bit of getting used to,' I thought.

We'd already been told that we wouldn't be allowed to run on it before the ref blew his whistle the next day. Walking on it in our normal shoes was one thing, but they didn't want a single stud marking it until the ref led the players out at ten to three. To me that was ludicrous. It meant all eleven of us would be forced to jump around in the dressing room, doing high kicks, stationary sprints, anything we could to get some blood flowing through the veins. By the time we stepped into the tunnel our muscles would still be cold.

Nothing could prepare a player for running on that luscious green turf, as the history books proved. The year before, Nottingham Forest had beaten Luton Town 2–1 in the final but that wasn't why it was remembered. There was a record amount of stoppage time for injuries that day as players went down like flies on the springy surface. Worst of all, goalscorer Roy Dwight was carried off with a broken leg after thirty-three minutes. In the 1952 final Arsenal lost Walley Barnes to a twisted knee, which was blamed on the pitch, and then three years later Man City's Jim Meadows suffered the same thing in the same part of the park. The following year Bert Trautmann broke his neck, although he famously played on.

So that was four games which had been ruined by a combination of an unusual playing surface and the rule that banned substitutions. To a man, the organisers, the FA, and the players must have been praying there'd be no repeat this year. It was one more thing to think about as I prepared for the following day's game.

Something was obviously on Dally Duncan's mind as well while we were there, and he called Derek Dougan over.

'About bloody time!' I thought. 'He's going to drop him.'

'I'm a bit concerned about that leg of yours, Derek,' Duncan said.

'Nothing wrong there, boss, I'm fine.'

'Well, you look like you're walking a bit odd to me so I want you to do a fitness test.'

The Wembley groundsman was there to make sure we didn't whip out a football or anything like that and mess up his precious turf but he said he didn't mind us running up the touchline.

'OK, Derek, let's see you run to the corner flag and back,' the manager said. Dougan just nodded then set off at a decent pace.

'That's got to be hurting him,' I said to Ally. 'He'll never get through the sprints.'

But those sprints never came. Dougan was a terrific player but he didn't really rely on his speed and the manager was happy enough to see him cover the ground. Normally for a hamstring test you get told to do ten sprints, like I had been made to do. Dougan wasn't asked to do one. He just jogged back to the bus and that was it: test over.

All the way back to the hotel the lads were buzzing with how it would feel to actually play on that amazing pitch the next day. We tried to imagine what it would be like when the stadium was full. Old Trafford was one thing, but a packed Wembley was meant to be something else. We couldn't wait to find out.

That night was when the atmosphere really changed. We'd been keeping a lid on our emotions to a large extent but by then the lads were kicking around on autopilot. Nobody could concentrate on anything so Ally suggested a night out at the dogs in Haringey.

'Do you think the boss will go for that?' I said.

Sure enough he did. He knew we didn't drink so that wasn't a problem, and it might do us good to relax.

'I'm sending Jack Weddle with you, though,' he warned. 'If anyone steps out of line – I'll be hearing about it.'

I don't think anyone really won any money that night but that wasn't the point. It was a team-building exercise. We were eleven blokes together and the next day we would be facing the opposition as one. And we were ready.

At least that's what we thought.

What we didn't know was that one of our crowd wasn't thinking about being part of a team at all. In fact that person had already written his transfer request back at the team hotel and had left it for the manager to find.

On the eve of the biggest game of our careers, and on a night when we were all bonding as a unit, one of our number was already thinking of getting out. It didn't occur to him to put the club first. It didn't occur to him to think of his team-mates and help them out. He just wanted what was best for him.

And his name was Derek Dougan.

Even though we'd had a dress rehearsal the day before, getting up and setting off for Wembley that day was a whole new experience. Ally MacLeod ate my breakfast as usual, but apart from that everything else seemed different. Before we set off Dally Duncan called us together and said he had something for us from the directors.

'We're getting some readies at last, are we?'

'Nothing like that, son. You're all getting one of these.'

Suddenly the trainer appeared holding a brand-new tracksuit in the Rovers colours.

'You've got one of these each, lads. Come and get them.'

Believe it or not, we were all very happy with this. We'd never had a

Rovers tracksuit before. We had our shirt and shorts and that was it. That's how tight the club was – they actually made us grateful to be getting a new piece of kit.

When we all got on the coach we were dressed the same – there was even a tracksuit for the twelfth man, who always travelled with us in case someone fell ill on the journey. But that wasn't the only thing that was different about the journey. This time we had a police escort.

Whipping our way through north London, not stopping at traffic lights, was a completely new sensation. It made me feel like royalty. And the closer we got, the more intense the feeling. Eventually even our coach got caught in traffic and I began to notice the pavements getting fuller and busier.

'They're not shoppers,' I realised. 'They've turned out to see us.'

It was just like I had seen on my sister's television. Hundreds of thousands of people lined the streets just to give us a wave. Most of them didn't even support Blackburn, they just loved the FA Cup and wanted to be part of it, just like us.

Everyone on the bus was really souped up. I never suffered from nerves but there was no denying this was a big game – the biggest I'd ever played. I looked around at the other faces on the bus. Harry Leyland, John Bray, Ronnie Clayton, Matt Woods, Mick McGrath, Louis Bimpson, Peter Dobing, Derek Dougan, Bryan Douglas and Ally MacLeod – they were all going through their own emotions, all trying to keep it together. Apart from Dougan, we were in the shape of our lives, we'd been working towards this. We were on a knife-edge. The level of anticipation was awesome. We knew we had to keep calm, keep focused. As much as I wanted to stand up and wave to all the fans out there, I knew I couldn't. But it was hard.

At half past one we turned into Wembley Way and it got even harder.

'Bloody hell, there're the Twin Towers!' someone said, and I felt a lump in my throat.

It's funny, I'd seen exactly the same building the day before and, yes, it had looked spectacular. But seeing it now, with the coach wading through a sea of people, was out of this world. That's when it hit me. That's when I realised I was going to play at Wembley.

Play in the biggest game in the world!

When the coach reached the stadium it didn't stop. Giant doors swung open and we just drove straight inside. It was like a James Bond movie. Then suddenly it was all systems go. We were shown our dressing room – we got the supposed 'unlucky' one – and then we were taken down the tunnel to have a look at the pitch. There were already thousands of people in the stadium and the noise when they saw us was incredible. I couldn't wait to get out there and hear the real thing.

Back in the dressing room, though, things didn't go to plan.

We all sat down on the benches, with our tracksuits over our kit, and tried to compose our thoughts. Dally Duncan normally said a few words at this point, and then Ron Clayton, the captain. I could usually take or leave whatever the manager said but this time he had my full attention.

'Lads,' he said, 'I need to tell you that this morning I received a letter. It was Derek, here.' He pointed at Dougan. 'He's asked for a transfer.'

What?

I couldn't believe what I was hearing. No one else could either. In a few seconds the place went from silence to a murmur of confusion to outright shouting.

'He's done what?'

'Chuck him out!'

'Drop him, boss!'

'You bloody traitor, Dougan!'

The air was blue and faces were red. My mind was all over the place. 'Why's he put in for a transfer now of all days? Is he being malicious? Does he want to wreck everything for us? Is he just that stupid?'

All I knew for sure was that Derek Dougan was a pillock. He didn't care about anyone or anything apart from himself. Because he was a laugh, a bit of a character, and he knew where the goal was, we'd put up with it. But now he'd shown his true colours and we all wanted him thrown off the team.

A strong manager would have done exactly that. But this was Dally Duncan.

'Dougan plays,' he said.

'But he's not even fit!'

'Dougan plays and that's the final word!'

So that was our preparation for the biggest game of our lives. It took the shine off everything. When we walked out to meet the royal party on the pitch before the match I, like the rest of the team, was still fuming. We had called Dougan every name we could think of.

The Wolves players must have wondered what the hell was going on.

When we stepped out of that tunnel we were met by a solid roar of sound and everything else went clean out of my mind. A hundred thousand voices all going off at once will do that to you. It was actually mind-blowing and as I lined up to shake hands with the dignitaries I wasn't thinking about Dougan. I was trying to drink in the occasion but it was almost too big to get my head round. And I had another problem.

It was a blindingly hot day – and we were all sweltering in our new uniforms. But, as Dougie had said, 'If I've got a tracksuit I'm going to wear the damn thing,' and we all agreed. But as I stood there in the afternoon sun I was really regretting it. If you look back at the film of the day you can see we were sweating buckets – and the Wolves lads, in their shorts and tops, were loving it.

I noticed a few cameras around the ground and thought of my mam watching the match at home. She'd never come to see me play and she wasn't going to start now, but at least it was being televised.

I looked up at the players' area of the crowd and tried to spot some familiar faces. Somewhere in that mass of cheering bodies were my dad and Jimmy, Bill Dean and just about every other relative I had. James Gibson, from Wigan Boys Club, was also there somewhere.

And most important of all, so was Pat. She was there, pride of place, with the other players' wives and girlfriends. They were our biggest fans and I knew I'd hear their voices soon enough. They always made themselves heard.

Finally, at three o'clock on the nose, Mr Howley the referee blew his whistle and the place erupted. If the noise when we'd come down the tunnel had been huge, this was something else. I thought the walls were in danger of coming down. For the first minute or two I really had to fight to concentrate on the match. The atmosphere was out of this world.

I could see that Wolves had their tails up, right from the off. They put out a strong team: Malcolm Finlayson, George Showell, Gerry Harris, Eddie Clamp, Bill Slater, Ron Flowers, Norman Deeley, Barry Stobart, Jimmy Murray, Peter Broadbent and Des Horne. But we were pretty handy as well and, as we kept reminding ourselves, they'd been fighting on two fronts, trying to keep the League within their grasp as well. We'd only had this match to concentrate on for the last six weeks.

I didn't play in my usual position in that final. Bill Eckersley was our usual left back but about three weeks earlier he'd stunned us all in training. He just turned up one morning and said to the manager and the lads, 'I am retired. I won't be coming in again.' And that was that. He'd just thrown his hat in and walked out of the game. He had seventeen caps for England and even at thirty-five he was still a very good player, but he'd had enough.

We all sat there, stunned, for a few minutes. Then the manager called me over.

'You'll be playing in Bill's position for the cup final,' he said. 'So you'd better get used to it now.'

So that May day I lined up on the left-hand side against a fella called Norman Deeley. He'd played a few games for England as well and he was pretty nippy but I took one look at him and knew I had the measure of him. He was a tiny lad, about twenty-seven but only 5'4", and I knew he wouldn't give me much trouble. One 'crunch' from me and he'd be in my pocket for the rest of the afternoon.

I was right. I had him frightened half to death right from the start. About twenty minutes in I got him in a tackle and I really hurt him. He was getting away from me so I just clogged him, perhaps a little unfairly, but not by the standards of the day. We didn't have yellow cards then, and to be sent off you'd have to really deserve it, so I got away with that. But I could see Deeley was in pain and that was exactly what I'd intended.

'He's finished for the rest of the game,' I thought. 'He won't bother me now.'

To be honest, we needed all the help we could get. Watching Dougan limp around up front was embarrassing. He should have declared himself unfit but he was too arrogant, too selfish for that. Louis Bimpson was a lovely lad, and a great big, galloping centre forward. But he was no Taffy Vernon and boy did we need a player like him now with Dougan no use to anyone.

But then things got worse.

Stobart put a low cross into the box and I saw Harry Leyland come for it. But before he could get there, Mick McGrath stuck out a foot and – *bang* – it was in the net. We were an own goal down. Now we really had to roll up our sleeves.

'Come on, lads,' Ronnie Clayton said at the restart. 'Get them to half-time then we'll give them something to think about.'

It was a solid plan – but it didn't work out like that.

In the forty-second minute, a fifty-fifty ball came in between me and Norman Deeley. I thought he would still be trying to get there ahead of me, even after the crunch I'd just given him. He was that type of player. So I set off, determined to win the ball.

And I did. I got there seconds before Deeley. But that was when I realised he had no intention at all of racing me for that ball.

He was going for me.

As I was running I heard a loud crack and felt my knee suddenly burn with pain. It took a second to realise what had happened and by then I was going too fast to stop. Still moving, I looked down and saw my injured leg lifting through – and it was bending the wrong way below the knee. Instinctively I flung my hands down to hold it and threw myself over before I could put any more weight on it. If it had touched the ground it would have snapped in a dozen more places.

I was in agony and I knew I was out of the game.

Eight

DID WE WIN?

We were a goal down and already as good as playing with ten men. And now I was out for the count.

Norman Deeley had got me good and proper, about a foot over the ball. There was no question in my mind that he had meant to do it. This was revenge for the tackle I'd made on him. The lads came running at once as I was rolling on the turf. They'd all heard both bones snap and they knew as well as I did that I was done for. I thought I was going to black out with pain, but at least help was on its way – or so I thought. Actually my agony was just beginning.

If somebody breaks their leg now, the first man to reach him on the pitch will have an injection ready to kill the pain. Then they have back-bracing stretchers that keep everything in place, or sometimes even little golf carts to transport you as comfortably as possible. We didn't have that then, not even at Wembley. A physio strapped a few yards of Elastoplast around my leg, which was absolutely unbearable, and then two fellas hoisted me on to this old canvas stretcher with two poles running up the side to bear the weight. Every step they took I swung into one of them and the sensation just made me want to be sick each time. You could hear a pin drop in that stadium as I went off and the last thing I wanted was everyone to hear me screaming, but I'd never felt pain like it.

But that was just the start. These days there'd be an air ambulance on standby for an event like that, but I knew that if I was seen by a doctor in under half an hour I was doing well.

The fellas took me into the dressing room and laid me down across one of the slipper baths, so I was suspended where my body sagged through the canvas. I could see what they were thinking – but it meant that my leg was pushed in the air, and that was the last thing I wanted. There was nothing else anyone could do for me until the ambulance had made its way through the Wembley traffic.

I had completely forgotten about the match but suddenly I was surrounded by the lads. It was half-time. As if things weren't going badly enough for them, imagine walking down the tunnel and being met by the sight of me on that stretcher. I would have done anything to not put them through it. They had to go out there and fight for their lives in the second half – but how could they focus on anything when they had to sit and look at me?

I know now that seeing me like that absolutely knackered them. It knocked the stuffing clean out of everyone.

I couldn't stop thinking I'd let them down. Ally MacLeod had to drop back into my position and cover the whole left wing on his own. We had a tight defence but it was going to be tough.

The second half kicked off and my ambulance still hadn't arrived. Eventually, though, one turned up and I was taken to the hospital in Wembley. I felt every bump on every road on the way there – and still no relief for the pain. Finally we stopped and the doors were yanked open. A doctor in a white coat was standing outside the hospital.

'I was watching you on television at home, David,' he said in a Polish accent, 'and as soon as you went down I grabbed my coat. I knew you'd be coming here.'

As he spoke the doctor was running his fingers along my broken leg. Even that hurt like hell but then he said, 'I've got something here to help you' – and he showed me a needle full of morphine.

Wow, that stuff really works. Within five minutes I felt like I could get back on the pitch. I couldn't believe what all the fuss had been about.

Now things had calmed down they wheeled me into the hospital and straight into the X-ray room. Even before the results came back the doctor said, 'I'll be operating in ten minutes. Your leg needs setting immediately.'

I went under the knife at half past four – the match at Wembley was still going on.

The doctor was the last person I saw before I went under and the first person I noticed when I woke up. I was being pushed along the corridor to a private room and he was there next to me.

As soon as I opened my eyes there was only one thought on my mind.

'Hello, Doc,' I said. 'Did we win?'

He shook his head and I knew it was bad news.

'You lost 3–0.'

The tears shot out of me. The floodgates just opened. All the emotion that had been building up in me all day, all the tension, all the anger with Dougan, the battle with Deeley and then the agony of the injury, it all came pouring out in one torrent of tears. I thought, 'Shit, we've lost the cup final. We've lost it.' It is so hard to explain the emotion but I didn't know what else to do. I just cried.

What he didn't tell me was that Norman Deeley had scored two of the goals. I think that would have pushed me over the edge!

I'm sorry to say I can't remember that doctor's name but I would like to thank him here for the wonderful job he did resetting my tib and fib and for the speed with which he handled everything.

Funnily enough, the effort of that little outburst sent me back to sleep again. The next time I woke up I was in bed and sitting at my side was James Gibson.

I remember him saying, 'Dave, can you hear me? How are you, lad? How are you feeling?' and for a few moments I couldn't remember where I was. Then it all came back to me, the match and, most importantly, the score. Mr Gibson was good company and about ten minutes later my dad walked in. They'd both left the stadium as soon as I'd gone down and it had taken them that long to find me.

About an hour after that I had another visitor – Pat. She'd seen everything and feared the worst. But without mobile telephones and with transport a problem she'd been stuck with the rest of the girls in the crowd before she could get away. She had a bit of a cry when she saw me, but I assured her I was fine.

A short while after I heard a commotion in the corridor. The door flung open and there were half a dozen friendly faces all anxiously peering round looking for me.

'All right, Crunch?' Ally said. 'How are you feeling?'

'A damn sight worse now I've seen your face!'

Derek Dougan hadn't bothered coming, of course. He hadn't dared. But I noticed my good mate Bryan Douglas was missing as well.

'Where's Dougie?' I asked. If there was one man I knew I could count on to support me it was that fella.

'Haven't you heard?' Ronnie said. 'His wife's gone into labour.'

'But that's meant to be next week,' I said.

'She must have been jealous of you getting all the attention – she's in another hospital in town. Dougie's there at the moment, then he'll be along later.'

Sure enough he turned up later and we had our usual giggle. He'd had a little boy, so he was filled with smiles even though the rest of us were moping around feeling sorry for ourselves. When he walked in the door I could see he was carrying something.

'It's your shirt, Dave. A souvenir – and I've got your medal as well.'

I forgot about the medal. There's probably only 2,000 people in the world who have FA Cup medals. Unfortunately mine says 'loser' on it and not 'winner', but I was still happy to see it. And I couldn't believe they'd managed to get permission to keep the shirts. The club had printed special 'Blackburn Rovers, Wembley, 1960' messages on the back so they were real collector's items. Ron and Dougie both signed mine and it's still hanging in the snooker room at my house.

When it came to the evening though, nobody wanted to go out to the banquet the club had organised. In the end I persuaded them all to go.

'Your wives will be expecting you,' I said. 'They deserve a night out even if you don't!'

Dougie's wife obviously couldn't go and I wasn't going to make it either. But I was shocked when Pat said she was staying with me.

'I can't go out enjoying myself with you lying here,' she said.

'Don't be daft. They don't let visitors stay late anyway. There's no point you moping around on your own in London.'

I told her not to feel guilty. She argued for half an hour but in the end agreed.

Before Ronnie had left I asked him about Dougan.

'He's gone,' he said. 'He picked up his medal, waved to the crowd, got changed and sodded off.'

It was a sad state of affairs. People come and go in football all the time but there's a wrong and a right way of doing things. It was like that then and it's like that now.

I like things to be done in the right manner – as you'll see later on. Years later I had a lad at Wigan called Pascal Chimbonda and he put me in mind of Dougan. We picked the lad up from Marseille for £500,000 and he did very well for us, voted best right back in the PFA's Team of the Year. I think that must have clouded his mind. On 7 May 2006 – fifty-six years to the very day from that cup final – Wigan lost a thrilling game to Arsenal in the final match of the season. Immediately after the match Chimbonda walked up to the manager, Paul Jewell, and handed over a written transfer request. He didn't even take his boots off, he just did it right in front of everyone else. Paul did his nut and I did too.

That's not the way you do things. You've got team-mates to think of, your manager and your fans.

Had he come in and said, 'Chairman, can I go to a bigger club?' I would have said, 'Yes, of course you can.' I will say that to any of our players. If you want to go to a bigger club, I don't blame you. Just be up front, ask the question, and if we can do it, we will. We let Bainesy – Leighton Baines – go to Everton. Aston Villa, who were challenging for Europe, came in for Heskey and that was OK as well. I don't believe in holding players back. If a big club comes in for them I just do not believe in trying to hang on to them against their will. I think Manchester United would have come for Chimbonda eventually. Alex Ferguson had virtually admitted as much. I told Chimbonda that, but he wanted to get down to London with Spurs didn't he? He wanted to be a big time Charlie down there.

While I was in hospital, I had dozens of visitors and hundreds of cards – with one notable exception. Not one person from Wolverhampton

Wanderers bothered to get in touch. Not one player and not one official. They didn't send flowers or even a note saying, 'Sorry about the injury – good luck for the future.' Dally Duncan told me that Stan Cullis, their manager, hadn't even bothered to ask him after the match how I was.

And I know why.

They knew Deeley was well out of order for that tackle. And they also knew it could cost me my career. They all knew he had gone way over the top of the ball, it was a totally illegal and cowardly attack. If that tackle had happened today, Deeley would have been annihilated. The media would roast him. But you could get away with it then, and to this day not one of that team has ever spoken to me about it.

The worst thing is, I've seen stories written saying that as I was stretchered off I waved to Deeley to show no hard feelings. What a load of cobblers. He knows what he did. And he knows I wasn't waving at him. If anything, I was telling Dougie to keep the lads fighting.

The next day Pat came in to tell me about the night. They'd all had a meal then gone on to a show. I was sorry not to be there but I was glad she'd gone. Now I had to persuade her to go home. Once again she didn't want to leave me, but staying in London wasn't at all straightforward. And, I said, 'Someone needs to run the shop.'

On the Monday morning I was moved to another hospital in London to see a specialist. This fella was a pioneer with broken legs, the number-one thinker in the business according to the docs at Wembley. His theory was that you shouldn't lie in bed with a broken leg because you're doing more damage than good. He wanted you to get up and have movement because he said the bone would repair itself much quicker if you've got blood flowing. He was right, as it turned out, but this was very new science at the time, very radical, and it took me aback.

The first thing the specialist did was take a new X-ray to see what was going on under my plaster. He was pleased with what he saw.

'They've done a good job there,' he said. 'A fantastic piece of surgery, actually. I'm not going to touch it but I'm going to build up the plaster on your thigh and I'm going to carry all the weight on your hip.'

I nodded, doing my best to keep up.

Then he said, 'After I've done that, tomorrow I want you to walk.'

I understood that all right!

I said, 'You want me to what?'

'I want you to walk tomorrow.'

I looked at him like he was mad but he just smiled and got on with the plastering. Even though the break was just below the knee, he took it right up my leg until it covered my thigh. His intention was to put all the stress and all the weight on the hip. When you put the foot down, it was the hip that bore the brunt, nowhere lower.

That was the theory, anyway. The next morning he wanted to put it to the test. At that stage I still thought he was joking. I'd never heard anything so ridiculous as a man walking two days after he's broken his leg.

'Good morning, Mr Whelan,' he said. 'Time for our stroll in the park.'

I said, 'No way, I can't do that!'

Still smiling, he gave me a pair of crutches and a dressing gown and off we set. On the way down in the lift he said, 'Just to let you know, when we are in the park I'm going to take your crutches away. All I want you to do is take a stride. That's all.'

'If you take my crutches away the only thing I'll be doing is falling on my backside.'

'No, you won't. Trust me.'

When we got into the park I still expected him to say he was joking, but he wasn't. He took my crutches away and so I had to stand there balancing on one leg. 'If the lads could see me now,' I thought.

Then he said, 'Come on, man, what are you waiting for? Take a step.'

I put my good foot down first to get some momentum, then swung my plastered left leg through and felt it touch the ground. As soon as I could I got my right leg back down again before the pain hit me.

But it didn't come.

'You've done it!' he said. 'Well done. That's all I wanted to see. You can have your crutches back now.'

'Thank goodness for that!'

I'd proved to him and, more importantly, to myself that the maths behind the plaster had worked. I'd just put all my weight on a broken leg and I didn't feel a thing.

He kept me in until Wednesday and then I was allowed to sign myself out. A couple of porters took me in an ambulance to the station and then they stretchered me on to a train. I'd never travelled first class before, not on Blackburn's money, but I had a bit of luxury that time. I was lying down the whole way because I couldn't sit up and I did my best to sleep. When I was woken up by one of the porters I couldn't believe what I saw. The train was in Blackburn station and there must have been about a thousand people waiting there.

I thought the Queen must be in town. It took a few seconds for the truth to sink in.

'Are they waiting for me?'

'Of course they are,' the guard said. 'You're a hero.'

That was a surprise. I thought, 'I don't want all these people seeing me stretchered out of the train.'

I said to the porters, 'Sorry, lads, you've had a wasted journey – hand me those crutches, will you?'

I hobbled down the steps and immediately the sound of the crowd cheering did more to lift my spirits than any medicine. It was a lovely moment and I'm convinced it helped speed up my recovery. It had certainly got me off my backside, which the doctor would have been chuffed to bits about.

For that moment I felt I could even have walked without the crutches, but turning up at home I realised just how ill I was. Getting upstairs to the bathroom and the bedroom was the first problem. With plaster running from hip to toe, there was no way for me to climb the stairs normally – I tobogganed up and down on my backside, which took for ever. In the end Pat set up a bed downstairs for me. I hated putting her through all that but there was nothing I could do.

Every day she went to run the shop and I did my best to fend for myself, but everything took such a long time. I also noticed a pain in my instep that was getting worse. I had been home three days when it finally became unbearable.

It was the middle of the night and I hadn't slept a wink because my foot had been throbbing. Eventually I couldn't take it any more. It felt like it was ready to burst.

I woke Pat up and said, 'Something's wrong, this hurts too much.' She called an ambulance and I was taken into A&E at Blackburn Infirmary. Everyone there knew me so a doctor came out immediately to see what was wrong.

'What's up, Dave? How's your leg?'

I told him what had been going on, he took one look and said, 'Your plaster has got to come off.'

I was booked in for the morning and given some painkillers to help me grab a few hours' sleep. By the time I woke up, the club doctor, Dr Burke, had arrived.

He was as officious as ever and started saying, 'What's wrong? What's wrong?' but not really caring about the answer.

I said, 'I've got severe pain in my foot, Doc, and the doctor here says my plaster has to come off.'

He puffed himself up to his full height and said, 'Nobody is touching that plaster. That's been put on by a specialist in London. No one touches that without his say-so.'

I think he expected that to be the end of the matter but the Blackburn doctor looked him straight in the eye and said, 'Dr Burke, with the greatest respect, this is Dave Whelan here. I don't think he'd be complaining of pain if it wasn't very, very serious.' Then he turned to me and said, 'Dave, you've got two choices. I can take that plaster off and find out what's wrong. Or I might be cutting your leg off by tonight.'

I said, 'What do you mean?'

'I think you're developing gangrene. It's the only explanation for pain building up like that. I think the plaster is cutting into you.'

'What are you waiting for?' I said. 'Take the plaster off now!'

Still Dr Burke wasn't having it. 'I forbid you to touch that,' he said. 'It's been applied by the world's leading bone specialist.'

'Ignore him, Doc,' I said. 'Just do it. Please!'

'Right,' Burke said. 'I won't be party to this. I'm off.'

And that was it – he just walked out.

I was taken into an operating room and told to relax. Suddenly I heard a high-pitched buzzing noise from behind me and then a nurse stepped round my bed and handed the doctor a circular saw. Relax? It was like something you take trees down with.

I thought, 'One slip from this fella and he'll take my leg off whether I need it or not!'

Cutting a piece of plaster that runs right up your body is no easy matter. He had to run the spinning blade all the way up one side and then back down the other – but one jog or a cough and he would go a fraction too deep and into my skin. He knew that, and so did I.

I was so tense lying there I didn't breathe, let alone move my leg, and eventually he took the top plate off. He had a poke around at my ankle and said, 'You're very lucky. Another few hours and you would have lost the bottom part of the leg.'

I looked down and my foot was entirely black. It had gone septic and gangrene had set in right across it where the plaster had broken the skin. I felt sick in my stomach. The pain was bad enough – but losing my leg? What use would I be to anybody like that?

'Will it be OK, Doc?' I said.

'You'll be fine as soon as we get some antibiotics into you.'

When I'd calmed down and the drugs had been administered he explained that I'd been unlucky. There had been nothing wrong with the plaster that the Polish surgeon had put on, but the weight of the extra plaster on my hip had gradually pushed the whole thing down every time I used my crutches and eventually it had pierced the skin. That's how the infection had got in.

'There's no doubt in my mind that you would have lost your leg,' the doctor said. 'It might have been in four hours, it might have been six. But by this time tomorrow you wouldn't have had anything below the knee.'

That doctor at the infirmary was supreme, and what he put himself through to get my plaster back on was extraordinary. He said I needed to have my leg perfectly still in the air while the nurses coated it with plaster. Then it would have to be still for another five minutes while everything dried. And the way I was going to achieve this was by him holding my leg perfectly still in the air.

I thought, 'You'll be lucky holding it steady for that long.'

But he only did.

He got hold of my leg, either side of the break, and lifted it so the nurses could get to work. Only when they'd done everywhere apart from where he was gripping did he shift. I don't know if it was fifteen minutes or thirty. All I know is he didn't budge an inch while that was going on, not one iota. A fantastic man.

I was let out the next day but I knew I still had about four months ahead of me in plaster. I thought, 'What the hell am I going to do with myself during that time?'

Obviously there was the shop, but what I really enjoyed with that little business was all the buying from the wholesalers. Being stuck behind a counter all day wasn't really for me but I couldn't see how I could do anything else with my leg in plaster. After a few days of only seeing the shop walls I knew I had to get out.

'Where are you going?' Pat asked me when she saw me trying to get my coat on one afternoon.

'I'm going to the cash and carry. It's Friday.'

'And how are you getting there?' she said.

'I'm going to drive.'

The look on her face was a picture. OK, I wasn't really sure I could pull it off, but I had to try. We had an old Ford that was big enough to bring all my stock back in, so I hobbled out and weighed up the situation. Using my crutch I managed to get the seat tilted back so I'd have enough room to let my left leg hang straight. Then I climbed in and started the engine.

'This'll be fun,' I thought, and gave the accelerator a few revs with my right foot. Then I planted the end of my crutch on the clutch pedal and pushed it in. Leaning across with my right hand, I put the car in first gear and accelerated fast. Before I knew it, I was moving. The car must have looked like a kangaroo bouncing along the road, but that was good enough for me.

I'm sure Pat expected me to walk back into the shop, hat in hand, and admit defeat. But I'd actually managed to get the car going and I drove all the way to the wholesaler's and back like that. It was totally illegal, of course, but you could get away with more things like that in those days. The police weren't as interested in motorists as they are today.

Life wasn't all bad though. I was as proud as punch when Pat announced we were going to have a family and there was not a happier man in Blackburn when our son, Paul, was born at Queen's Park Hospital. I wasn't there at the birth, although I arrived within half an hour. It's no use saying that I wanted to be there, because I didn't. I'm afraid that didn't appeal to me at all, and at the time I think I would have been considered odd if I had gone.

Having children changes your life for ever. It's not just the practical things, having to get used to a house full of nappies. But now you have a reason to work even harder. You're not just providing for yourself or your wife, but you've got a little fella depending on you. If I needed more incentive to get back to playing football, that was it.

As the weeks went by the plaster came off and I was allowed to walk without a stick. Finally I went back for light training and before I knew it I was selected to play in a pre-season reserve game. Personally I thought it was a bit early for me, but Blackburn, like a lot of clubs, had a history of rushing players back.

I looked at the fixture list and my heart sank: we were playing Preston at Deepdale – and I'd be up against the maestro, Tom Finney. I hadn't played a game for months and now I had to go there and mark the best player who had ever lived.

Before the match I had a nice surprise when Tom came over to me and said, 'How are you, Dave? How's your leg recovering?'

I said, 'It's doing OK, I think. I'm just easing myself back in. I could do without playing against you though!'

Tom laughed. 'You'll be all right, lad,' he said. 'Good luck.'

I thought, 'Good luck? It will take more than that against him.'

The game kicked off and I held my own against the other lads but then came the moment I'd been dreading. Tom had picked up the ball on the halfway line and he was flying past our boys. He got to me and without taking my eyes off the ball I stuck out a leg. I've lost count of the amount of times I'd done that against him – and usually I'm left with my leg in thin air because he's danced past me. But this time was different.

I felt my boot connect with the ball.

I'd actually tackled Tom Finney!

You can imagine how I felt after that. I started flying into tackles with other players and really sank my teeth into the game. A few minutes later

I saw Tom coming at me again. Once more he got too close and I won the ball. 'How on earth did I do that?' I thought. And then I realised – he was letting me. Sure enough, another ball came over and I got it off him again. There was no other explanation. The man was letting me have it every time.

After the match I sought him out and said, 'Hey, Tom – you deliberately let me take the ball off you in that match. You normally skin me alive. What's going on?'

He looked to me and said, 'You need some confidence, son, and if you can get some confidence out of today's match it will do you the power of good in the future.'

I was bowled over by that. I thought, 'What a gentleman.'

Whenever I've seen him since I remind him of it and say, 'Tom, you're such a good sport, it's unreal. That was unnecessary and it's something I will never forget.'

Normally football is a ruthless game but he is not a ruthless man. He let me take the ball off him three times in a row because he thought it would help my rehabilitation in the game. It didn't matter to him that he looked like he couldn't beat me. He knew and I knew the truth and that's all he cared about. But he's a true gentleman; always has been and always will be. It was a great shame when he retired soon after because the Preston manager wouldn't let him do lighter training than the younger lads. At thirty-eight, I think he deserved it.

I managed to get through that match but I didn't make it back into the first team. Once the season kicked off I found myself playing with the A team, the B team or wherever a place needed filling. It was pretty soul-destroying watching my mates turning out for the first eleven and knowing that I should have been there. But I had to be honest with myself – my pace was nowhere near as electric as it had been, and for a defender that was crucial. In his prime, Derek Dougan could do a hundred yards in ten seconds and I was always able to race him over the first forty because I was lightning from a standing start. But I lost that with the injury. Look at Michael Owen – he's still a great player but his pace isn't a patch on what it used to be before his injuries.

Every Saturday when I wasn't picked I remembered the tackle that had done the damage. That wasn't the memory I wanted to have of Wembley but it was the only one I had.

The hardest part for me was knowing that I didn't deserve to be in the first team, either. In hindsight I know that I shouldn't have been playing at all at that stage. These days you don't whip a lad's plaster off and have him in matches so quickly. You have weeks, months of gym work, ball training and non-contact treatment. Rushing players back too soon is just asking for trouble because they either overcompensate for their injured leg by putting too much stress on the other leg, risking new injuries there, or they ignore their own body and ask too much of the fragile bones.

And that's what happened to me.

I was playing against Sheffield Wednesday in the reserves and I took a kick in the leg from their winger. I felt it come in and knew immediately that he'd got exactly the spot that had been broken before. Sure enough, that was me done for. It didn't break but it cracked. We both heard it. And that meant another six weeks in plaster.

I couldn't believe it. I wasn't a nice person to be around for a while after that – for the first time people started talking about me retiring from football. I can honestly say the thought hadn't entered my mind before. People have injuries all the time. I was only twenty-four. Who retires at twenty-four?

I'm a believer that a positive attitude can help you in all sorts of ways, and it was only by truly believing I would play again that I got through all the pain of the injury. You can't afford for one moment to think you're not going to make it back, otherwise the life drains out of you and you might as well call it a day.

When the plaster came off the second time I wasn't properly healed and I had a pronounced limp. That was when the club secretary came to see me with a proposition.

'David, we want to give you a testimonial match to help you in your retirement.'

'My what?' I said. 'I'm not retiring. I'm going to play again.'

The first time I came back I believe they rushed me too hastily. This time, though, it was me trying to prove a point. I wanted to get back into the game as quickly as possible to prove them all wrong.

It was around the same time that another realisation hit me. If Blackburn didn't think I could play again, there was no reason for them to keep paying my wages. Contracts weren't the same in those days – the players had virtually no rights at all. A club owned a player and they could choose to pay them or not and there was nothing the lad could do about it. These days you hear threats from chairmen and managers about letting a wantaway player 'rot in the reserves' but financially that never makes sense because they couldn't afford the wages to be wasted like that. In those days it happened quite often.

I realised I was lucky to have been kept on the £20-a-week salary but my timing could have been better. In 1957 Jimmy Hill had been voted PFA chairman and in 1961 he won his fight for the maximum wage to be scrapped. From that moment on, players could negotiate their own fees directly with the clubs. There weren't agents like there are today so players would walk in and negotiate face to face for themselves. People like Ally MacLeod, Bryan Douglas and Ronnie Clayton went straight up to £40 or £60 a week while Johnny Haynes became the first player on £100. My money, of course, didn't budge. If anything I was lucky the club didn't put it down. As far as negotiating strengths went, I didn't have a leg to stand on – almost literally.

Over the years I'd been on the receiving end of Blackburn's tightness but in that circumstance I have to say a big 'thank-you' to them for standing by me. I just hoped they'd let me have the chance of thanking them on the pitch.

Funnily enough, I had reason to thank a future benefactor of Blackburn as well. Jack Walker was a local lad whose family ran the largest steel business in the area. One day he would own the club but back then he was just a passionate Rovers fan – and a very wealthy one at that. Whenever I used to see him out and about in town or at Ewood he would slip me a five-pound note just to see me through the hard times. A wonderful man, Mr Walker, and I wasn't the last to benefit from his generosity.

I still had money coming in from our shop, of course, but I felt there could be more. I took on a lady from the Mill Hill area to help out and I began to spend a bit of time at Blackburn market. One stall in particular caught my eye. It was selling a lot of the same stock as I did in my shop – but for about half the price.

'How are they doing that?' I wondered. There was only one way to find out.

Fortunately the traders, two brothers called Bill and Albert Howarth, recognised me and so I didn't have to make too many introductions. But I said, 'I run a little grocery shop and I buy things at the same price you're selling them at. How the hell do you do that?'

No successful businessman gives their secrets away but Bill Howarth was a thoughtful man so he said, 'Look, Dave, I'll supply you stock if you want and we'll go from there.'

So I started taking boxes of Andrews, toilet rolls, cleaning products and all sorts of things at way below the official wholesale prices. As time went on, they began to educate me in the rudiments of market trading and let me work alongside them on the stall. They taught me about margins, about when to buy, when to sell, depreciation, everything you could possibly need to know. They said, 'You want tuppence in the shilling, so that's sixteen per cent gross margin.' I lapped that kind of information up. I was good at maths at school but only the basic stuff. I could never do trigonometry and all that, but for numbers I had a sharp brain. If you said something was twenty-nine shillings a dozen, I knew that was two and five each and I knew that I wanted to make sixteen per cent on that, so I wanted 5p on it straight off, in old money, to get that sixteen per cent gross profit.

I had the natural flair, I just needed the Howarths to show me how to use it.

I then looked at my own business in a completely new light. I thought, 'I need to be making sixteen per cent on every single item in here – am I doing that?'

And the answer was no.

My shop was taking around £400 a week gross – but the Howarths could make that in one day. The biggest problem I had was with cash flow and all the customers owing me money. Everyone would pay up eventually but sometimes I'd be carrying debt worth hundreds of pounds, and that's not healthy. You never had debts like that on the market. And best of all,

all transactions were in cash and with no receipts. To me as a part-time shopkeeper that was a lesson in life. I knew I had to have a taste of that kind of business.

'Why don't you open your own market stall?' Bill said one day.

'Well I can't do it here because you run Blackburn,' I said. 'But no one in Wigan sells half the things you do. I think I'll give it a go there.'

As soon as the idea entered my head I knew I had to pursue it, but there were problems. The first, of course, was Pat. We lived in Blackburn, that's where our family home was. I would have to uproot her to take her back to our home town, but even though I was sure she would say yes, perhaps the market was too much of a gamble.

I thought, 'I'll sell this shop here and buy another one in Wigan and then start looking at the market from there.'

The second obstacle was the football. That was harder to overcome. I was trying desperately hard to play myself back into contention for a first-team place and realistically I could only do myself justice if I stayed local. While I began to investigate shop sites in Wigan, however, my decision was made for me after one night against Blackpool.

I was playing in the A team, just trying to get some speed back in my legs after nearly eighteen months out of the spotlight. Darwin Football Club, where the A and B teams used to play, wasn't the best ground in the world but even then I was struggling. I'd come back too soon and my body was letting me know it. Every time I kicked the ball, if I didn't time it to perfection it sent this pain right through me. When you're fit you don't realise the strain it takes to clump a football. But when you're out of whack it's imperative you kick it cleanly because if it comes off the end of your toe or something, you really feel it. That's what I did at Blackpool. I kicked it off my toe and it sent such a jolt into my bone I fell over clutching my leg.

Nothing was broken and I got back up again but I knew I was making a mistake playing that game. In the end the Blackpool trainer went over to our bench and said, 'I think you should haul him off.' Afterwards he said to me, 'You've got some bloody guts, you have. No way were you fit to play but you were really trying. I respect that – but for your own sake don't rush it.'

I was moping back in training the next day when the manager appeared on the touchline. I hadn't seen him for a while and he was smiling.

'Hello, boss,' I said. 'Come to look me over?'

He laughed. 'Actually I've come with some news. Jimmy McGuigan's had a look at you. He'd like you to go and play for him at Crewe. What do you think?'

What did I think?

I'd been busting my guts out to get fit for Blackburn and here was my manager trying to offload me somewhere else. There was no doubt about that. The fact he was even telling me about the offer revealed to me that I didn't feature in his plans for the future. After all, he had never mentioned it when Matt Busby had come in for me a few years earlier. That's how it worked then. My last match for the first team had been in the FA Cup final, for God's sake. In my mind I was a First Division player on the way back from injury – and Crewe Alexandra were in the Fourth Division.

On the bright side, it gave me an excuse to sell the Mill Hill shop and start anew in Wigan. Crewe wasn't too far from my old town and the train and road links were superb. In pure footballing terms I might have been taking a step down, but the possibilities for my business interests were endless.

'This is just the beginning,' I told myself. 'And I can make it work.'

Nine

WHEN CAN I TAKE IT?

1963 was a year of new beginnings. My daughter Jayne was born and it was when I really got the taste for making money through selling. And that was only really possible because of my move to Crewe Alexandra.

Taking that step down the divisions at the age of twenty-seven was a blow to the ego, I don't mind admitting. Even off the pitch it was a rude awakening. I'd got quite used to everyone in Blackburn giving me a wave in the street or popping into the shop for a chat. Most of the people in Crewe didn't know me from Adam.

I still have wonderful times when I go back to Ewood Park or if I'm out in a restaurant with Ron or Dougie. It's amazing how many people remember us playing for the club. I swear half the folk who come up and say hello aren't even old enough to have seen us play, but they're still so polite and respectful.

It's not just in Blackburn that I get that sort of reaction, though. I was in France recently with my grandson for his twenty-first birthday party and a fellow in the hotel tapped me on the shoulder and said, 'I have to tell you something while I'm in here.'

I thought, 'Oh yes – what's this going to be?' The chap was getting on. He was my age, seventy-odd.

He said, 'I was at the cup final when you broke your leg. I cried my bloody heart out when we lost.'

I said, 'I cried my heart out the same as you.'

Even if I didn't get on with everyone at Blackburn, at least I knew them all. I had a comfort zone there which took a bit of leaving. The other thing I noticed straight away was the drop in conditions. Rovers didn't have very good training facilities compared with the rest of the First Division – but what Crewe had to offer was diabolical. They used to borrow a school field if the kids weren't using it or just play outside in the dirt. Things were a lot tougher than I could ever have expected.

Then there were the players. I was used to playing with full inter-nationals – I even lined up alongside a captain of England in Ronnie Clayton. At Crewe I was starting matches next to electricians, drivers, part-time engineers, because most of them did something in the afternoons. Peter Leigh, the left back, was a good player who was at City before he joined the Railwaymen, but he'd train in the mornings and clean windows in the afternoon. Everybody did something to make extra money, including me, of course.

The names of the players still trip off my tongue because we had a great spirit there. Johnny King, Barrie Wheatley, Eric Barnes, Stan Keery, Kevin McHale, the Welshman Chris Riley, Billy Haydock, Peter Leigh, Frank Lord, Geoff Hickson and the two Scottish lads, Peter Gowans and Willie Mailey, were all there when I arrived. Mick Gannon, Keith Stott, Alan Bradshaw and Tommy Lowry arrived soon after. They were good lads. They were all prepared to work. When the money isn't the reason you do something, sometimes you try harder. These boys loved their football and they gave that club their all.

Jimmy McGuigan was the manager and I liked him from the off. But if I'm honest, tactics and things like that weren't quite at the level I was used to. Crewe's trainer had never played football at any level and while he was a hundred per cent committed, there was only so much he could teach anyone. To be fair to Jimmy, he was very quick to ask me for my advice. 'How would Johnny Carey do this, Dave?' he'd say. Or, 'Do you mind taking a session? Show the lads a few new tricks?'

When you've played for a successful team you can't help picking things up, so I helped him as much as I could. I was full of ideas and tried to foster different ways to do things, working on them, moulding them,

My father, Jimmy Whelan, in uniform in 1941.
Dave Whelan personal collection

My mam, Maggie Whelan, aged eighteen.
Dave Whelan personal collection

5 May 1950: aged fourteen, being presented with the Lythgoe Cup by Wigan's Deputy Mayor. I was captain of Highfield Secondary Modern's football and rugby league teams.
Dave Whelan personal collection

The familiar
Clayton Street
entrance to
Wigan Boys Club
in Wallgate where
my life was
changed.
*Wigan Archives
Service WLCT*

Playing with the Wigan Boys Club Brass Band, 1953.
Wigan Archives Service WLCT

In the blue and white strip of Blackburn Rovers as a seventeen-year-old, 1954.   *Colorsport*

Pouring tea for the team at Blackpool's Norbreck Hydro Hotel as we enjoyed our First Division status, December 1959.   *Howard Talbot Photography*

Ewood Park, October 1958: the first of my two 'lucky' goals against Preston's Fred Else, after a pulled muscle meant I was moved up front.
Howard Talbot Photography

Clearing off the line with a header when the ball got past Harry Leyland during our 2-1 victory over Man City, April 1959.   *Howard Talbot Photography*

Serving in our shop in Blackburn, watched by my wife, Pat, and our fifteen-month-old son, Paul, April 1960 – just weeks before the FA Cup final. *Howard Talbot Photography*

Trying on new hats for Wembley with Ally MacLeod, Bryan Douglas and Harry Leyland, April 1960. *Howard Talbot Photography*

The proudest man on earth: in
my 'Wembley' Blackburn strip.
Howard Talbot Photography

Blackburn Rovers' FA Cup final team. *PA Photos*

The match gets under way: Harry Leyland saves as I look on. *Colorsport*

Walking out onto the Wembley turf in our new tracksuits, 7 May 1960. *Colorsport*

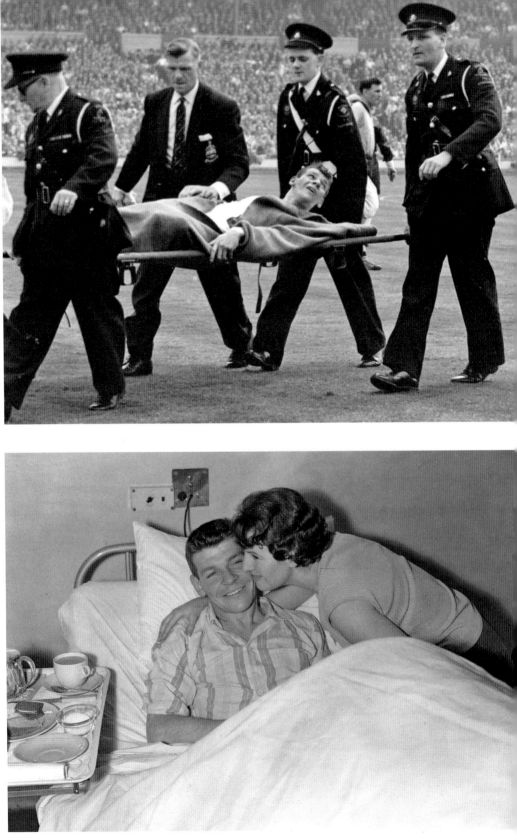

Recovering in the Royal London Orthopaedic Hospital.   *Offside Sports Photography*

The end of my dream: stretchered off just before half-time after Norman Deeley's diabolical challenge. *Colorsport*

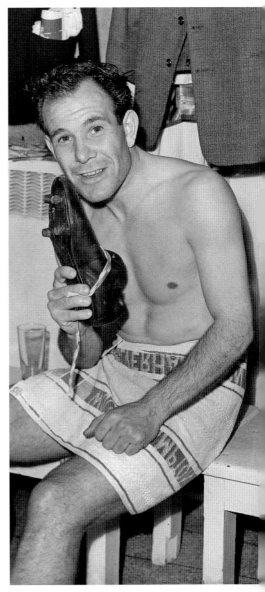

Norman Deeley showing the boot that scored two goals in the final – and put me in hospital. *Colorsport*

A new beginning at Crewe Alexandra, 1964. *Colorsport*

With Sir Alex Ferguson at the official opening of the JJB Stadium, 4 August 1999. *PA Photos*

Arjan de Zeeuw holds off United's Dwight Yorke as Wigan take on the treble winners in the first official game at the JJB. *PA Photos*

A dream come true: celebrating promotion to the Promised Land of the Premier League with Paul Jewell, 8 May 2005.
Colorsport

I promised Wigan Athletic fans that I would give them Premier League football and with that day's victory over Reading we achieved it.
PA Photos

The happiest day in the JJB's history.
PA Photos

A stadium fit for the Premier League: my way of putting something back into the sport that gave me so much. *Rex Features*

The controversial Carlos Tevez holds off Wigan's Emmerson Boyce at the JJB, 28 April 2007. *Getty Images*

The day the Premier League got it wrong: Paul Jewell celebrates our win over Sheffield United but, with West Ham escaping a points deduction, distraught Blades fans and their manager Neil Warnock face an unjust relegation.

Offside Sports Photography (right) *Colorsport* (bottom)

Steve Bruce shares a joke with Arsène Wenger, 11 April 2009. *PA Photos*

The one amigo:
fans' favourite
Roberto Martínez
returns, this time
as manager, and a
new era begins,
16 June 2009.
PA Photos

A new name in sports retail and a new name in football: from 1 August 2009 the JJB became the DW Stadium. *PA Photos*

trying to give them the benefit of my experience. I hadn't been there long before I had everyone training the way I was used to. A short while after that Jimmy McGuigan made me captain.

'You're driving the team anyway,' he said. 'We may as well make it official.'

The other thing that helped was the fact I was back in my usual position of right back. There was a lot more that a right-footer could do with the ball on the right flank. Over on the other side your natural movement is to knock the ball into touch, which isn't always the right thing to do.

The last couple of months of the season really went in our favour and we started moving up the table. Barrow, Chesterfield, Lincoln, Hartlepool, Chester, Darlington, Workington, Mansfield Town all gave us two points. Out of the last fifteen games we scored twenty-two points out of a possible thirty.

'That's championship-winning form,' I thought. 'We could do something here.'

For the final game of the season we had Exeter at our place and 9,807 fans piled into Gresty Road. It didn't matter what division I was in. I wanted to win that match as much as I'd wanted to win the cup final.

The game was tight, but I was relentless in encouraging the team forwards. I even strayed across the halfway line myself a few times – that's how desperate I was to win. Just when I was losing a bit of faith, the ball fell to Frank Lord. Now Frank was one of those forgotten players. Like me, he'd taken a nasty leg break that had stopped his top-flight career. But if he'd been left alone he would have played for England, no doubt about it at all. He holds the record for the most hat-tricks scored for Crewe – eight – and he later went on to play for Rovers and scout for Manchester United. Years later he even helped me out as caretaker manager at Wigan – but more of that later.

The question at that moment, though, was: did he have the nerve to do what was needed right now when the pressure was on?

'Come on, Lordy, put it away,' I yelled.

He looked up once, waited for the keeper to go down then slotted home. We'd done it. Victory was ours. Crewe had been one of the founding members of the Second Division and since then had only ever gone down. I'd been at the club for half a season, most of it as captain, and I'd led them to the first promotion in their history. As the lads carried me and Lordy around the park on their shoulders I thought, 'It really doesn't get any better than this!' The whole town celebrated that night and for the first time since I'd left Ewood I felt like I belonged.

Just as I experienced at Blackburn, though, it's hanging on to your new status that's the hard part because you're suddenly facing twenty-odd new teams. That's hundreds of new players to mug up on, new pitches to get used to, sometimes even new tactics you run into and have to respond to.

It was hard going. In those days the FA didn't publish the League tables until the season had bedded in nicely, unlike today when you get a list after one match. But the first table they did print made unhappy reading for all of us. We were rock bottom and in danger of being cut adrift. It was the same the next week and the next. When you only win two of your first fifteen games, you can't expect much more.

17 September was a big game for us because we were away at Coventry at a time when Jimmy Hill was managing them. We'd actually won our previous match against Bristol City and so on the way there the mood was good. 'The Sky Blues are there for the taking,' Jimmy McGuigan said. 'Let's show them what we're made of.'

Show them what we're made of? They bashed us off the park. It's a miserable feeling when you've lost 5–1 and we all felt sorry for ourselves on the way back. But that wasn't enough for some people. Crewe, like Blackburn, always sent a member of the board along to away matches to enjoy the host team's hospitality and to foster relations in case any transfers needed to be done. The chap who had come with us that day – who I won't name, for his family's sake – was a right so-and-so. He knew bugger-all about football but that didn't stop him tearing into all of us on that home journey.

'You're a bunch of lazy bastards,' he was shouting. 'You're not fit to wear the shirt. Tell me why I shouldn't get rid of the lot of you.'

We all sat there in silence but not out of respect. The man was such a joke there was just nothing to say. He'd never played the game and he never would. What did his opinion matter? Even Jimmy McGuigan looked ashamed sitting next to him. He knew as well as I did that we weren't lazy – we just weren't good enough. We were a Fourth Division team who had got lucky. We were doing our best but resources were scarce and it wouldn't be long before we were back in the lowest league.

Halfway home the coach pulled over as usual at a pub so we could go to the gents and maybe get a swift half in before the rest of the journey. It was a different culture to Blackburn because Lordy and the boys all liked a drink. So, it turned out, did the director.

Of course, once he'd got an ale inside him, the complaints started off again. Eventually he calmed down, though, and said he was off to the toilet. He put his half-finished beer down on the bar and staggered off. As soon as he was out of sight, Frank Lord picked up the beer, whipped his John Thomas out and peed into the glass. It happened so quick I couldn't take it in at first but then I just could not stop laughing. He filled it right to the top and even managed to get a lovely head on it with a drop of beer from his own glass. Then he put it back on the bar and we waited.

The daft old sod came out and before he could say a word, Frank said, 'We'll try harder next time. Just to show no hard feelings I've got you another pint.'

'That's very generous of you, Frank. I'm glad you're taking my comments on board.'

With that he raised the glass to his lips.

At that point you'd think the bloke would smell something or he'd notice that he had a dozen or so men, including the manager, biting their lip or staring at their shoes to try not to laugh. But he didn't. He opened his mouth and downed it in one. At the end he just said, 'Right, that coach is leaving in two minutes whether you lot are on it or not!' and he marched out of the bar.

'Thank Christ for that!' I thought and we all exploded with laughter. One more moment of holding it in and I'd have had an accident.

That was typical of the sort of thing players get up to when they're united. You only need one bad apple to spoil it for everyone, as I knew to my cost, but when the whole crowd was pulling in the same direction it was a wonderful feeling. That little trick did more to make us stick together on the field than any amount of shouting from that idiot. As a bonding exercise I can't think of anything better – but if any of the Wigan lads think of trying it on me they'd better know where the door is!

I had another run-in with the same fella a short while later. It started when Jimmy McGuigan called me into his office.

'Got a problem, boss?' I said.

'Yes and no, Dave. I've got an offer to go and manage Grimsby Town and I'm going to take it. The only problem is, the board of directors won't let me leave until I've found a replacement. I'm recommending you to be the manager here. What do you say?'

I said, 'I don't want to be the manager, boss.'

'You don't? Why ever not? You're virtually running the place anyway.'

I said, 'To be honest with you, I don't need the hassle and I certainly don't need the money. I'm taking too much cash on the markets and any spare time I have, that's where I have to spend it.'

I felt guilty turning down that opportunity, especially as it put the boss in a bit of a fix. The director tried to change my mind but I said the same thing to him: 'I'm making too much money in my other business to give it up for this.'

And it was true – but getting to that stage had not been easy. In fact, if I were a superstitious man, I would have said that things were conspiring against me when I arrived in Wigan to open my stall. Everywhere I turned I was met with objections.

The day that I joined Crewe I was in the process of selling the shop in Blackburn. I'd found premises in Pool Street, near where I grew up in Poolstock, and had made an offer, but best of all was the fact that we could actually afford a separate house. No more living in a couple of rooms above the office! I think there was a little bit of overlap, but within a fortnight of leaving Rovers, Pat and I settled into a lovely little house at 310 Poolstock Lane that had set me back £1,100. We were so happy at the chance of living like a normal family without the aromas of bacon slicers and cheese counters wafting into our living room.

From a football point of view, the train to Crewe was about thirty-five minutes – perfectly manageable. But the M6 motorway had just opened then so I could also drive to work in about forty-five or fifty minutes. I soon realised that that was what I preferred, so I splashed out on my first really nice car: a dark blue Jaguar 2.4 litre. That was some motor and I began to actually enjoy my trips into Gresty Road.

The shop was really just to keep things ticking over and to give Pat a business for when she wasn't looking after the children. What I really wanted to do was get into the markets. I wanted to do in Wigan what the Howarth brothers did in Blackburn.

Now, Wigan did not have a market as such back then. There was an old market hall which had hosted a Friday market for 300 years, but nothing went on during the rest of the week, and nothing ever outside in the big town square. Most exciting, from my point of view, there was no one at all selling things like patent medicines and toiletries – no one doing razor blades, sanitary towels, Anadin and all the stuff the Howarths had trained me to deal in.

I sensed my opportunity and rushed to see the market superintendent, a fella called Len Dutton.

'Hello, Dave, how can I help you?' he said, shaking my hand and welcoming me into his office.

I said, 'I would like a stall to sell patented medicines and toiletries.'

He shook his head. 'You're not the first to ask to do that,' he said, 'but it's not allowed.'

'Not allowed?'

'No. It's in the statute books. There's an Appropriation List at the town hall with all the items that can be sold in this market.'

I'd hit my first brick wall.

'Do you mind if I check this out?' I asked.

'Of course not, but you're wasting your time.'

On the way to the town hall I mulled it over. There must be some mistake. Even in the 1800s wild herbs and pressed flowers would have been sold as remedies in that hall and market square.

I arrived at the hall and saw a girl on the front desk. I said, 'I am a ratepayer in Wigan, I live in Poolstock Lane, and I would like to see the Appropriation List of things I am allowed to sell in the market.'

She said, 'I've never heard of such a thing.'

I said, 'Neither had I until today, but I know it exists so would you mind going out the back and finding out who has it please, because I would like to see it.'

She disappeared for a few minutes. When she returned she was smiling. 'You're right. There is a list and I've just spoken to the clerk's assistant and she says could you come back tomorrow and she will have it ready for you?'

I could barely sleep that night through anticipation. All my hopes were pinned on that list. I couldn't wait to see it.

When I returned the next day the clerk had been as good as her word and there it was. Dated something like 1810, this regulation had the power to make or break my business dreams. If I didn't find what I wanted on there I might be uprooting my family again. I scanned anxiously down the column of small, spidery old writing until I spotted what I was after.

According to that council document I could sell any medicine and all accompanying bathroom accoutrements. The only restriction was that Sunday was out of bounds. Well, that didn't matter.

'Could I have a copy of this, please?' I asked the girl. A few minutes later I left that building with such a spring in my step. That photocopy could be dynamite for me.

I went back in to see Len Dutton and said, 'Len, I've just been to the town hall and I've got a list of things I can sell on Wigan market and on what days I can sell them. Have a look at this,' and I handed it over. He scrutinised it like a bookie with a winning ticket, looking for evidence it was forged. I'm sure he thought I'd written it myself.

Finally, he said, 'It looks like you're right – you can sell toiletries any day apart from Sunday. Just give me a day to verify it but it looks like you're going to be fine.'

I said, 'OK, I'll be back tomorrow.'

Twenty-four hours later I was back in his office and he was still scratching his head. 'Nobody I've spoken to even knew that document existed,' he said. 'But it's certainly genuine. Now – you know there's a waiting list for a stall in the market, don't you?'

I said, 'That's fine. I don't want to go in the market.'

'You don't? Well, what do you want then?'

'I want two stalls directly outside the main entrance of the market hall,' I said.

He looked at me like I was mad, but he wasn't going to argue and lose twice in one week. The next Monday I got permission to miss training for once and I turned up with my sister Pauline and a vanload of stock I'd bought cheaply from the Howarth brothers. We set up the stalls and waited.

I know Len Dutton didn't understand why I wanted outside space when everyone else was indoors, but I had my reasons. The market hall is in central Wigan and the bus stops were all at the top of the shopping arcade. To get inside the market hall everyone would have to pass my stall – and as I was the only one there they were sure to notice me. About half past eight the first bus pulled up and within minutes we were flooded. In five minutes we'd seen more faces than the shop got in a day.

It was magical.

I thought, 'There's no going back now. This is my future.'

Once again, though, it wasn't quite that easy.

We had been going for about twenty minutes when I noticed the faces at the front of my stall weren't holding out pound notes and toiletries. What's more they were men and not women – and they all looked ready for a rumble.

It was like a scene from the old Wild West. A deputation of about fifteen of the more established market traders from inside the hall had marched out, with the chairman of the markets committee, to tell me in no uncertain terms that I was going to stop trading there and then.

I'd been expecting some sort of confrontation, but this was a bunch of grown men who'd seen too many Westerns. I said very calmly, 'If you could please stand to one side so my customers can still be served, I'll happily have a chat with you.'

'There'll be no more serving here!' the chairman of the group declared with the bravery of someone controlling a mob of big lads. 'I don't care if you are a fancy footballer, you've got no more rights to sell this stuff out here than anyone else. So pack up your stall before we pack it up for you.'

I strung them along for as long as I dared, but in the end I realised I was losing customers while I messed around with these fellas. I still had the documents from the town hall so I waved them under the chairman's nose and said, 'According to this piece of legislation laid down in 1810, not only do I have the right to trade here but I can sell toothbrushes, painkillers or whatever I like. And if you don't believe me, take it up with your MP.'

Fifteen gobs smacked shut at the same time. There was silence around the whole stall – even my customers were waiting to see how this one developed.

'Hmm, it looks like you might have a point here,' one of the blokes said. 'Of course, we're going to have to check it.'

'I've checked it thoroughly already,' I beamed, 'but if one of you fellas has time to waste in the town hall, be my guest.'

To be fair, the next day the same bunch of traders one by one came up to me and apologised like men. I appreciated that. 'You're bloody right,' one of them said. 'How come no one else knew about these rules?'

I shrugged. I hadn't known about them either, but it's not in my nature to take no for an answer. Not when there's a shilling to be made and a customer waiting.

Pauline found the arguments of the first day a bit too exciting but for me the thrill came at the end of the afternoon when I counted up the takings.

'How much do you reckon we've got, Pauline?' I asked her.

'Well I must have taken a couple of hundred,' she said. 'Four hundred?'

'Not even close. Seven hundred pounds! In one day!'

It was incredible and all of it was at my sixteen per cent margin as a minimum. And as for overheads, they were non-existent. I was paying fifteen shillings in rent – 75p in today's money – and that included rates and everything. I didn't have any heat or lighting on the stall but even so, what a bargain.

We had a bit of a celebration that night and I came to a few decisions. I couldn't play football and run the shop and the market so I would do the buying for both, Pat would run the shop and hire my mam and Elsie to help her out, and I would go into partnership with Pauline and her husband Colin to run the market, because it was obvious there was plenty of money in it for everyone. That night over one of my rare pints of beer we toasted the launch of Whelan & Taylor's market stall.

'Here's to many more years,' Colin said.

'And many more pound notes!'

Our next decision was to add another member of staff – our dad. He was still singing in the evenings, of course, but both Pauline and I were really happy we could give him a wage so he didn't have to slog his guts out in the mill all day. It was a stroke of genius getting him involved as people used to hunt him out for a chat like they did me in Blackburn. It was funny to watch, because when he was around I was Mr Nobody. He was the star in Wigan, not me.

When he saw how well we were doing my brother Jimmy decided to throw in his job and get his own stall. I trained him up in Wigan then went around the markets for him till I found a nice patch in Warrington. He set up there on his own but I did his buying.

We all got into a nice little rhythm. Jimmy in Warrington, us in Wigan. I would go and train in the morning then come back for about half past one and help out. Mainly though I was in charge of buying and I would spend a lot of time hunting around for the best suppliers. Then one day I struck gold. I heard of this outfit operating out of Manchester.

I was told just two things about them, but they were two very important things.

The first was that they could supply what I wanted for the right price.

And the second was that they would do anything for a pound note, the crisper the better.

I knew I had to make a good impression on my first visit so I got myself down to my local Barclays branch. I said to the chap behind the glass, 'I would like £1,000 in brand-new £10 notes.' They'd just put a new tenner into circulation and I thought it would be a nice touch. But the man said, 'You'll have to see the manager about that. I don't know if we've got that many.'

I said, 'Give over, you're a bank. You must have boxes of them.'

The manager turned up and of course he was only too pleased to help me out. The look on that teller's face as he had to count them all out for me! He looked even angrier when I then counted them back, very, very slowly.

It was an impressive note, there was no denying that. And I had a hundred of them, all crisp and beautiful.

I got myself up to Manchester and found myself sat around a table in a warehouse with my new suppliers. After the introductions were out the way I reached into my pocket and placed, very carefully, the bundle of brand-new notes on the table in front of me. I sensed the room go silent. 'I've got their attention now,' I thought. 'They know they've got a real player on their hands.' Then I started listing the things I wanted. 'Anadin, Wilkinson Sword razor blades, Beechams Powders, Dr Whites, Andrews Liver Salts – all the big patent medicines.' For as long as I spoke, those lads' eyes did not leave the pile of money for one second. I kid you not.

Then it came time to negotiate a price. These fellas were sharp as arrows but they were fair – and even their worst price was better than anywhere else. Because I wanted to buy in big numbers, though, I got a very healthy reduction before we even started. Having those pound notes staring up from the table at them seemed to work in my favour.

Beechams Powders in those days used to sell at two and three. I used to sell them at 1/11 and buy them for eighteen shillings per dozen. So I was making five pence a go. That's twenty per cent – a very good deal. With something like the Wilkinson Sword, which was brand new, that would go for two and eleven in Boots, but I would do it for two and six – half a crown – and still get my margin. We didn't have a recommended price in those days, just a retail price, and so technically I was selling below the manufacturer's stated amount. But the numbers I was shifting, no one could have complained, I thought.

The better we did, the more money I took up to Manchester. At first I would stuff all the stock into my Jag. Then I began driving a van up there. Soon, though, I was nipping up in my car to do the deal and Colin or my dad would follow later with a lorry then take it back to a warehouse I rented.

I was really happy to have been able to help my family out by bringing them all in on the action, but there were a couple of other fellas I wanted to do something for as well. I got on the phone to Bill Howarth and told him about my deals. He said, 'Bloody hell, Dave, you're getting it for less than us! You really have learnt the ropes, son.'

So after that I started supplying them as well. I never charged a mark-up, not for the Howarths, because I owed them so much. But they'd give me their order and I'd negotiate a deal and then they'd pay me later. With the extra numbers I was able to nail the prices lower.

After twelve months of being back in Wigan business was booming. We were pulling in a couple of thousand a week clear profit and life was good, really good. Then one day I was driving up to Manchester for my weekly meeting and I drove past the same Rolls-Royce dealership that I saw every week. Normally all the Rollers were tucked up inside the building, but this time there was a car parked on show outside.

I had to take a look. It was a Phantom, stunning blue and about a dozen miles on the clock. In those days there was a nine-month waiting list for one of these things – you didn't just buy them off the peg. But this one certainly looked like it was for sale.

I stuck my head inside the showroom and said, 'Is that car for sale by any chance?'

The salesman leapt up. 'You're in luck, sir – it's just arrived but the order's been cancelled.'

I said, 'How much is it?'

'£10,300.'

I said, 'How much will you give me for my Jag as part exchange?'

He ummed and ahhed and came up with about £800.

'Fine,' I said. 'When can I take it?'

'You can take it as soon as you pay for it.'

I said, 'Well I'll be taking it right now then,' and I heaved a briefcase full of notes on to his desk. 'I'll just count you out the money while you sort out the paperwork.'

The look on that salesman's face! Up until that point I could tell he thought I was a wind-up merchant. How many people must he have seen every day pretending they could afford a Rolls-Royce? But I really did have the readies with me, and more besides.

I was covered for insurance so that only left a tax disc. The police weren't so hot on that sort of thing back then, so I took a risk and drove it out without one. I still had to buy for the market so I nipped back home first and picked up some more cash. Pulling into Poolstock Lane I felt like the king of the world. I saw some kids playing in the street and their mouths actually dropped open when they saw me pull up. I couldn't help laughing. Twenty years ago that was me playing in that street. And now look at me!

I got back up to Manchester and I was halfway through my order when the boss came in and said, 'Someone's got a lovely motor outside. I wonder whose it is.'

'I think you'll find it's mine,' I said.

He cracked a wide grin. 'Nah, I mean the Rolls-Royce that's parked out there.'

I said, 'So do I. I bought it this morning!'

The look on those lads' faces! I could tell the boss was thinking, 'We're not charging this guy enough if he's driving one of those,' but we had a decent laugh about it.

It was the same story at Crewe the next day. I stuck the Phantom outside the club building and gave a blast on the horn. One by one all the lads looked over and then they came running. When they'd finished calling me all the names under the sun they all wanted to have a ride in it. We had a bit of fun then got on with training. We were just getting ready to leave when the chairman walked into the changing room.

'Have we got visitors today, lads?' he asked. 'Because there's a fantastic Rolls-Royce parked out there.'

All the while he was speaking he was giving the place a once-over, trying to spot the millionaire in our midst.

Then one of the team said, 'It's his, boss,' and a dozen fingers pointed my way.

The poor old chairman was speechless. As far as he knew I earned £22 a week playing football. He'd seen my Jag but plenty of players in the First Division had nice cars. A Roller, though, was a different league altogether. He only had a little Austin himself and so he said, 'How on earth can you afford that?'

I said, 'I have a couple of business ventures elsewhere,' and left it at that.

'Well they must be doing all right for you, that's all I can say.'

My days at Crewe were a complete joy from start to end. What had frustrated me about their amateurism when I first joined now made me warm to them. The club's solution to the problem of Jimmy McGuigan leaving was absolutely typical of them. I came in one day and the chairman said, 'I'd like you all to meet your new manager.'

He opened the door and a chap called Ernie Tag stepped in.

We all knew Ernie – but he wasn't a famous footballer. He was the newsagent who ran the paper shop along the street!

But do you know what? He did incredibly well!

Jimmy McGuigan was that desperate to take the Grimsby job that he had begged Ernie to help him out. It was the last thing he wanted to saddle himself with, but he was a supporter of the club so he said he would give it a go. I must admit I found taking orders from a man more used to marking up copies of the *Daily Mirror* than to marking opposition players very awkward, but Ernie was a good egg and he used to listen to my advice an awful lot. If any of the lads ever stepped out of line with him, Frank Lord or myself would set them straight. You need good people in football and Ernie was definitely one of those, and in fact his record over the years turned out to be marginally better than Jimmy McGuigan's.

In Ernie's first season we had Terry Harkin banging in a record thirty-five League goals, so that gave us a solid foundation. We were in the Fourth Division but we were more than holding our own.

I enjoyed working with Ernie and I was still having fun on the pitch. But I had to admit, it was getting harder. I wasn't as quick as I had been even when I'd joined Crewe and at the end of matches now I was ready to lie down. Five years earlier I would have been up for another game if it kicked off there and then. But it does take it out of you more, and even though thirty is far from old, when you've got whippets of lads who are nineteen, twenty, you're really made to feel your age.

For me, though, it was worth the effort because I still enjoyed it. When you don't depend on something for a living then you can have fun with it. The day football becomes just a job then you have to get out because it will hurt you in the end. I saw it happen to others. Even now I can watch a player and say, 'He is iffy.' That means he doesn't want to graft for ninety minutes because he's not up to it and his heart's not in it any more. You can tell the ones who won't work, who can't work.

Of course, if he's got ability then maybe that's acceptable. If he's truly outstanding then the rest will carry him and wear his deficiencies. You never saw Stanley Matthews fight. You never saw Tom Finney fight. But could they play! You would carry them for ever because they had been touched by the Lord and they could play even into their thirties, or fifties in Stan's case.

I was no Stan Matthews but I would go to war for my team on that pitch. For ninety minutes my life was on the line. That's what it meant to me to play professional football. It wasn't about the money. It was the passion. Everything was going well coming into the final quarter of the season and then I got a sharp reminder of how fragile life can be.

We were home to Cardiff. I was playing right back and the corner came in. I went to head it as usual but it didn't happen like that. Their big striker came up at the same time but he was late. I got the ball – and he got me. It was a pure accident – but I fell to the floor unconscious. When I came round they were carrying me off on a stretcher.

As I was taken inside the dressing room to have a proper check-over, I remember saying, 'I'm all right, I'm all right.' But then I put my hand to my face and got the shock of my life. 'What's happened to me?' I thought. 'My cheek's disappeared.'

From my chin to my eye socket it was just flapping skin. The bone had vanished. Where the hell had that gone?

Peter Leigh came running in just after to see how I was. He said, 'Don't worry with 999 – I have to drive past the hospital on my way home.'

By the time we got to Crewe Royal I was hurting. Whatever adrenalin I had from the match had well and truly worn off. My head felt and looked inside out. We got straight to the front of the A&E queue and a doctor asked what the trouble was.

I was surprised he couldn't see for himself, but I said, 'I was playing for Crewe Alex tonight and I got a head in my face.'

He turned me this way and that and then said, 'You need some tablets.'

'Tablets? Doc – have you not noticed, there's a great hole in my face. My cheekbone's disappeared. Tablets won't cure this!'

But he wouldn't be told. 'I think that it'll be all right by tomorrow,' he insisted.

By the time I left I could barely talk, so Peter took me all the way home. Pat screamed when she saw me. 'What on earth has happened to you?' I don't blame her. I looked like the Elephant Man going home that night.

I swallowed a painkiller and managed to get to sleep. But about four in the morning I woke up in absolute agony. My face was pulsing, going throb, throb, throb. And the slightest movement was like a punch in the jaw. I gulped down another tablet but nothing changed.

At eight o'clock I had to give in and went to Wigan Infirmary, where a doctor saw me instantly. 'What the hell's happened here, Dave?' he said. Even as he spoke, he was getting me into a wheelchair and running down the corridor towards the X-ray room. By the time that was finished he said, 'You're in surgery in fifteen minutes.'

My operation was very delicate and called for a specialist dental surgeon. He had to get his instruments inside my mouth, behind the cheekbone, then physically knock it back out. It's just like it sounds – tap, tap, tap, until he gets it lined up and as smooth as possible. Of course I didn't feel a thing under the anaesthetic, but when I came to it felt like I'd been punched in the head – and I suppose in a way I had.

I was told I couldn't eat for about ten days – no solids at all in that time – but considering how much it hurt to move my jaw there was no danger of me tucking into a sandwich just yet.

Once everything calmed down I saw the specialist for a check-up. He hadn't had time to talk to me before but now he asked, 'Why didn't you get this done at Crewe Royal? Why did you leave it so long to come here?'

I told him about the painkillers and he was shocked. 'Dave, I don't want to worry you,' he said, 'but I could tell instantly that you had a depressed cheek fracture. And what that means is if that bone had touched your brain you were a dead man. One shake of your head too vigorously and that would have been it.'

I thought of how lucky I'd been and over the next few days I felt a strange feeling beginning to take hold of me. I realised something was missing but for a while I couldn't put my finger on what it was. Then I realised.

I wasn't desperate to play football again.

'Is this it?' I wondered. 'Have I had enough?'

I thought about it some more and realised, 'Yes, I have.' It was taking me so long to recover from injuries and I was picking up more and more little knocks that I knew my heart was no longer in it. When you start thinking like that there's only one way you can go.

I thought, 'That's it, I'm retiring.'

That Cardiff game, after 115 appearances for Crewe, was my last match.

As one door closes, of course, another one opens. I was out of action for six weeks with my jawbone wired up, but eventually I eased myself back into the markets and after that I never looked back. Football had given me the best years of my life, but from the moment I retired from Crewe, that's when my real business life kicked in.

Ten

OBJECTION, YOUR HONOUR!

When you spend all your life dreaming of one thing it's a surprise when your destiny turns out to lie in some other direction. For as long as I could remember, all I'd wanted to do was play football. But that side of my life was now over. In fact, from the moment I hung up my boots, I didn't go to another football match for six years. A lot of ex-pros go through this – especially when, like me, they've retired through injury. It's too hard sitting up there watching other people doing what you should be doing, and you don't – you can't – enjoy it. You go from living and breathing football to wanting to get as far away from it as possible.

These days it's often only players who work for the media who still go along. When Kevin Keegan came back as Newcastle manager he admitted he hadn't seen a match for a couple of years – and that's about average, I would say.

The one thing you do miss, of course, is the adrenalin. Waking up on a Saturday morning and knowing there was a game coming up gave me such a thrill. There was nothing like it. The whole day was built around that moment at three o'clock when the referee blew his whistle. I absolutely loved that feeling, and when it disappeared from my life I was left with a massive void. I couldn't explain it to Pat or to any of my friends because it sounded daft. Only other ex-footballers knew what I was going through.

For some people it's also tied in with the fact that they don't have 50,000 people chanting their name every week. With others it's the realisation that their livelihood has dried up. More than a few of these guys have turned to the bottle because of it.

I was lucky. I did actually have something else to do with my time – and it was making me a lot of money.

My market stall was booming. The other traders would stand there scratching their heads saying, 'How the hell are you getting away with those prices?' But the people who travelled from all around to get their cheap toiletries, medicines and baby foods from me all eventually went into the market hall, so everyone benefited.

The one advantage the other lot had over me, of course, was that their business took place indoors. As soon as it rained or turned a bit chilly I noticed a downturn, so I decided to give the stall a bit of a make-over.

We erected wooden panels on the sides and over the top so everyone was protected from the elements. Best of all, though, my dad climbed up the nearest lamp-post and ran a cable from the electricity supply into my stall – so now we had power and lights and even an electric till! That was a stroke of genius, and as soon as we'd done it I asked for permission from Len Dutton.

'But what if he says no?' Pauline worried.

I said, 'He might. But it's easier to apologise than to get permission.'

When you've had a bit of success you're always going to attract attention – and not always in a good way. I would find that out again and again as my business grew but the first inkling I got it was happening to me was when I received a letter from a solicitor. It was on behalf of Boots the Chemist.

I thought, 'Oh, blimey, now the big boys are taking notice of me. I must be doing something right.'

Not in their eyes, though, I wasn't.

Boots had complained to the Pharmaceutical Society of Great Britain that I was selling patent medicine from a market stall. They also objected to the fact that I was offering goods below the retail price. Before I knew it, I had a date set in Wigan Magistrates' Court.

Boots turned up with a crowd of people. There were advisers for this, lawyers for that. I don't know what half of them did, but I'm sure they weren't cheap.

On the other side of the aisle there was a table for the accused. That's where I sat – on my own.

'Mr Whelan, who is representing you?' the magistrate asked.

I said, 'I'm representing myself, your honour.'

'Very good. How do you plead?'

'I plead not guilty.'

Boots put their case and then it was my turn. I said, 'It's not a market stall. I've got full running electricity, walls and a ceiling and it's open as many days of the week as Boots. It's true I remove my stock at night because of security, but to all intents and purposes it's a shop.'

The magistrate said, 'There's only one way to settle this – I need to see this stall or shop.'

An hour later we had the whole courtroom down at the market watching my father doing a roaring trade with the local shoppers.

'OK,' the magistrate said, 'I've seen enough. Back in the court in one hour.'

When we got there he threw the case out. 'Mr Whelan is operating as close to a shop as he can manage, and I believe that is a respectable place to be purveying patent medicines.'

Boots didn't like that, of course, so they appealed and took me to the High Court in London. This was much more serious and, if I wasn't very careful, much more expensive. Everyone said I needed to get in a proper solicitor but I thought, 'I'm not paying for that. We could be down there for weeks.'

Before I went into the courtroom, a solicitor for Boots came up to me and said, 'Who's representing you?'

I said, 'No one. I'm representing myself.'

'You can't do that.'

I said, 'This is an English court of law and I'm an Englishman. English law says I can represent myself, surely.'

He smiled. 'No you can't. This is the Appeal Court. It doesn't work like that.'

'Bugger,' I thought. But I said, 'Well, there's no one else with me so I'm going in.'

'Fine,' he said, 'but you'll lose.'

This was a much grander affair than the Wigan courts. There were three judges and a lot of wigs and fancy robes. Once again I went through the same conversation.

'Who is representing Whelan & Taylor?' the middle judge asked.

'Me, sir. Dave Whelan.'

'I know who you are but I said who is representing you?'

'I'm representing myself, sir.' But I knew what was coming next.

'This is the Appeal Court, Mr Whelan. You are not allowed to represent yourself.'

I tried to look like I knew what I was doing and I gave the same speech I'd given the fella outside.

'With all due respect, your honour, I thought that in a court of law an Englishman could defend himself against charges brought against him. Surely that's the law?'

I fully expected to be chucked out right then and there, but do you know what? The judges put their heads together then said, 'We think you might have a point . . . Recess for ten minutes,' and off they went to chat about it.

When they reappeared the main judge said, 'You're English, you're in an English court of law, you can represent yourself if you want, so carry on.'

'Thank you, sir,' I said, but inside I was punching the air. It was like that moment Tom Finney had let me take the ball off him just to boost my confidence. At that moment I felt confident I could take anything Boots could throw at me.

If anything, I was a bit too confident.

Boots started with their case, this time emphasising that I was selling aspirin and Anadin, all cut-price, and that my 'shop' was actually a market stall, one I'd simply dressed up to call a shop.

There was a programme on television at the time called *Crown Court*, so I'd picked up some of the lingo. After a while, unable to sit and listen to their accusations a second longer, I leapt to my feet and yelled, 'Objection, your honour!'

The whole court fell silent and the Boots brief just stared at me openmouthed.

The judge leant over his bench and said, 'Mr Whelan, you can't object in an Appeal Court. You've got to listen to what the other party says before you have your own say.'

I didn't know that. 'Sorry, sir.'

But twenty minutes later I was on my feet again.

'Objection, your honour – it's not true! If I was hearing those words I'd say I was guilty as well!'

Well, that kicked off a right buzz around the room, and the judge had to bang his little hammer for order.

'Mr Whelan, you are trying my patience. If you stand up one more time I will not hesitate to throw you out of this court, and you will not get a chance to represent yourself. Is that clear?'

'Perfectly, sir.'

By then I'd lost a little of my nerve, but when it came time to mount a defence I quickly got into my stride. I rattled off all the reasons why Wigan court had voted in my favour in the first place and I added, 'They don't care if I'm a shop, a market stall or a hole in the wall. The only reason they're bothered about my market is because I'm doing better business than them and they want to stop it.'

After a while the judges disappeared outside to mull it over. When they came back in I had no idea which way it was going to go but the Boots team looked more than pleased with themselves.

The main judge spoke. 'We find that Mr Whelan has a very good case. Without seeing his shop, we are happy to go on the word of Wigan Magistrates' Court, and we endorse their ruling that it is a shop. However, on the question of selling patent medicines below the retail price, we find him guilty because he has admitted as much.'

I'd won one and lost one. The big factor, though, was how I was going to be punished. With that verdict the judges were within their rights to stop me trading. But he said, 'We are therefore fining Whelan & Taylor the sum of £200.'

You've never seen a guilty man look so relieved. That was peanuts to me and I'd be back in Wigan doing it again tomorrow. The Boots side weren't happy with that at all, and their man was on his feet again.

'We'd like as is customary to request that the guilty party pay our costs.'

'That's going to be a fortune,' I thought, but I didn't dare say anything until I was asked. Then I said, 'Your honour, since I won the original case in Wigan I don't think it's fair to have to pay for them to drag me down here, although I'm happy to pay my own costs.'

The judge didn't even consult on that one. He just said, 'Each party must pay their own costs. Court dismissed.'

I had to laugh. My only cost was a bit of petrol to get down there. I didn't have a solicitor, I didn't stay in London overnight, I hadn't even bought myself any lunch yet. On the other hand, Boots must have had a bomb to pay.

I have to admit we started to enjoy the good life. My wife isn't at all flashy by nature but we began to spend a bit more time doing things as a family and spending a bit of money. Pat and I liked to have a wander round antique fairs, and now we had a bit of cash in our pocket we could buy one or two things. Something that caught my eye as soon as I saw it was this huge suit of armour. It needed a bit of a polish but I thought, 'That will look superb greeting people at our house.' Pat said I was mad, of course, but it was one of those things you see and you just have to have. It reminded me of the *Ivanhoe* and *Camelot* films I watched as a boy, and as I could afford it I thought, 'Why not?'

We began taking nice holidays as well. I was the first person in the Whelan family ever to go skiing, which I really enjoyed for those moments when you stand at the top of a mountain and think, 'OK, I'm going down there as fast as I can.' After a few years out of the game, that was the closest I'd come in a long while to feeling the rush of a Saturday afternoon. It wasn't the same, but it was close.

Business gave me thrills in other ways, of course, and I felt great satisfaction watching the market business grow and develop, especially as I now had another stall inside the market hall. Between that, the original stall, the shop and my little warehouse I had a dozen staff working for me. I realised one day that I was getting itchy feet though. Things were a little too comfortable and I had fallen into a rut. Life is never the same two days running when you have small children but I needed a bit more than that in my working day. I began to think about new ways of taking my business forward. The market was definitely an improvement on our corner shop, so what did that leave?

Then out of the blue it came to me: the supermarket.

Lennon's were one of the first in the land to open supermarkets and they'd got a store in Wigan and another one in St Helens. I went and had a look and I thought, 'This is the future. I need to be part of this.'

Before then all grocery shops were just like mine – you would go in and tell the person behind the counter what you wanted – tin of beans, a pound of butter, a slice of gammon, whatever – and they would fetch it for you. There was none of this helping yourself or browsing through stuff to check the ingredients or anything like that. So having a place where you could actually wander around and look at things was a breath of fresh air, and of course it took a bit of getting used to, like everything. But I knew that eventually people would want to select things themselves and actually see the vegetables they were buying.

As soon as I saw Lennon's I knew that was it.

Sometimes when you work hard enough a bit of good fortune comes your way. I happened to mention to the fella I bought my electric till from, who worked for National Cash Registers, that I was thinking of changing business, and he came straight back to me with a fabulous offer.

'NCR are having a sales conference out in Miami for four days,' he said. 'How would you like to go over there and hear what we can do for you?'

Well, you don't get an offer like that every day of the week, do you? This company paid for me to fly out and listen to their sales pitch, but most of the time was my own so I turned it into a frantic research trip. I went in every supermarket I could find, because of course America led the way in these things. Lennon's didn't have trolleys then, only baskets, but you had them in Chicago. It was incredible seeing how they'd taken the same concept and made it work so well. Every supermarket I went in was packed with customers, which just made me even more determined to enter the game. I couldn't wait to get back home and get cracking.

I set up a new company called WDS Ltd as soon as I got back. To run a private company in those days you'd typically have one hundred shares and if you were the sole proprietor you'd own the lot. I only took ninety-five per cent of the shares in WDS, though. The rest I put in the names of

Bill and Albert Howarth. I didn't ask them for a penny and I didn't ask them for permission – it was just my way of saying thank you for their help in starting me off.

Then I began hunting around Wigan for a suitable space, but it was a slow process and every day that went by felt like I was missing the boat. Then just as I was getting frustrated I discovered the perfect place right under my nose. An old warehouse of about 6,000 square feet became available in the Market Square, right opposite my stall. The rent was £4,000 a year, about £80 a week, which was a huge step-up after what I'd been paying, but the space was incredible. I had three huge floors to trade on and I didn't have to shift my stock at the end of the day!

The ground floor was for food retailing only and I set it all up exactly how I'd seen it in America. The same shelving, the same positions for everything, the same feel. I got the local joiner to build me six wooden checkouts, and of course plugged in NCR's latest tills. I installed a butcher's counter which looked very white and clean but the big innovation at the time was refrigeration, so I took a small loan from Barclays and had a vast cooling system put in my dairy counter. That was something America was doing before the UK and I knew it would catch on like wildfire. To be able to sell frozen and fresh food was a retailer's dream.

Lennon's had been my inspiration but my place was very different by the time we'd finished kitting it out. They were a small supermarket that still felt like a corner shop. I had gone all out for customer choice and great value. My philosophy from day one was pile it high, sell it cheap – and the customers absolutely fell in love with that.

I didn't want to just concentrate on food, though, so the upstairs floors were devoted to just about everything else. We sold baby clothes, prams, cots, glassware, china, cookers, fridges, you name it. I wanted to offer everything under one roof – we were one of the first in the land to sell white goods alongside tins of beans. Funnily enough, though, one of the few things that didn't sell in huge numbers was sports gear. Being an ex-pro, I thought that putting a few Mitre footballs and the latest boots on the first floor would be an instant winner. They sold, but not in any great numbers. I scratched my head on that one, but one day I'd work it out.

While the transformation was taking place I started to think about drumming up business. I had no doubts whatsoever that the shop would be a hit once word got round and people had experienced it for themselves, but I wanted to start with a bang. I needed to come up with something to grab attention on our opening day – *but what?*

Then just as I was leaving the house one day I walked past that suit of armour that I'd bought and inspiration struck. You could see your face in the polished metal now and I thought, 'If I enjoy seeing that thing every day, I'm sure other people would as well – but who can I get to wear it?'

I couldn't wait to get hold of my father that day. I said, 'I've got you a new suit.'

'Oh thanks very much. Where is it?'

'It's back at the house – will you come and try it on after work?'

When he saw what I had in mind he burst out laughing, but he was always game for anything so he said, 'If I can get in it, I will wear it.'

Somehow he squeezed his legs inside, then we lifted the rest of it on. You'd think it had been made for him. I had a sandwich board to hang around his neck, which read 'Whelan's Discount Store, Opens Thursday', and then I sent him out on the streets.

I was meant to be supervising the finishing touches at the supermarket but I couldn't resist watching my old man clunk up and down the streets around the Market Square. Wiganers couldn't believe their eyes. I saw people walking into lamp-posts, coming out of their shops to have a look – one fella crashed his bike staring so hard. It was a hysterical sight but it worked. It got attention. Kids dragged their mums around the town just to catch a glimpse of him, and all the while he was telling folk about the shop. He was such a great talker – no one could speak to him without ending up at the supermarket.

Eventually I left him to it and got back to my shop. A couple of hours later there was a commotion at the front door. All the fitters and painters were laughing and pointing – because there was our knight in shining armour hopping up and down like a Morris dancer.

'Are you all right, Dad?' I asked.

'No, I'm bloody not,' he shouted. 'Get this thing off me – I'm bursting for a pee!'

That suit of armour is very special to me, and it caught Paul Jewell's eye twenty-five years later when he came to my house. I told him, 'If you get Wigan promotion to the Premier League you can have it.'

We were in the old Third Division at the time so I thought it would be safe for a few years yet, although obviously I wanted him to succeed. It was the last thing on his mind that day we made it, but I had the suit all wrapped and delivered to his house. He was speechless but touched I'd remembered.

My dad's good work paid off. When we opened that Thursday the queues were already forming outside. I'm not an emotional man but the feeling I got watching person after person taking their loaded baskets to the checkout really moved me. I thought, 'I've done it, I've got it right.'

And I had. On top of the rent it had cost me about £12,000 to refurbish that old warehouse and transform it into Whelan's Discount Store, not counting the salaries of my twenty-four new staff. But at the end of that day I had to pinch myself. We had just over £7,000 in the tills. Seven grand in one day – and, I promised myself, that was just the beginning.

For a while I continued to buy for the market stalls as well as the super-market – but it was harder now because the Manchester mob didn't handle food. I could get everything else from them, but for edibles I had to use a wholesaler. I signed up with Taylors of Westhoughton, but I knew right from the start that I had to get away from that set-up as soon as possible. The way you make money in business is to get rid of all the middlemen you possibly can. You have to buy at the cheapest price – which means straight from the manufacturer – and you have to buy in bulk to get the big discounts.

So my next ambition was to get a warehouse where I could house enough stock to make bulk buying worthwhile. The old mill where my dad used to work, Eckersley's, had stopped trading by then so I bought a large chunk of warehouse space in there and hived off a little area to use as an office. You had to climb up steps to get there because I think it must have been the old foreman's office and he needed to see the shop floor. I didn't have much in the way of furniture but I got an old bench where a girl used to sit and help me out with telephone calls and a bit of typing and that suited me fine. I preferred to be out and about anyway.

Once I had the warehouse sorted I could go direct to the likes of Heinz and Birds Eye and get much better prices. Funnily enough, though, it was through something else that I started to do the best business.

One of our big sellers was bread. I used to sell a loaf for a shilling – five pence today but twelve pence in old money. Everywhere else it was one and thruppence. The big baker in Wigan was called Rathbone Brothers but I couldn't get the right price from them so I had done a deal with another baker, Hall's, instead – and boy was that paying off. I was paying eleven pence a loaf and selling for twelve so that was an instant penny profit on each one, which soon added up because we were selling hundreds of loaves a day. People started to queue round the block every morning just to get their hands on one at that price. It was an irresistible saving for folk and I had delivery vans from Hall's coming in and out all morning. As one unloaded, there'd be another one waiting behind it. It was a constant procession because customers would come from all over Wigan to buy their bread from us.

Rathbone didn't like this. He rang up and asked to see me. A market trader getting asked for a meeting with a retail god like him was unheard of, so I said, yes, of course I would see him.

'Right, when can you come over?' he asked.

'Oh no, Mr Rathbone – if anyone wants a meeting with me they have to come to my office.'

He was a bit put out by that because he was used to getting his own way. But the next day it was him and his associate who were climbing up the wooden staircase to my little office. They got straight to the point and said Rathbone's would like to start supplying me with bread as I seemed to be doing all right selling it.

I tried to downplay my pride that he was asking to work with me – and not the other way round. 'Of course, it all depends on the price.'

'I think you'll like our price,' he said, 'but the main thing is we don't want you selling our bread for a shilling. It's one and three everywhere else and we can't have you going lower.'

I scratched my chin at that one. 'Did you see the sign above the door as you came in, Mr Rathbone?'

'Aye, I did.'

'Well you'll have seen it was my name and not yours – so it'll be me who decides what price I sell at in my own shop. I think that's the end of the meeting, gentlemen.'

Then he started sweating. 'Let's not be too hasty. Let's talk about it.'

'There's nothing to talk about. We do a deal and I sell at a shilling if I want to, or you clear off now.'

'I'll think about it.'

I knew then that I had him. A month later he came back and tried to get me to go up a penny but I held firm. In the end he resigned himself to losing. 'How many loaves do you want?' he asked.

I made him jump through a few hoops but it was a good relationship for both of us. Rathbone's in Wigan really was the name, and so to have them in my shop was untrue. It was like Warburton's – an ace name with an ace product. When they started supplying us, sales went even higher, sometimes hundreds a day. And if people were coming to us to buy a loaf, they never left without picking up a basketful of other essentials as well.

With my new shop heaving every single day I started to look for a new site. That was the other thing I'd spotted in Miami – chains of stores in the same area. England at the time only had Boots and a handful of others, but not much at all in the area of grocery. I was about to change that.

These days you have property directors at all the big companies and their job is to source new locations. I would eventually get chaps in to do this for me, but in the early 1970s I was on my own. I would drive around the area just looking and looking. Then one day I was in St Helens' Sutton Lane and saw an old railway depot building at the end of a disused track that looked pretty much wrecked and unloved.

I got out of the Rolls and had a nose around. The train track used to come straight into the building so the engineers could work on the engines, and even get underneath to clean them. Despite that and all the large holes in the roof designed to let the steam escape I fell in love with that place. I got straight on to British Rail in Liverpool and made them an offer. The very next week, with a thirty-six-year lease fixed at £400 a year, I started the business of transforming the building into my vision.

More than once over the next six months I wondered if I'd bitten off more than I could chew, but we persevered. The floor was replaced, the holes repaired, and state-of-the-art shop fittings began to be installed. I'd kept abreast of the latest innovations in the USA so I was happiest of all when we took delivery of all these vertical fridges with large glass doors. Customers could see exactly what was for sale with them – and more importantly they could reach it too. It sounds weird now, but that piece of hardware alone gave me a total buzz.

Compared with today it was probably an eyesore, but to me then that store was a thing of beauty. It was state-of-the-art, it had the newest technology behind it and I'd ploughed every penny I had into it. More than once I found myself standing outside just admiring it.

The whole project didn't just require a huge cash investment – it needed an investment of faith as well. The location itself was a huge gamble because there were no other shops near by. I was actually creating one of the first out-of-town stores in the UK, even if we didn't call it that. Cars, though, were becoming more and more popular and I could see the future of retail would be shaped by that.

It was a nervous time when we opened it finally but I needn't have worried. The place boomed, it absolutely took off. Next I opened another one in Bolton and after that I converted an old cotton mill in Manchester. This was my most ambitious project yet, because at 50,000 square feet it was the largest – one of the biggest in the country. I was always looking for new ways to get customers in front of the goods so I installed a narrow walkway that let mums push their prams up this gradual ramp to reach the non-foods upstairs. Anything I could think of I did – and it all seemed to pay off.

For a while life seemed a bit too good to be true. Then two episodes occurred which reminded me that you can become an expert on anything but there are always lessons to be learnt about people. Human nature is a funny thing, and I was about to discover it the hard way.

The first incident was another court case. It wasn't Boots this time but Cow & Gate, the leading manufacturer of baby foods. They didn't have a problem with us not being a 'proper shop' like Boots had – they just hated us selling their stock so cheaply. The retail price was still king then, so technically we were selling illegally but the day the court order arrived I wasn't bothered. You just think, 'We're only trying to save people money, we've nothing to fear, nothing to hide. Let's get stuck into them.'

There was big interest in our case because it was the first to challenge the retail price law, and a lot of manufacturers of other goods suddenly started paying attention. We sold everything at discount – that was the whole point of the store, that was its name! Pushchairs were another controversial one, though. Silver Cross prams were the Rolls-Royce of baby kit. They used to sell even then for something like £29.99, which was criminal for a young family, but with babies you've got to have the best you can afford, haven't you? The makers used to play on this, so there was uproar all round when they saw our undercutting. Every single company stood shoulder to shoulder with Cow & Gate because if we lost we'd have to put everyone's prices up.

Representing myself against Boots had paid off, but I was warned against trying my luck a second time so we brought in Roger Lane Smith, who had a company in Manchester. He was top-drawer for us and the judges threw the case right out of court in under three hours.

It had taken six months of our time and a hell of a lot of money but we'd won the day – and our costs back. As a result of that case the recommended retail price was brought in, so producers could never again demand the price you sold at. We hadn't done it for Rathbone and we would never have to do it again.

Roger Lane Smith went on to become a very close friend of mine and an invaluable work associate.

The other episode that occurred in the 70s was a visit from the tax man. This wouldn't be the last time I was investigated – but it was the most traumatic because I quickly learnt that people I thought I could trust were behind it.

It started when I got a call from Fairhurst's, our accountants. They said, 'Dave, the Inland Revenue are here going through the files. You'd better get over quick.'

I flew over there and this fella who liked the sound of his own voice a bit too much told me I was to be the subject of a full investigation because of 'information received'.

'What kind of information?'

'I'm not at liberty to divulge,' he said imperiously.

He asked me a bunch of questions and pretty much accused me of siphoning off cash from the business. It ended with him saying he would be in touch when he'd concluded his investigations – but it didn't look good for me.

The next few weeks were very unpleasant. I didn't know what he was talking about but he seemed pretty sure of his evidence. Then a large parcel of documents arrived at the office. It made very interesting reading.

Inside the package were copies of all my correspondence with the Revenue – as well as lots of 'information' about me supplied by other people. I felt sick as I went through it. One fella I'd had to let go from the shop had written in saying, 'You should check Dave Whelan out. He takes stock from the warehouse and sells it for cash.' There were others from names I didn't recognise who said things like, 'He drives around in a big Rolls-Royce so he must be up to no good.' The worst one of all, though, was a piece of vitriol from a man whose name I recognised at once.

The previous year Pat and I had bought an apartment in Majorca. We'd met this fella out there and had always been friendly with him and his family. But now here he was saying, 'Dave Whelan throws money around like confetti and he's got a giant yacht moored out here.' A yacht? It was a two-man dinghy!

I have to admit I was a bit choked by all this, and Pat had to give me a talking-to. 'There are some very scary people out there who are jealous of other people's success,' she said.

On the bright side, it was obvious that I wasn't meant to have received these letters, so I made copies and stopped worrying about my next meeting with the Revenue. When it happened, I was seen by a chap from their head office in Birmingham. He was even worse than the last fella. I let him tell me what sort of a person he thought I was for a while but eventually I had to say, 'There's something I'm very unhappy about.'

That stopped him in his tracks. 'Oh yes – what's that?'

I threw the letters on the table. 'I resent the fact that you're sending these everywhere.'

He went green. 'Where the hell did you get those?'

'Your office sent them to me. You can have them if you want – but of course I've kept copies.'

'It doesn't change anything,' he blustered, white as a sheet by now.

I pointed to another letter. 'I think this one changes quite a lot, actually.'

He read the letter I'd selected. It was from his own boss.

'"This man obviously earns a lot of money and he declares a lot of money. As far as I can see there is very little evidence apart from public speculation. Be very careful about what you say."'

'Apparently even your own boss thinks you're on thin ice with this one,' I said.

He went quiet. 'I don't like this one bit,' he said. 'Number one, I apologise for the letters. Number two, I'm going to drop the case.' He turned to his oppo. 'There is no case to answer here as far as I can see. Come on.'

You'd think I'd feel better after that, but knowing that the only reason I went through it in the first place was because of other people's spite left a very sour taste in my mouth. Later on I took a great deal of satisfaction from calling the guy who used to work for me.

'Hello, it's Dave Whelan here,' I said.

'Oh, hello, Dave. What do you want?'

So I told him I knew about the letter. I just wish I could have seen his face. People are very strange animals at times.

By 1978 I had eight supermarkets and a wonderful bottom line. Even though the percentage on food was a lot less than sixteen per cent, because I was selling in such quantities it was still very healthy.

Supermarkets then used to operate a lot differently to how they operate now. You could get by on twelve per cent gross margin but your wages-to-sales ratio should not be more than three per cent. When Kwik Save first opened, Albert Gubay used to operate at two per cent, but he used to make suppliers come in themselves and put all the food out so he didn't need staff to do it. So McVitie's would come in and put their own Digestives or Ginger Nuts on his shelves for nothing. If you wanted to sell frozen food, you had to provide the refrigerated cabinet. He was absolutely ruthless but very, very successful.

Because of his lower wages-to-sales ratio he could go rock-bottom on his food prices – like Aldi do now. He was probably operating on nine per cent gross margin but because he had big sales, as long as he was finishing up with two or three per cent net he was fine.

I used to operate on eleven or twelve per cent in the food part, but with the non-foods I got it up to fourteen per cent gross. I had four per cent wages to sales but that still gave me a decent profit. Another great operator, Morrisons, used to have fifteen per cent gross margin. Now it's about twenty or twenty-five on food. But the wages to sales have come up too, to about eight or ten per cent, along with all the other overheads.

In those days, if you made more than £100,000 you were advised to turn your company public. We'd already been well over this amount for some time and so Roger Lane Smith suggested I think about becoming a PLC. It's a big move but basically it means you get a lot of investment to fund expansion – and with seven supermarkets already that was my plan. He took me into Manchester to see the old Slater Walker Company, a big commercial bank, but from the moment I sat down in their office I started having doubts.

The fella I saw was pinstriped, a real well-dressed city type with a cigar and braces and everything. He looked exactly how you would expect – but he came up with a load of questions I hadn't been prepared for.

'What's your gearing like?'

I thought to myself, 'The only gearing I know about is when you bash your balls changing gears on an old Raleigh bicycle.' But I said, 'I don't know what you're talking about.'

'Your gearing – what are your liabilities to your assets?'

'Er . . .' I didn't know that one either.

Then he said, 'What's your leakage like?'

I knew that one! I said, 'We've got no leaks since we fixed the roof at St Helens.'

'I don't mean holes in the roof – I mean how much do you lose to shoplifting?'

It was all getting a bit too much for me so I turned to Roger and said, 'I don't think I'm ready for this yet. I don't understand half of what this gentleman is asking me. I'll have to read up on it.'

The banker agreed. 'I think you've got it in one there, Mr Whelan. I suggest you go away and do a bit of homework.'

On the way home I resolved to throw myself into building my business as I had been doing. But a few weeks later I got a call from Ken Morrison and everything changed.

Morrisons supermarkets were legends in Yorkshire but they had no branches over our way in Lancashire. Ken Morrison had been along to look at our set-up and had liked what he'd seen. And he should know because that man is the absolute king of the supermarkets. So when he rang and said, 'Will you pop over to have a meeting?' I was there like a shot. This wasn't like talking to Rathbone's bakery – whatever Ken had to say was worth travelling for.

I went over to their offices in Thornton Street, Bradford, and instantly got on with Ken. He doesn't mince his words and neither do I. He had a cup of tea rustled up for me and before I'd even taken a sip he said, 'I would like to buy your supermarkets. Are you willing to sell?'

It had never occurred to me to try to sell but you have to recognise an opportunity when it arises and at least listen to an offer.

I said, 'Yes, I'm willing – at the right price.'

'I was thinking about one million quid.'

'I was thinking about two.'

Ken had a chuckle at that. 'Two million? You've only got seven supermarkets.'

'I know, but I've also got the land and planning permission for another one just outside Wigan. That's a gold mine just there.'

He thought about it and offered another £250,000. 'And then I'm finished.'

I couldn't very well drop from £2 million to that, so I thanked him for his tea and said I'd be off right after I'd used the gents.

I was still at the urinal when the door opened and someone else came and stood next to me.

'Will you take 1.4?'

It was Ken.

'You're persistent, aren't you, following me in here!' I said. 'But no, 1.5 is as low as I will go.'

He took a deep breath and said, 'OK, you bastard. One and a half but you've bloody squeezed me to death.'

How about that? We finished up, washed our hands then shook on it – all before we left the room. Then he led me back to the office where the rest of his team still were. They were all surprised to see me come back in.

'Right, ladies and gentlemen,' he announced. 'There's a deal on the table, it's all agreed. All you solicitors can bugger off.'

I had no doubts that he would keep his word, and just when he said it would, the money arrived in my bank account. Ken's like that – nice and direct.

But he's a shrewd fella as well. Before it all went through he had to send the auditors in to value the stock and check on the creditors and generally go through your books. While that was going on I offered to give him a tour of the business so he knew what was what. We went around Wigan first and I took him in the warehouse, then we went to St Helens. I was a proud man showing him around. The shop looked fantastic and I could tell he was impressed. What really caught his eye, though, were Easter eggs. We'd just put Cadbury's eggs on sale in a basket at the end of the aisles at rock-bottom prices. He raised his eyebrow at that.

'A bit low, isn't it?'

'It gets people pouring in and then we've got them.'

While we were talking he picked up one of these eggs and spotted a big dent in it, where someone had picked it up and dropped it. The foil was still intact but when he shook it you could hear it was broken.

'I hope you're not counting this in the stock,' he said with a perfectly straight face. 'I want it knocked off.'

He called over an auditor and said, 'Chuck this away and get it off that list.'

I was trying so hard not to laugh but I thought, 'Two can be ruthless,' so I said, 'Whoa, that's my stock you're talking about. Give it here' – and I started eating it myself. 'Do you want a piece, Ken?'

'No I don't!' But he was laughing as he said it.

Ken was one of a kind and definitely top of the pile – he still is. The finest retailer for a very long time.

Once the deal had gone through there were two very important things I had to do. The first was to pick up the phone to the Howarths.

'Hello, Bill. I've sold out to Morrisons. I'll make sure you get your share.'

He congratulated me but he didn't even ask about the money. A lot of people would have latched on to that right away, but Bill just accepted I would do the right thing – just as he'd done the right thing with me. He used to pop in to see me from time to time, which was his right as a shareholder, but he never once interfered and he certainly never tried to liquidate his asset by selling to anyone else.

I had a relationship with them that was very special, so it filled me with great pride to write that cheque for £75,000. Only once they'd received it did they get back in touch.

'We don't deserve this,' Bill said.

'Of course you do, and more. You're the ones who taught me two plus two is four.'

'But you're the one who did the work.'

There was one other person I had to have a chat to as well, and that was Pat.

'What are you going to do, love?' she asked.

'For the first time in my life I'm going to do absolutely nothing,' I said. And that was the day I retired. I was forty-two years of age.

Eleven

MY STOCK'S FLYING AWAY!

Retirement's a double-edged thing. It's nice not working – but having nothing to do is a completely different matter.

When Morrisons took over the Discount Stores I got out of markets and sold the shop as well. I handed over Whelan & Taylor completely to my sister and I stopped buying for her and Jimmy. 'This is me finished – I'm going to enjoy doing absolutely nothing.'

Pat had other ideas.

On my first day as a free agent she said, 'Do you fancy going into Southport for a look round the shops?'

'That'll make a nice change. Why not?'

So off we went. I'm the sort of person who goes shopping about once a year, generally around Christmas. That trip to Southport was nice enough, but the next day Pat said, 'They've got some lovely new shops in Manchester – why don't we take a ride over there today?'

Out came the Rolls once again.

And that's how the week went on. Monday Southport, Tuesday Manchester, Wednesday Wigan, Thursday Bolton, Friday Liverpool. Driving home I thought, 'Five days in a row of shopping – if I do this for a fortnight I'll turn into a cabbage!'

We got home and I sat Pat down. 'Retirement's not for me, love. I'm going back to work.'

'Are you sure? What will you do?'

'Well I'll not be shopping again, that's for sure!'

A few weeks later I was playing golf with a chap called John Bradburn. He was an old rugby union player but in those days he taught geography at the local grammar school. He also owned a bait-and-tackle shop that dabbled in other sports goods. I'd originally got talking to him on the market one day and he'd asked if I'd come in and do a bit of football coaching if I ever had the time. 'I'd be happy to, John – when do you want me?'

I did that a few times on and off and eventually started having the odd round or two of golf with John as well. We were on the back nine one day when he mentioned he was thinking of getting rid of his shop.

My ears pricked up at this. 'You're selling up, you say? How much are you asking for it?'

'I reckon it's worth £22,000 – more for the stock,' he said. 'Are you interested?'

'I might be. I'll have a think about that.'

The shop, JJ Bradburn, had started out in 1903 as JJ Broughton, whose owner was also an ex-sportsman. Then it had been bought by JJ Braddock and finally John Joseph Bradburn. I'd driven past it plenty of times but only been in once or twice when I'd tried my hand at fishing. As a sport, though, fishing bores me to tears. Nothing happens. Even so, I thought, 'I can imagine myself getting into sports retail – it's an obvious step.'

I paid £22,000 for the shop and another £12,000 for the stock and started to think what I was going to call it. For as long as I could remember, kids in Wigan used to say, 'I'm going to JJ's,' so I knew I needed to keep that somehow if I could, but I wanted the name to sound a bit fresher, to have the Whelan mark on it.

After scratching my head for a few days I thought, 'JJ Broughton – JJ Bradburn – both JJB. There's my name right there.'

So that's where it came from – and to think years later 'JJB' ended up being voted one of the top ten most recognisable brands in the UK.

Going back into work was exciting but very strange for me because the shop was so small and I'd been used to running hundreds of staff across multiple sites for so long. I did employ a couple of assistants but it was my plan to be there every single day. That's an absolute must when you start out in a business. You have to work the shop floor and get a proper grasp of everything. You need to see it in action, feel it and smell it.

The shop was set out in the old-fashioned style – there were glass cabinets and shelves around the place but if you wanted to buy anything you had to go to the counter. I'd spent the last few years making money out of getting away from that principle but I decided to see how it worked out.

That first Monday morning I was like a kid in a sweet shop. I had the fire back in my belly and even though the sales I was making were tiny compared with trade at the Discount Stores or on the markets, I was happy to be back in business. We had a few customers before lunch and I thought, 'That's all right. Things will pick up soon enough.'

Most of our trade was fishermen and a lot of them just wanted bait. John Bradburn had installed a large fridge in the basement and it was filled chock-a-block with Benny Ashurst's maggots. We sold them for five pence a scoop and got through thousands of the tiny things every week, most of them just before the weekend.

We'd been going about a month when a lad and his dad came in for some supplies for their day's fishing.

As I went downstairs to get their bait I heard an odd sound that I couldn't put my finger on. I assumed it must be something to do with the fridge, because that was capable of all sorts of weird noises.

It turned out I was right – but not in the way I'd expected.

I picked up the little scoop and a plastic box and opened the fridge door. How I wish I hadn't! There was a terrific buzzing and about a million bluebottles shot up at my face!

I ran upstairs and yelled, 'My stock's flying away!'

I discovered that the electricity had failed in the basement over the weekend and because I'd had no need to go down there for a few days it had gone unnoticed. But it was obviously long enough for the maggots to get warm enough to change into flies.

I decided there and then that maggots had no place in JJB – fishing was out, and I was going to take the shop in a new direction.

*

Thinking that night about ways I could improve JJB, I remembered what it was that had started my transition into supermarkets – going to America. If it could work for one side of retail, why not for another? I booked a big family holiday to Miami and New York and promised myself that by the time we'd got back, I would know exactly what to do with JJB.

The moment I set foot on American soil I could sense the answer was just around the corner. Little did I realise that I already knew it – and had applied it to my supermarkets years ago.

My eyes were opened in the first minute of walking into a sports shop over there. They had a lot of different stock but the main difference was where they put it. It wasn't locked behind glass. Everything was on shelves on the shop floor.

I stood there for about thirty minutes and I watched the same story unfold time after time. A mum and her lad would come in for something – it might be trainers, shorts, anything. But while she's looking for the cheapest version, he's wandering around picking up a basketball and bouncing it on the floor. It doesn't matter if they've only popped in for boot studs – the second that boy has got the ball in his hands and he's felt what it must be like to play for the Harlem Globetrotters, he's not putting that ball down.

Sale after sale after sale went on like that and it was exactly the same in every other shop I went into. Then I decided, 'That's the way to do it. Kids should come in and pick up a cricket bat or a football or boots. You need your customers to physically handle things. They need to get a feel for it, they need to fall in love with it – and they need to leave the shop with it.'

As soon as I'd cracked my problem I couldn't wait to get back home to put it into action.

It really was a controversial move. People in Britain were just getting used to supermarkets letting them put their own shopping in trolleys. No one was doing it in any other type of shop. Wigan had two sports stores, mine and Oliver Somers, and for as long as anyone could remember, they'd been identical. Everything you wanted to buy had to come from upstairs before you could try it on. It was a ridiculous way of doing things if you think about it now, because customers had to know what they wanted before they went in. There was no browsing or random purchasing. So many missed opportunities, I realised, but that was about to change.

I put the 'closed' sign on the door and spent a week converting the shop entirely into self-service. I had trainers, boots and shoes covering the back wall so you could see every single type we had. If you said, 'This in a size eight, please,' it could be in your hands in seconds and you would be able to stroll around the shop in it. The tills were at the back as well, so people had to walk past everything to pay and they'd have to pass all sorts of special offers and bargains on the way. And I put changing rooms right there in the middle of the clothing section. I thought, 'I don't want anyone not buying a top because it's too far to walk to try it on.' So they were there, slap bang in the middle of everything, and a member of staff would help you carry stuff in there if necessary – and watch to make sure the same amount came out of course!

Everything I did had been pioneered in America and I was about to pioneer it in Great Britain.

The question was: would it work?

I'm not kidding you – it absolutely boomed. I don't know how many arguments it caused among families, but it was the same wonderful story day after day. Boys would come in, bounce a ball and not be able to put it down.

'I want it, Mum, I want it.'

Bang – sale done.

Girls were the same. We had hockey equipment, netballs, something for everyone. If they could get hold of something, play with it in my shop for a few minutes, the next thing you know they're imagining themselves as Bobby Moore at Wembley, Bill Beaumont at Twickenham or Björn Borg on Centre Court at Wimbledon. It was an incredible transformation.

Understanding who your customers are really is a crucial part of retail. You might have the best cigars in the world, but unless gentlemen smokers are passing your shop those cigars are not shifting anywhere. I made that mistake with the supermarkets when I tried to put sports in there. It had always bothered me why footballs and boots and the like hadn't been a winner in the Discount Stores and now I knew why. Mums are the ones who frequent supermarkets – if they can get along without the nippers then they will, because no child likes being dragged up one aisle after another. But it's youngsters who drive the leisure business. They're the ones who know the brands, they're the ones who have the sports obsession. It's them that you need to be seeing picking up that cricket ball and bowling like they're Ian Botham.

Even if they do come shopping for a piece of kit, mums are only interested in value. They don't want brands, they just want what's cheap. It's their children who care what colour something is, how many stripes it's got, who's wearing it on the television.

Little did I know, though, that it wouldn't be long before the adults would soon be coming in with as much enthusiasm as their children. The late 80s and early 90s were a boom period for fitness – Jane Fonda's work-out videos were flying off the shelves, jogging was really getting popular and people in general started looking after themselves. In Wigan they all started coming my way – and I knew if I could get them there, I could get them anywhere.

That's when I knew I had to expand. I'd done it before with the supermarkets – I could do it again with JJB.

The first thing I did, though, wasn't to open another store – although that was definitely in my plans. I needed to maximise the potential of this place first. A building became empty at the back of me, an old fruit warehouse owned by Owen Conroy of Wigan, so I snapped that up. That let me shift things around a bit in the shop, and I put the menswear section and what was left of my fishing stock out there, but the main thing it allowed me to do was build two squash courts behind the shop. Squash in those days was relatively new. People were just picking up on it and it was starting to become the game that businessmen played in their lunch hours. Private clubs began to spring up all over the place but you needed membership even to get in the door. My plan was to have it ticket-only and it worked. My squash courts were the first in the land where you could walk in and buy a ticket or book without membership.

It was a gamble of course, because I'd never done anything like that before. But was I confident? Absolutely. When I'd coached John Bradburn's pupils they'd shown me this fives court they all loved playing on. Then I'd been on a holiday in Bournemouth and come across a squash court in our hotel. I'd never heard of the game before, but here I had a go and fell in love with it. It was exactly the kind of fast-moving game I loved.

We charged a pound a court – 50p per person – for forty minutes and it took off like nothing I've ever seen. Within weeks of opening we regularly had queues of people on a Monday morning wanting to put their name next to a time for that week. Of course, to buy that ticket they had to come into the shop, where we would be selling squash gear and everything else they might need. It generated a lot of flow through the store and we became the place to go for a while. I opened up a back entrance as well, so when the shop shut at six o'clock, customers could still get into the courts. We had a changing room, showers – and of course a little display selling sports gear there as well. I couldn't believe how the sport took off and a few years later I bought a cinema that was being closed and converted that to another half a dozen courts. Then I did the same in other towns like Bolton, Manchester, St Helens. We ran leagues from all of them, which kept people interested, and we even began to charge membership – £10 to join, £2 to play. That game was a money-making machine for me. It was an amazing time and I got in at just the right moment.

It was hard to believe it all started from the same premises that had stood there selling maggots and the like since 1903. In fact that store and the squash side of things in particular just kept on growing until the drink-driving laws tightened up in the UK. As soon as that happened the game was killed, not just in Wigan but throughout the country. It had always been seen as a sociable sport, and players would have a game in the evening, then a pint or two in the bar. When driving became a problem so did playing and gradually people drifted away.

That's when I really decided to press on in the retail side of things – and that meant opening new shops.

Expansion is expensive. The profit is definitely there in the long run, but the cash-flow problems when you first start up can kill a venture before it even opens its doors. Fortunately, when I'd gone into JJB I did so with about a million pounds from Ken Morrison in my bank account. The plan was to invest all this in the business without borrowing a penny. That let me open my second store in Oldham, then another one in Manchester.

Now I had a problem, though, because you can't be in three places at once. That's when the real big changes started to come in and I began to hire very talented people to help me out. One of the earliest guys I employed was a lad called Winston Higham. I realised early on that JJB needed to stand for something wherever it opened, and I have to say Winston was responsible for doing a lot of the ground work in the early days. He was the first designer I'd ever hired and he was brilliant. He had a say in how the shops looked, the way things were set out. He gave us the identity we needed.

Funnily enough, his real name wasn't Winston but he was a devout fan of Churchill so the name stuck.

I also got in managers for each store and they ran the day-to-day operations, but I spent a day or two a week in every single outlet. You can't afford to let anything slide when you're starting out and while I still only had three stores it was manageable for me.

On the markets I'd had the Howarth lads to guide me and in supermarkets I'd quickly learnt the need to cut out the middlemen and get a warehouse. I'd sold that to Morrisons but I thought it was worth putting a call in to Ken. If any man could be a role model, it would be him. By the time he retired in 2008, Morrisons was a £13 billion company, and he'd rightly been knighted for his services to Britain.

'We're not using Eckersley's Mill,' Ken told me. 'You can have it back if you like.'

Perfect. It was a giant space and it meant I could buy in bulk, store it there and ship to each shop as and when. Central distribution was paramount. It was convenient but mostly it meant I could get greater savings when I was buying – and that shook a few people up.

When I took over JJB, I have to admit almost total ignorance about the brands. I'd heard of the big names, of course, like Adidas, Puma, Slazenger and Dunlop, but I didn't know what was selling and what wasn't. That was the one thing I had to do before any other – work out who was dominating the market and get in bed with them right from the off. Nike weren't even around then, which is amazing considering their position today, but there were plenty of others for me to get to know.

While everyone in food retail buys in bulk, the sports manufacturers had never come across anyone in the UK doing it because there were no chains. A lot of business was done at trade fairs, which were held around the country and in Europe, particularly Germany. You'd get hundreds of one-man bands turning up to these events and Adidas and Co. would sell to them all individually. Then I arrived on the scene and started ordering for three shops. Then ten, then twenty and more and more. When you're buying that much stock you suddenly become a lot more important to the seller – and at first they didn't like that. Not one bit.

When I started out I had the same terms as everyone else, but I didn't know the ropes then. I didn't have a grasp of the margins companies worked to, so I was led by what John Bradburn had been doing and what the sales reps told me. When I got settled I started selling off trainers or footballs at discount prices and the suppliers didn't like that at all, but I was shifting so many they only complained so much. I used to knock £3 off their shoes then and watch them fly out the door big-style. It gave me a few headaches with the suppliers but that sudden injection of cash flow lets you do incredible things.

As I learnt the game I started to apply my knowledge of other areas of retail. In food you aim for a ten-day stock turnover – that means something comes in and out within ten days. When I entered the sports market, the average shop was doing all right if it turned over its stock once a year. Absolutely amazing.

That's where my instincts and my experience kicked in. I thought, 'I have got to get this down to twenty, twenty-five days minimum or I'm just wasting my time here.'

I treated everything as food. I bought fresh and I sold fresh if I possibly could. I didn't want anything sitting on my shelves for more than a month.

In some cases it was absolutely critical and I don't know how shops were getting away with not doing it in the past. Tennis was still a big game in the 1970s – I'd even started playing it myself – but balls then weren't sold in the pressurised canisters like they are today. They'd arrive in a cardboard box, and every day they sat in your shop they'd be getting softer and softer. After six weeks they wouldn't be fit for a dog to chase, so they had to fly in and out or they weren't worth touching.

With more pound notes flowing in I could be bolder with my suppliers.

I was already getting good discounts for buying 500 pairs of shoes instead of fifty, but there were more areas where savings could be had. I started with the fella from Adidas. He knew as well as I did that cash was king.

'How much will you give me if I pay within thirty days?' I asked him.

'That's two per cent discount. That's standard.'

'What about if I pay in fourteen days?'

That got him thinking. 'I'll give you five per cent if you can manage that,' he said, 'but nobody else can.'

'I can do better than that. I'm going to pay you, in full, within ten days of delivery. And for that I want ten per cent discount.'

He had to ask his boss on that one, but I knew the answer before he even came back to me. Of course he could. It was the same story with Mitre, Puma and the rest. Everyone wants better cash flow. It's what drives shops and world economies alike.

As I began to get to grips with my suppliers I started pushing on again on the expansion front. It went well – until I got to Liverpool. You can't operate in the North West without going into Liverpool but the problem was the city already had a very successful and established sports shop. Jack Sharpe's had been there since the 1930s and they were quite famous. I wasn't worried about the challenge of going head to head with them – but my suppliers got very funny about it.

One by one they came up to me and said, 'Dave, it will be very difficult to supply you if you go into Liverpool. Jack Sharpe's been our customer for years.'

'But he doesn't buy a fraction off you that I do.'

'I'm just saying, you're putting us in a difficult position.'

In a way it was a bit like the situation I'd had with my tax investigation. The reps I worked with were driven by an element of jealousy – they resented my buying power and they could do without me getting stronger. Of course, when Jack Sharpe heard I was sniffing around his patch, he was straight on to all of them.

'If you supply JJB in Liverpool, you can forget about any business from me!'

I don't know where he would have got his kit from if they'd taken him up on it, but it was enough to rattle the big boys. I thought about it for a while and weighed up my options.

'Do I really need the hassle?' I wondered. But, on the other hand, was I really going to let these people tell me how to run my business?

No, I wasn't – and I had the perfect solution.

I went round to Jack Sharpe's and saw his son, who was running the business. I said, 'I've got four shops now and I'm coming to Liverpool, that's a promise. I don't want to open in opposition near you – so I want to buy your shop.'

The suppliers lost their little game with me that time but everyone else came out of it a winner. Jack Sharpe's were happy to get a good price. I was delighted at stealing a business as established as theirs – and the people of Liverpool would be over the moon once I'd shown them what a proper sports store should be like.

Like all of the other shops in the industry, Jack Sharpe's was old-fashioned, with everything hidden away behind long banks of counters. I thought, 'Once I've made this place self-service it's going to be a little gold mine.' And I was right – but first it needed some work.

The first thing I did was stick a 'sale' sign in the window and mark everything down thirty, forty or fifty per cent. I wanted all the old stock out of that building as quickly as possible. There were two reasons: number one, I didn't want to have to pay for storage while I converted the shop. Number two, the sudden injection of cash would go a long way to paying for the work in the first place.

I completely revamped that outfit, and not just the downstairs. I had a beautiful staircase put in and that led up to the offices, which were also transformed. It was the make-over of the year – and it only took two weeks to do it, start to finish. At the end you've never seen a prouder man than me. Now, though, I had to make it work.

I needn't have worried. Business doubled in a month, trebled in six and by the end of the first trading year it was completely unrecognisable from the enterprise that I'd taken over. Liverpool as a community really embraced that shop and they gave me a message: 'This is the way to expand. Buy established businesses on sites where customers already expect to find a sports shop.'

*

So that's how I went on for a few years. Manchester, York, Bolton, Warrington – you name it, if there was a successful shop in that area, I was looking to acquire it. And once I had, Winston Higham and his team would move in to transform it into a JJB.

I couldn't have been happier.

Even though JJB was doing so well and I was kept busy day and night by my plans for it, I couldn't resist following a hunch when one occurred to me – especially if I thought it would give me some of that all-important cash flow to pour into buying new shops.

It was 1980 and I had gone into Ashton-under-Lyne on the other side of Manchester to look at possibilities of opening there. I noticed they had something called a roller-skating rink, which I'd never heard of before, so I went over to have a look. It was shut during the day and the sign on the door said it would be open at seven. I thought, 'Roller skates are sports goods – I need to see what goes on in this place.'

A few nights later I returned with a couple of friends to see what was what. I thought I'd turned up at the wrong place – it was absolutely heaving with people. Kids, teenagers, grown men and women – there must have been 500 of them in that building, all whizzing round and round on the wooden rink. Everyone lined up and got a pair of boots with skates already attached at the bottom – which was an innovation at the time – and they were off.

I could see that this was no flash in the pan – and I knew that it was exactly what a town like Wigan was crying out for.

The building that my warehouse was in, Eckersley's Mill, had a huge canteen area which used to feed its thousands of employees in the old days. I got hold of that space and started transforming it immediately. We put down 14,000 square feet of reinforced maple – the single most expensive thing I've ever bought, I think, because the floor has to be sprung – and installed an area with things for kids like Slush Puppies and confectionery, and a bar for the adults. Then I started doing a bit of advertising and I even got hold of some local dignitaries to help out with the launch.

In April 1980, Councillors Harry and Marian Milligan, the Mayor and Mayoress of Wigan, stood next to me outside the main entrance and declared the Wigan Roller Rink officially open. Then we stood aside and watched as 750 people poured in. It was the same the next night and the one after and every single one after that. We opened at seven but the queues would start forming from six when people knocked off work or got back from school.

Just like with squash courts, it was the right thing at the right time. Dancing was dying out after the whole disco phase but people still needed somewhere to go at night. Youngsters still had to have a place where they could go and chase the opposite sex – and on roller skates they had to chase them pretty hard! Every night you'd see boys and girls holding hands as they went round together. Another night they might be with different people, but that's youngsters for you.

Everywhere I went in Wigan people would be talking about 'the Empire Skate Building', as they were all calling it. I've never seen a response to anything like it before or since. And where there is demand, of course there's money. It was a pound to get in but then most of them wanted to hire boots as well – so that was another pound each. And then there were the bar takings on top of that. We were open seven nights a week and two lunchtime sessions at the weekend.

It was a magnificent operation and best of all, every single penny was cash. There were no cheques, not a penny on account, and nothing to pay purchase tax on. All those sorts of things were like leeches on cash flow but we avoided all of them. In the first week I took £7,500 on the door alone.

I knew I was on to a winner and looked at doing the same elsewhere. Some premises came up in Warrington, freehold for £60,000, so I bought them and opened my second Roller Rink. It was exactly the same success story, right from the word go.

I probably could have done all right out of skating if I'd only concentrated on that, but a few years later I got an offer I couldn't refuse for the businesses. A lady I knew from Blackburn called me one day and said, 'Are you interested in selling?'

As I've mentioned before, I'm always willing to listen to offers. No businessman shuts a door without listening – no good businessman, anyway.

This lady ran a jeweller's shop among other things and was pretty successful. These days she does a lot of after-dinner speaking and cancer work, but she was always a good, sharp businesswoman.

So she came across and about twenty minutes later we'd done the deal. She wanted them that badly, and I could see how much could be done with the amount of pound notes she was offering.

I don't know if it was a particularly good purchase for her in the end, because like so many other things, the trend for roller skating passed to some extent. I didn't see it coming and neither did she. She had a few very good years and developed the business, then she turned the rinks into go-kart arenas, which was the latest craze. Funnily enough, if you opened a rink now, I think the time is right for it to do very well again. These things are cyclical. They come and they go. You just have to wait for the next generation to come along.

When you're dealing in cash, you don't have half the red tape that affects other business transactions, and I was able to pour a substantial proportion of my takings from the Roller Rinks straight into JJB. It meant I could open another six or seven a year on top of what I was already doing.

Business really was flying. I was tremendously happy with the way things were working out and I had a great team working with me. Our property director, Barry Dunn, had started sharing with me all the hunting about for new premises, and David Greenwood came in on the financial side. When you're the size that JJB had grown to in such a short space of time, you're only as good as the folk working with you. And I knew that in those lads and the rest of my staff I had excellent people.

Things couldn't have been better. I was in charge of a business that had grown to more than a hundred shops and I was loving every minute of it. 'But,' I asked myself one night, 'where do I go from here?'

The answer, I realised, was the place I'd failed to understand before: the City.

Twelve

I'LL TOSS YOU FOR IT

One of the great things about being your own boss is you can act on your instinct. At JJB I had a boardroom of very experienced people but I was the one who owned the shares. I called the shots. I would take advice, but at the end of the day it was my decision that mattered.

That meant I could open stores in the places I fancied. It also gave me the power to appoint people I thought could make a difference to our business. In 1983 I hired a young lad called Duncan Sharpe.

Duncan was a golfer from Hull and very good at the game. But the professional tour is a very hard nut to crack. There is so much competition and he was always finishing just outside the top four. I think he knew in his heart of hearts that he would never make it to the very top of the game, so he was happy to accept my offer of employment. He upped sticks from Hull and moved just outside Wigan. Fortunately for Pat and me, his wife moved with him – because he was married to our daughter, Jayne.

Jayne had met Duncan while she was studying at Hull University and we'd been out with the pair of them a few times when we'd visited her. We knew it was serious. Then out of the blue one day I got a call from my secretary. She said, 'There's a young man to see you on some urgent business.'

It was Duncan.

He came into my office and he actually asked for my daughter's hand in marriage. I knew Jayne was mad keen on him so it was not a hard decision. But I really admired him for his old-fashioned manners, and that's when I thought he'd do well in my company.

I also realised that if he worked for me we'd get to see more of Jayne!

We were living in Standish then, so the wedding took place at our local C of E church. There are few prouder moments than when you walk your daughter down the aisle. I knew I was handing her over to a good man, though.

Like everyone who comes to work for me, Duncan started off in a store. It's essential that every single employee gets a feeling for what our core business is all about, and the only way you can get that is to do your time on the shop floor. You need to see how everything works, how we operate. Selling, retailing, dealing with customers – everything starts there. Duncan excelled at every post he tried and so then I brought him into the office and put him on to buying.

Buying and selling is something that you're given a gift to do. It's called being streetwise. You have to know instinctively when you're buying something for the right price and what you can sell it for. The same rule applies if you're buying one item or one million, and simple as it sounds, there are very few people who can do that well. Most successful entre-preneurs normally haven't been to university. You get the odd one, but mostly it's the lads who are streetwise who think of an idea or do something and make a hit of it without help from anyone. And Duncan was one of these fellas.

I started him on buying shoes and that went well, so he moved on to clothing, which is much more difficult. Some people have accused me of nepotism, for promoting my family. But they don't understand business. If Duncan had failed in any area, he would have been out, just like anyone else. If anything, there was more pressure on him as my son-in-law to prove he was there on merit. And, I have to say, it worked. Every area he went into, he excelled at, and within ten years he was chief executive of JJB.

I was opening stores left, right and centre in the 1980s and they were getting bigger and bigger. We were the first to offer a proper American-style sports 'superstore' and customers just loved it. They'd come in and spend a whole morning or afternoon wandering around, trying clothes on, testing the equipment, you name it.

There's more to opening a new branch than just the staff it employs. Every time you expand you are stretching your resources and so adjustments have to be made to keep on top of new developments. A shop will need a manager, and he will need an area manager overseeing him. I won't give an area manager more than ten shops to look after – any more than that and he'll struggle to spend adequate time in any of them and before you know it things slip beneath the radar. He has to know every corner of those shops, spot instantly if someone isn't working or stock is old or dirty. So ten, for me, is the maximum. Then you have regional managers who will have forty shops in their brief. Then you have more deliveries to make, so you need extra drivers, new trucks – and eventually we even had to invest in a brand-new warehousing facility. And all this needs to be controlled from staff at head office, of course, so you start bringing in people there as well. So every time I opened a new store, I knew there were adjustments that had to be made to every inch of the company.

Not all my new ventures were on such a grand scale as the superstores, though. Those really catered for mass-market sport interest. Getting people through the doors who were interested in things like skiing, hiking and climbing was difficult. That's why I opened a string of shops called Alpine Sports, which catered exclusively for them. That did really well for us and in 1988 Blacks Leisure made us an offer for the whole business. I was happy to talk to them because they had something I wanted. There were eleven shops in the country called Howard Sports and they were all on very good sites. I bought them in exchange for Alpine Sports and converted them to the JJB brand.

Opening eleven new JJB stores just like that was a real eye-opener, and if anything it just propelled our expansion plans. I spent at least half the week out on the road looking at sites. Barry Dunn, our property guy, was doing the same. Between us we were identifying dozens of potential new locations – and it was my plan to fill every single one.

I have to say, it was working as well. The year we achieved a million-pound profit was a landmark for me. No sports store had ever made anything like that kind of money before. In supermarkets I'd been aiming for £100,000 – that was the target. But JJB blew those ambitions out of the water. And it kept getting better. From one million to three million to six million. By the 1990s our profit was double that. We were a seriously wealthy company with a seriously healthy future. But could I keep it up?

The Howard Sports deal showed me the opportunities available if you picked the right business to invest in. In 1989 I received a phone call from a friend.

'Dave, I'm thinking of selling my shares – do you want to buy them?'

It was an offer out of the blue and potentially it could take me into a whole new stratosphere. But I wasn't sure so I said what I always do: 'I'm interested in hearing what you've got to say. Let's have a meeting.'

My friend was a chap called Martin Edwards and he wasn't phoning to sell me a sports shop or anything like that. The company he owned was in a different line of work.

It was called Manchester United.

Martin had a house near our apartment in Majorca so we knew each other pretty well. We had dinner whenever we were all over there together and one day he revealed he was thinking of selling his shares in the club.

Surprised, I said, 'You can't do that!' and thought that was the end of it.

Then a few months went by and suddenly this fella called Michael Knighton was all over the papers saying he was going to buy Man U. Remember him? He was the one who came on the pitch at Old Trafford taking penalties and doing keepy-uppies. About a week before the deal was due to go through Martin rang me:

'I can't believe this fella – he's done all this publicity and suddenly he hasn't got the money. Are you sure you're not interested in buying them yourself?'

So the next day I went to a meeting at Old Trafford – it was pretty lively. My old Army pal Bobby Charlton was there, Martin was there, of course, but I was gobsmacked to see Knighton round the table as well.

He'd offered to buy Martin's fifty-one per cent holding for £11 million as part of a takeover bid worth £20 million – but his backers had pulled out.

Despite this he started outlining all his big plans for the club, and as we sat there listening, I began to wonder why I'd been invited. Was the deal off or not?

Eventually I piped up. 'I've got an idea. I will buy your fifty-one per cent and I will combine it with JJB and we will put one company together.'

By the time we disbanded we were all buzzing with excitement – apart from Knighton, of course, who could see a massive opportunity drifting past.

But when I got back to Wigan I began to have a few doubts. There was no denying that Man U would be a tremendous club to own and I was convinced that with the right backing it could become as big in the 90s as it had been in the 60s. But I was running JJB and that could actually prove problematic.

I thought, 'If I've bought Manchester United, no fans from any other club will buy anything from us.'

It was a real concern. I could picture my stores in Liverpool with stones flung through the windows in protest.

I knew I had to pull out but I didn't want to let Martin down again. When I rang him back with the bad news I had an idea for him.

'Look, Martin, I'll get into too much bother with City and Liverpool fans if I come on board,' I said. 'But why don't you float it on the market instead? You'll get a lot more for your shares in the long run.'

'Do you think I will get away with that?'

'I've no doubt you'll get a good reception from the City,' I said. 'No doubts at all.'

'All right then, I'll investigate that.'

A few weeks later we spoke again. 'I think we're going ahead,' he revealed. 'I think we're going to the market.' Two years later United floated with a valuation of £18 million. In 2005 it sold for £790 million. And to think I could have had fifty-one per cent for £11 million!

It doesn't pay to have regrets in business, but you have to learn from everything you do, good and bad. I did the right thing at the time for JJB, and that was the most important thing. But watching United suddenly have all their money worries wiped out by going to the market was certainly an eye-opener for me.

Cash flow – I've said it before – is the driving force of any expansion plans. It's no good being rich on paper. Without fierce cash flow you have your hands tied behind your back in everything you do. Opening a shop demands a huge investment up front. First of all there's the building purchase or lease, then you need £20,000 for the refit plus another £50,000 worth of stock. And that's before staff wages or promotion. Yes, you can move stock from other branches but it has to be bought in the first place, so you are talking a frightening amount of initial outlay. The pressure was on for each branch to make money within four weeks of opening. If it didn't, the next launch could suffer from lack of funds. Without careful supervision, one shop's poor cash flow had the potential to have a domino-like effect on the rest of the business. If one fell, they were all in danger of tumbling.

We had around a hundred stores all over the country and I had some big decisions to make. Did I want to stick with what I had and develop more slowly? Or should I take the plunge – get investment and really go for it?

I went for it.

Going to the market is a huge decision. A lot of people make it without realising just how much their lives will change. Suddenly you're not your own boss any more. You've got the whole City looking over your shoulder, scrutinising your every move. It's a straitjacket on your activities. You have to report twice a year, you've got to give trading updates twice a year, and you end up actually hiring dozens of people just to deal with that side of things. In many ways it's a complete distraction and a lot of businesses fail because they can't live up to their new fiscal responsibilities.

On the upside, though, is the prospect of investment beyond your wildest dreams.

We first went to the City in 1992. Our profits were in the millions and as far as I was concerned, all our ducks were in a row. When the fellas in suits had a look, though, they only gave us a share valuation of £1.49. Not so long ago I'd been confused by talk of 'gearing' and 'leakages', but now

I knew a lot more about going public – and I wasn't impressed. I mulled the offer over with Roger Lane Smith and the board but I knew in my heart that the valuation was too low and for the second time in my life I left a City firm empty-handed.

When I returned eighteen months later, however, it was a different story. Our profit was now £4.6 million and we had 123 stores and that impressed the money men. In October 1994 we were offered £2.14 a share, giving a market capitalisation of £64 million. 'That's more like it!' I thought.

When the financial dust settled, JJB received an immediate cash injection of £35 million. What's more, I got another £20 million for my shares. In the past I had always ploughed my profit back into the business. This time I was advised to hold back. 'You don't have to support JJB any more,' Roger advised me. 'That is what the share issue is for. This money is for you.'

I didn't have any plans to invest anywhere else. Little did I know, however, that an opportunity very close to home would be calling to me within a year. Before I could get distracted by that, though, I had a PLC to run.

Floating a company on the Stock Exchange is a complicated business. Just keeping up with the jargon was difficult, but I had very good advisers and they all said the same thing – I was going to make an awful lot of money, both personally and for investment in the company.

We floated at £2.14 and within eighteen months our investors were sitting on £12 a share. It wouldn't be long, in fact, before JJB was valued at close to £1 billion.

The downside from my point of view, of course, is that I no longer owned a hundred per cent of my own company. But with seventy-nine per cent I was easily the majority shareholder – and I had incredible investment at my fingertips. With that sort of power behind me I increased our expansion programme as far as I could. Within a year we were opening twenty-five brand new stores a year – just over two a month. Things really were booming. But we were aiming even higher.

With JJB now a national concern it gave us all new things to think about. When you sit down in an office in Wigan and plan a new shop, you really do have to ask the question 'Which part of the country is it in?' because that makes a difference on your profits. In the North West, for example, certain fashions might be stronger than in the South East, so you have to be alert to that. But there's another geographical factor that can make a large impact – and I had honestly never seen this one coming.

When I sat down with that pinstriped banker from Slater Walker in the 1970s he'd mentioned the term 'leakage'. I didn't know then but this basically means the amount of stock or money or profit lost through theft. Once I started opening stores all over the country I noticed two very odd things. Number one: leakages were three times worse in the South than in the North. But even more shocking was number two: the majority of all losses were from staff.

People I actually employed were stealing thousands from me!

You try to keep a smile on your face when you employ so many staff, but sometimes it's quite hard, walking around a shop floor and thinking, 'Some of you are nicking hundreds off me every week.'

It's a bit of a shocker when you first discover the facts. If you get £100,000 stolen in a year, £80,000 of that will be by staff. That's in every retail operation. Most of it takes place at the till. In a supermarket, the teller will see a relative in the queue and when she gets served, only a fraction of the goods will get swiped over the scanner. If you're a manager it's hard to spot. You'll see everything lifted off the conveyor belt and it looks fine – but really none of it is registering. It's either held too high to make a bleep or the teller's got their hand over the scanner.

Supermarkets lose fortunes that way, and I soon discovered sports stores did too. No manager can keep track of every employee's family, so you don't realise that it's Johnny's auntie he's serving at the till. You've no way of spotting that instead of £89.99 for that pair of Nike Airs, he's only ringing up half price. There are so many tricks like that and I'm sure they all think, 'What's a few quid to a company like this?'

What's really interesting is that the problem is worse the closer you get to London. In places like Wigan and around here, the levels of theft aren't that bad and in Scotland it's virtually non-existent. From Birmingham downwards it gets progressively worse, then you get to the outskirts of London, to places like Reading, and it is lethal. It seems to be a way of life for the staff there. If your shop has a turnover – not profit – of two million quid, which is nothing in a town like that, you're talking £60,000 straight through the door.

But then once you go the other side of the capital it gets better again. Kent, Cornwall, Southampton, places down there on the coast, are all very honest.

London presents all sorts of other problems for a retailer. You only open there because you have to – that's where the City is, that's where most of the media is, that's where you have to be seen to be.

In fact, it is the worst trading environment in the country. It's busy, it's exciting, but there's so much choice for customers that you can be over-looked, costs are so much more expensive and staff turnover is absolutely unreal. It's not worth giving anyone a name badge because they've quit before the ink's dry. Tell one of them, 'I don't like the way you're doing that,' and they'll put the thing down and just walk out.

'You can't talk to me like that,' they say, and they just disappear. They know there's another job in the next shop.

I've never got a penny profit out of stores in London and I know I'm not the only one. Fortunately, though, the capital remains the exception and things were working out better than ever elsewhere. We were so busy expanding, in fact, that I thought I needed help. It wasn't a new office – it wasn't new staff.

It was a helicopter.

With a business as successful as ours it's easy to lose track of how it began. For me, it was that single shop in Wigan. I knew what had to be done with that place and I personally oversaw the company's expansion for the first few years. Even when Barry Dunn was in place, I always tried to be involved in new sites. But with two, three and soon four shops opening a month that was becoming more and more difficult. The miles were too great to cover and dozens of JJBs were slipping through the net, opening to the public before I'd even set foot inside them. And that's not right. As chairman, as owner, you have to step inside, you have to smell it, you have to feel it – but before you do any of that, you have to see where it is.

And nothing helped me do that better than a helicopter.

There is nothing quite like a whirlybird for giving you a perspective on an area. From up there you can see the whole town in one glance. You can see exactly what rail and road links it has, how much traffic flow there is, and most importantly, you can count the chimney pots. How many houses are there near by, what's your local pool of customers going to be like?

Being airborne revolutionised the way I did business and I think it allowed us to get a lot more done, without question. And of course there's something special about being in a helicopter. You can't help feeling like you've gone up in the world.

The City slated us for buying it. 'It doesn't look right if company directors are seen being too flash,' I was told.

'I'm not being flash – this thing is an essential tool of my business.'

The investors might have turned their noses up but the chopper won a load of fans elsewhere. Not a lot of places have airfields right next to their shopping districts, so we used to land on school fields an awful lot. We'd phone ahead, get permission and make sure the area was clear. Then we'd come sweeping out of the sky, totally branded in JJB logos, land in the middle of the rugby pitch and 400 kids would come streaming out to have a look.

Even if the school was in session, the teachers would always bring the children out because it's not every day they get to see a helicopter up close. The first thing I did was always hand over a dozen or so Mitre footballs to the sport teacher to apologise for landing on his playing surface, then while I went off to do my work, we always left the pilot there to give everyone a little tour and talk. There isn't a boy alive who doesn't want to know what it's like to fly one of those things. It was an amazing feeling seeing the wonder on the children's faces when we came down and it was even better when we took off. They were all kept a very safe distance back but you could see the wind from the rotor blades whipping their hair all over the place and they loved every minute of it.

The helicopter had so many benefits, but the main one was its speed. A trip to Portsmouth, for example, was eight hours in a car – seven if you're lucky. But you can't do business after that sort of journey so immediately you're looking at an overnight stay and another eight hours on the way back. Compare that with a couple of hours in the air.

To succeed in business you have to cut out all the wasted time – and there's nothing like sitting on a motorway for costing you hours. I need my staff to get from A to B as quickly as possible. They have to be on site or in their office for the maximum amount of time, and that is why they were all given access to the helicopter. London from Wigan is an hour and ten minutes. Even Scotland is little more than a day trip. You're there in the morning, you can have your meeting and a spot of lunch, then back again by tea.

When we bought the chopper, though, it never occurred to me that I'd be using it for international trips. But that's because I hadn't thought of expanding into Europe at the time. When we did decide to go ahead, it was an absolute revelation. We were no longer talking about 200-mile trips – it was more like 400. And how better to do it?

JJB were doing so well in the UK that exporting our brand seemed a logical step. America is too far away and it's a market that has been the graveyard for a lot of English companies, so Europe was the obvious place to go. I was itching for fresh areas to expand into and I couldn't wait to get started.

I looked first of all at Germany because I'd been there so many times for trade fairs. But on closer analysis, I decided the market was a bit too different to the UK's. Customers behaved differently, the sports shop in society held a lesser value than I was used to. But Spain and Holland, our evidence indicated, were as close to us as you would get.

In reality we soon learnt they were both very, very different.

We had a lot of obstacles barring our way into Europe, and the biggest of all came from the manufacturers. JJB in England had all the big brands right where we wanted them – we were such a dominant buyer. But the last thing those suppliers wanted was us eating into foreign markets and knocking down their margins over there as well.

The solution was to cut them out of the equation. So that's what I did – I shipped the stock from Wigan. They didn't like it, but they couldn't stop me. And we were buying so much in England that it was nothing to deliver a little of that across the Channel.

We started in Holland with one shop in Rotterdam and another in Amsterdam. Everything went to plan. The local council welcomed us with open arms and the press couldn't give us enough publicity. As for the stores themselves, they were both fantastically laid out – two of our best ever, in fact – and absolutely jammed with stock that had been flying off the shelves at home.

'We can't fail,' I thought.

But we did.

I had thought the closest people to the English were the Dutch and the Spaniards. I soon discovered I was very wrong. The Dutch, as a nation, spend a fraction of the money that Brits do on themselves. And when they do, their tastes are very conservative – I'd go so far as to say dull. We had two shops packed with the latest colourful finery and shoppers just turned their noses up. Where was the old-fashioned stuff, where were the dull colours?

Before I realised how badly the Netherlands were responding, I'd already gone into Spain. Barry Dunn's contacts had pinpointed Barcelona, Majorca and Valencia as the best locations so I flew over with him to check out the proposed sites. I couldn't see anything wrong. In fact, 'They're perfect,' I said.

We opened in a blaze of glory and initially did very well. But eventually the lack of support from the suppliers began to bite. Spain back then wasn't used to having a chain of sports shops, so all the individual stores were being given all the latest Spanish kit while we were trying to pass on English stock. The differences weren't huge, but all manufacturers made slightly varied goods for individual markets – and we were losing out.

After eighteen months I'd had enough. The plan of dipping our toe in the international waters before pushing out big-time was shelved and I pulled the plug on all the European shops. But that didn't mean I lost my appetite for new avenues – not at all. If anything it just meant I would have to look further afield for my inspiration.

Once again I turned to America.

I never like to miss out on new trends and most of those in retail originate in the United States. I go there regularly to monitor their business, but it was when I was back in Miami that I fell in love with what one fella had done.

He'd taken a little multi-storey car park and converted it. A couple of levels were still for cars, but one whole floor was now a sports shop – and above that was a state-of-the-art health centre and gym. In fact the entire top floor had a basketball court in the middle and a running track around it so joggers could get their exercise at 200 feet up. It was a simple idea but absolutely fantastic. And from the crowds going in and out, I could see it was working. I was sold instantly.

'That is it!' I realised. 'That is where JJB should be going.' I immediately started making plans for doing the same thing at home.

Back in Wigan, I marched into the boardroom and declared, 'Have I got a winner for us!'

A sea of expectant faces stared back at me. They soon looked unimpressed when I said, 'Picture a JJB superstore with a gym below it. That is the future.' In fact, no one thought it would work. When you're the chairman and major shareholder, though, and when you believe as passionately as I did, you become hard to stop. But why didn't they see it? To me, sport goods and health go hand in hand. And I had never forgotten how successful my old squash courts behind the first shop had been.

A suitable site came up in Oldham and I was determined to push it through. I could see it now: an amazing shop on the top floor and an escalator leading down to the best health centre in town. We'd have Jacuzzis, steam rooms, swimming pools, quality equipment, gym glasses, luxury changing areas – everything you could possibly want.

We invested a fortune in that place and it looked fantastic. Even then a lot of people doubted it.

'It will never work,' one of our finance guys called Tony said. 'It will be shut within three years.'

'It will be making a million within one,' I said. 'Bottom line.'

We were soon shaking on a £100 bet.

Within ten months, though, Tony was knocking on my door. 'I've just seen the figures for Oldham. You've done it. You've made your million on it.'

Obviously we didn't stop there and health centres started springing up wherever I could place them. The second one appeared in Warrington, followed by another in St Helens. Soon there were a quarter of a million members across the country, all paying their monthly or annual subscriptions. When you think about 250,000 people paying £25–30 a month up front, that's £70–80 million a year straight off. It's a fantastic business and even today the fitness side is still the part of JJB that excites me the most.

When you've had a bit of success, it's strange how people pop up looking for favours. I got a call from Geoffrey Boycott one day which took my breath away.

'Listen, Dave, my grandson is very interested in table tennis.'

I said, 'Oh yes.'

'So do you think I could have a table tennis table?'

'I'll have a look for you,' I said and went off to check. Then a few minutes later I rang him back. 'Yes, you're in luck, we've got some in. I can do one for you at discount – £245.'

There was a pause.

'Ah, I wasn't thinking of paying for it.'

'So what were you thinking of doing?'

'I thought I could visit a couple of your stores and sign a few autographs and we could treat that as payment.'

I had a right laugh at that. I said, 'I don't want you to visit my stores. If you don't want to pay for a table then clear off!'

In 1998 we had 170 stores and we were getting bold. An announcement had been made twelve months earlier saying we wanted to have fifty new shops a year. In July I did a deal that meant we met that target in one fell swoop.

When you're a listed company it's hard to do anything without the financial press knowing about it. There are so many layers of people working on the corporate side of things that leaks inevitably happen. No one, though, expected to hear that two of the largest sports retailers in the country had become one. That had the phones ringing, I can tell you.

Tom Hunter started out selling trainers from the back of a van in Ayrshire but eventually his Sports Division shops became well established, especially up in his native Scotland. He still wasn't in our league, though – not till he did the deal with Philip Green.

Green is a celebrity billionaire now because he owns BHS, Top Shop and plenty of others. But in 1995 he was down on his uppers after a couple of unlucky deals. He worshipped at the same synagogue as the finance director at Sears, so he was in on the ground when Liam Strong put Olympus Sports up for sale. Green didn't have the money but he knew a man called Tom Hunter. Tom couldn't afford it either but he had the background that convinced Sears to give them a shot. Green eventually brokered a deal that gave Sports Division Olympus for £1 – as long as they took on the £30 million debt. As payment, Tom gave Philip Green shares in Sports Division.

So they got Olympus for virtually nothing – and JJB suddenly had a rival with more than 200 shops.

I didn't know either of them but this deal really grabbed my attention. I started looking into their shops and liked what I saw. Tom had started doing out-of-town stores like us and he had some nice areas, especially in the North and above the border. Eventually I'd seen enough and I rang Tom.

I said, 'It's Dave Whelan here. I'm interested in talking to you about buying your company. Are you interested in listening?'

And he was.

I knew then that he was a good businessman. If you don't listen to offers – even if you don't think you want to sell at that point – then you're stupid and you'll get found out eventually. Listening to people is how you learn. You might not go along with it in the end, but you have to hear a person out. Whatever anybody says, you have to listen.

Me, Barry Dunn and our finance director, David Greenwood, all flew up to an airfield near Ayr and Tom picked us up himself. We would still have to do due diligence and a full stock check, but for now I just needed to hear from him whether he was interested in selling – and for what price.

At that time Tom was making something around £30 million before depreciation – depreciation is something that comes off the bottom, like renewing your fixtures and fittings. But his cash flow was good. I liked that.

During that visit I realised that I wanted his business very much. He was so strong in Scotland that I couldn't see us growing there organically to match him in under ten years. He was also very powerful in the North of England. We got very close to completing a deal at the first attempt – but close is not enough. We fell out over the price of one property which he said was worth a million more than I valued it at. In hindsight it seems daft that a thing like that can hold things up – especially when I was still offering £278 million!

'Well, it looks like the deal's off,' Tom said, and I had to agree. We packed our briefcases and prepared to leave. There were no hard feelings – absolutely none. It was just one of those things. In the car on the way to the airport, though, I had a brainwave.

I said, 'Tom, listen – I'll toss you for it. If you win it's 279, if I win it's 278.'

'Done.'

'You know you're talking about millions here!' Barry said.

Tom tossed and asked me to call. Whenever I toss a coin I always shout 'tails'. I don't know why but I always do. This time the coin went up in the air and I called out, 'Heads!'

Don't ask me why – I just did.

But it was tails.

So that was the deal done – and the market never ever knew how it happened. The men in pinstripes don't take too kindly to that kind of thing, but they know it happens from time to time. Business is about considered risk-taking.

When we announced that deal it took everyone by surprise. Even Philip Green hadn't known about it until the night before it went through, after the markets had closed. That was Tom's decision, even though Green held a lot of shares.

Bringing Sports Division into JJB, and gradually converting all the stores to our brand, was an expensive business and so we had a share issue to boost investment. The advantage of this is millions of pounds to work with. The downside, of course, is that once again my holding in the company was reduced. But at around fifty-nine per cent I still massively held the controlling interest.

We got a lot of column inches about the Sports Division deal in the financial press and a few commentators suggested I'd paid over the odds – not by £1 million, but by a lot more. Looking back, I think I probably did go twenty million too much. But from where I stood at the time, I was overseeing an empire of more than 400 shops – and counting. What had begun in Wigan in 1979 was reaching out across the entire country.

Tom Hunter's business wasn't the only company I was keeping an eye on. Nobody can come into the same business as JJB and not be known in our office. You might be at a trade fair or another industry function and notice someone who is having a bit of success. That's when you think, 'He seems to be doing the right things – I'll go and have a look at his operation.'

A few years earlier I had become aware of a small business run by a fella called Mike Ashley.

These days Ashley is a household name, partly for having created Sports Direct, but mainly for the terrible press he's getting up at Newcastle. If he could do something wrong at that club, in the eyes of the supporters, he seems to have done it. For a start he's not a fan. He supports Spurs and everyone up there knows that. But the biggest mistake Ashley could have made was picking a fight with Kevin Keegan. Geordies bleed black and white blood and they support their own. In a popularity contest there was only going to be one winner on Tyneside – and it wasn't Ashley.

I admit, when he first bought that club I had a chuckle. I thought, 'He won't know what he's let himself in for.' Then he started appearing on the terraces in a Magpies shirt, just like a fan. But he's the *owner* of the club. You don't do that. You need to maintain a distance. In my opinion, when you go into a boardroom and the owner's wearing jeans and a replica shirt, it's giving out the wrong message. At Wigan all my match-day guests wear a tie. If they're coming to enjoy my hospitality, those are the standards. A chairman or owner shouldn't try to be friends with everyone. They should set an example.

I think the media have loved having Ashley in football – but when he bought the club in 2007 he took a lot of journalists by surprise. You hear all sorts of rumours in sport but no one had seen this move coming. For days afterwards the press ran stories along the lines of 'Who is Mike Ashley?' because outside the business world he wasn't a famous name at all.

But I knew him of course.

Like me he started out with just one shop, a little Sport and Ski business in Maidenhead, and then started expanding. That's when I decided to go along and take a look.

As soon as I stepped through the door I could see exactly what he was doing. 'Pile it high, sell it cheap' is the old supermarket slogan, and that's how he was operating, cutting the price of everything down to the bone. He was running with minimal service, low wages to sales and low margins but I could see the turnover was definitely there.

I had a decision to make. If I judged him a serious threat I would have to act. But he didn't seem to be doing much with Adidas and Nike, who were our big suppliers at that time, so I actually decided to walk away.

Looking back, when he grew to about six shops, I really should have crushed him.

There are ways and means of doing anything in business, but getting rid of a new threat is quite straightforward. Ashley was making his money by being cheaper than his competitors. That's really all he had going for him – it wasn't outstanding quality and it wasn't fantastic customer service. So all I had to do was be cheaper than him. Some of his stores were near mine – I could easily have gone half-price on everything for twelve months. That would have been the end of his unique selling point, the customers would flock to JJB and that would be it for his shops. And where he was operating and I wasn't? Well, I should have opened a store there and run that at half-price as well. Yes, I would have taken a hit, but in the scheme of things it would have been nothing.

And it would have finished Ashley off.

It sounds brutal, but I wouldn't have been the first major player to do something like that – and I wouldn't have been the last. You'd be surprised what goes on when a big business feels threatened.

But I didn't do it. The likes of Adidas and Nike and Reebok are really against going half-price with their products. They don't like it now and they hated it then, so I would have had a fight on my hands getting them onside. I decided the threat of Mike Ashley didn't warrant the effort.

I hoped I wouldn't live to regret my decision.

While my plans for national success in business steamed ahead, however, there was something else much closer to home that was crying out for my attention – and my time and my money. I was in charge of one of the most important PLCs in the country and I knew I couldn't afford to be distracted.

But then I couldn't turn down a plea from the people of Wigan either.

Thirteen

JESUS IS A WIGANER

When Martin Edwards offered to sell me his shares in Manchester United in 1989, the timing wasn't right but it did awaken a few dormant feelings. I'd successfully avoided the beautiful game for a long time up to that point, never going to matches and trying every other sport I could find rather than football. But just being in Old Trafford for that meeting got my blood pumping again. When you look out over a pitch, even when there's not a game on, you can't help being inspired. When I got a call a few weeks later from another old friend asking for help, I was in the mood to listen – even though I'd regretted it once before.

Wigan Athletic Football Club was formed in 1932 and spent its first forty-six years playing non-League football. Then in 1978 they made it into the Fourth Division, with Southport going the other way. Times weren't good, though, and it was while they were playing in the Lancashire Combination that I was approached by Stan Jackson, one of the directors of the club.

He said, 'Dave, things are a bit tight – would you like to come on board as a director?'

I said, 'I've got to be honest, Stan – when you've played professionally for fourteen years, there's no fun to be had watching football matches. That's why so many players drop out of the game. We miss it too much.'

'Look, Dave, just come along to a match and see how you feel.'

So I agreed and I went along to see Wigan play away at Droylsden. It was a horrible night – cold, rain sweeping in from all angles – but at least I thought I'd be looked after by the directors.

Was I heck.

I was given a ticket and that's it. The rain was pouring down and I can't remember how Wigan got on because I spent most of the match just glaring up at the directors' area where Stan and his cronies were all nice and dry.

The following Tuesday I went to my first directors' meeting. The board didn't waste any time getting to the point.

'Dave, we haven't got enough money to pay the players' wages this week. We need £640. Can you help?'

I looked round the table at this lot and thought how nice and dry they must have been over at Droylsden while I was wet to the bone. So I said, 'That's a bit rich, actually. You invite me on to the board to bail you lot out but you don't even have the decency to give me a ticket with a roof over my head at the match.'

There was a bit of nervous coughing and mumbling at this point, but I carried on.

'You didn't even give me a car park space!'

One of the six men went to say something but I stopped him.

'You've treated me very poorly but I don't like to see my local club in trouble so I will pay your wages this week. But that's it – I resign as a director as of now.'

And I walked out.

I didn't watch another Wigan match for years, but obviously I was delighted that they reached the Fourth Division at last. Then one day I got a knock on my office door at the warehouse. It was Stan Jackson. He actually had tears in his eyes as he told me, 'We're going into liquidation after Saturday's match. Is there any way you can help us?'

I'd already had my fingers burnt once but by now the Man U deal was still fresh in my mind.

I said, 'Who are you playing?'

It was Hartlepool United at home.

'OK, I'll come to the match and tell you how I feel afterwards.'

I took Pat along and funnily enough we had a seat in their little boardroom that time. I think we scraped a 1–1 draw but, my God, were they poor. There was one fella in the middle of the park who stood out, this lad they signed from Nottingham Forest, but apart from him they were rubbish. But it was a strange day because the quality didn't matter to me. I knew even as I shook my head in disbelief at some of the passing that I was getting that feeling again. A little bit of enthusiasm about the game was creeping into me even as we sat there. By the time they scored a goal I was cheering and I knew I was hooked. The light had come on again and I decided that I would try to help. But I knew I wasn't ready to go back as a director – if I was going to turn this club around it would be under my rules.

Wigan was owned by two fellas from London at the time – Nick Bitel and Stephen Gage. They wanted half a million for the club – 'That's what we paid for it and we just want our money back' – although it wasn't worth anything like that. I had just floated JJB and so I actually had a bit of cash in my bank account – going public had earned me £30 million.

When I did the deal in February 1995 I got everyone together, players, management and directors, and said, 'Sport for me is like business – you have to play to win. It is my ambition to take this club into the Premier League – so let's get working!'

The press soon got hold of that quote, so I was asked about it again. This time I was even bolder. 'I want to be in the top flight within ten years. That is my pledge to the people of Wigan.'

There were more than one or two smirks and the odd 'silly sod' thrown my way, and I can't honestly say I was totally convinced myself – not about the time-frame, anyway. But you have to aim for the top. If you don't, you can't expect anything other than mediocrity. And I will not accept that.

One of the reasons nobody believed my plans was because of our ground. Wigan had always played at Springfield Park and the place was showing its age. It was decrepit, with one seated stand and one standing. Both ends were open and there was no training ground – just a little patch of ash where the players could have a kickabout. I knew I'd have to put some money into developing it but there were more urgent matters to deal with first. By buying the club I'd stopped it going out of business but I could see that something drastic needed to be done. That has to start on the pitch.

I inherited Graham Barrow as the manager when I took over. He had played for Wigan at centre back in the Lancashire Combination and he was a very nice guy. It's natural in business to want your own appointments in place, but I believe in giving people a chance and so he stayed on while I settled in. It didn't take me long, though, to realise that things weren't as I would like them. I looked at the team and I looked at the way Graham was training them and I thought, 'I know I've been out of the game for a few years, but that can't be right.'

A crowd of 1,452 didn't exactly pack into the 10,000-capacity Springfield Park for my first game and it was then I knew we had a job on our hands. But I still thought, 'If we get it right on the pitch, the fans will come.' We finished that season fourteenth, which was perfectly respectable considering the mess the club was in when I'd arrived, but I had big plans for the future and I needed to do something bold. For the first time people started saying that Wigan was an 'ambitious' club – and in the summer of '95 we proved it with the signings of 'The Three Amigos'.

The arrival of Roberto Martínez and Isidro Diaz from FC Balaguer and Jesus Seba from Real Zaragoza made the entire Football League sit up and think, 'What the bloody hell is going on in Wigan?' It wasn't quite like Man City trying to blow £100 million on Kaká, but in our division it was close. It had never been done in the lower divisions before – no one had been so audacious as to bring over three Spaniards to fight it out at the bottom of the League. In fact no club had ever had three Spaniards full stop.

Of course, things don't go exactly as you'd like with foreign players. The contracts were signed up at a hotel I own, Wrightington's, and they didn't understand a word that was written down. One of the fellas from our Spanish shops had to come over with them to translate. We got them going on English lessons as soon as possible.

They were stunning players though and I knew with the right guidance they would do well for us. But was Graham Barrow the man to supply it, I wondered.

I don't think our supporters could believe their luck and our average gate went up by a few hundred for the start of that season. Everywhere you looked around Springfield Park there were sombreros, stuffed donkeys and anything else people had brought back from their summer holidays in Benidorm. These days you have the Arab headdresses at Man City and the Russian hats at Chelsea, but for us that summer Spanish fever was everywhere. The highlight came when we were playing away at Torquay in the FA Cup and Wigan supporters held up this big banner saying 'Jesus is a Wiganer!' That was all over the TV and newspapers for a few days afterwards.

Seeing those fellas run out at Gillingham on the first day of the 1995/6 season was a special occasion – especially as they, like the whole team, were wearing identical JJB shirts to those worn by thousands of shop staff up and down the country. I was getting publicity for both my companies and I couldn't have been happier, especially when Martínez scored on his debut.

'This is going to be our season,' I thought, and I wasn't the only one.

Football doesn't always work out the way you plan, though, and by October we were struggling. When Mansfield put six past us at Springfield Park it was time for some tough decisions. Graham Barrow had done his best but he had to go. He took the decision well because he's a good man. In fact, he is still a good scout, but he had the wrong team and he was the wrong man for me.

My old pal from Crewe, Frank Lord, stepped in as caretaker for a few games and he did well for us: he won two, drew one and lost one. Sadly, he died in South Africa in 2007. He did all right for us, did Lordy, but I needed someone permanent.

John Deehan had been the centre forward for Aston Villa – the fans used to call him 'Dixie Deehan' after the Everton great. He was at Norwich at the time I received his application and so I got him in for an interview. I thought he was very good and gave him the job.

We played all right for the rest of the season and came within a gnat's whisker of the play-offs. We needed a point from the final three games to guarantee a place but it didn't work out. I don't know if it was nerves or what, but we lost them all and it was another season in the lowest division that we started in 1996.

We had some cracking players that season and John Deehan really got the best out of them. Graeme Jones and Graham Lancashire were on fire in front of goal – in fact Jonesy was the country's top scorer – and the Spaniards and Ian Kilford were pinging in half a dozen or so each as well. By the end of the season we'd gone one better than the previous year and a play-off place was the least we could expect. But if we won our last match at home, we'd be promoted automatically.

It was so hard for me watching that match and not being able to do anything, but you have to have faith in your team. And they did it for us. They won the game – and with it the League Two title.

For the first time since I was a kid I knew what it was like to be a football fan again, because I really enjoyed that day. For that ninety minutes I wasn't the chairman, I was just like the rest of the crowd with my heart in my mouth and everything crossed. Once it was over, though, I knew I wasn't an ordinary fan and that in fact my responsibilities as owner had just increased. We'd taken the first step towards my dream, but now the serious work needed to start.

After years of Wigan being a rugby town with football way down the list, the Latics were finally getting some attention – and it felt great. But what I didn't know at the time was that our rugby league club was actually in a very bad way.

My old bread supplier, Tom Rathbone, Arthur Thomas and Jack Robinson had taken over the club in 1982, keeping the ex-Wigan star Jack Hilton on as chairman, and they'd done well. But in the mid-90s money was running out. They were struggling and they were going into receivership. Although I was involved with football, everyone knew I was a rugby player as a lad as well, so I was invited to go along to see if there was anything to be done.

'What's your plan to get out of this mess?' I asked.

'Well, we're thinking of selling Central Park to Tesco.'

'You're what?'

Central Park had been the home for that club for almost a hundred years.

I said, 'Number one: the fans will tear you apart.'

'Well, we've no option.'

'And number two: where do you think you're going to play when you've sold your ground?'

'Ah, we've thought of that – we're going to ask Bolton if we can play at their new Reebok Stadium.'

That was enough for me. I called an extraordinary general meeting and announced to the whole room my plan for the club.

I said, 'You cannot sell the stadium from underneath the club and have us going cap in hand to Bolton. Let me have controlling interest and I will rebuild Central Park.'

From the floor I could hear people calling out 'Yes!', 'Come on, Dave!' – you've never heard so much emotion, but that's how much the club meant to people.

We took a vote and the motion was carried by eighty-five per cent. It was decided. For the second time in a few years I was trying to save another slice of Wigan's history from extinction.

But then it all went wrong – very wrong.

I had another meeting with the board and they announced, 'We've done the deal with Tesco's. They're buying Central Park for £10 million.'

I said, 'You can't do that. The shareholders voted that I would buy the club and redevelop the ground.'

'Our shares say that we make the decisions.' And they were right. They'd issued themselves 120,000 debenture shares over the years to reflect all the money that had been put into the club – so when it came to decision-making, they held all the power – and full voting rights.

That was it – our club had no ground. We were genuinely looking at the end of rugby league in Wigan.

I knew I had to do something. But what? Then I realised: I was powerless while those debentures were still around.

'I'm buying you fellas out,' I said. 'If I can find a way to fix this, I will.'

I don't know where the press got it from, but by the time the deal was reported it was being said that I had sold the ground to Tesco. That is categorically not true. The board had done it – and after I'd got support to take the club over and redevelop the ground. But, people said, 'You're the new owner', 'You're the one getting the £10 million from the supermarket', 'You're the one who's come out all right'.

I'd never had a bad press before, and certainly not in Wigan. I owe everything to my town and I'm always looking for ways to put something back. I had to get the real facts across.

Even £10 million doesn't go far for a club like Wigan. For a start it was drowning in debt. Then those debenture shares had to be acquired. Most galling of all, the local council owned a 'ransom strip' around the ground – about four yards running down to the river – so they took £2 million from the Tesco deal. By the time everything was paid off we only had £2 million in the bank to build a new ground. Peanuts. Absolute peanuts. It wouldn't even pay for the drawings.

I knew then what I had to do. Springfield Park was too antiquated for a football club with ambition like ours, and now Wigan Warriors needed a new home as well – and fast. I could see only one solution. 'I'm going to build a stadium for both clubs,' I said. 'And I'm going to do it myself.'

I found a patch of land out in Robin Park and went to Wigan Council. I thought, 'They made £2 million out of that ransom strip – hopefully they'll help me out here.'

I opened negotiations with Lord Peter Smith, who backed my idea for a new stadium. He also convinced the rest of the council to get fully behind me and they let me have the land on a long lease. I engaged Alfred McAlpine builders and plans were drawn up for a 25,000-seater, exactly three years after I bought the Latics. Then I got the price. I was committed but it knocks you back when you see it in black and white. The bill for just constructing the stadium was more than £35 million. Fitting it out was another £8 million, and that's on top of all the other costs. Figures quickly reached £65 million and to date, with Premiership wages and all the costs that go with eating at the top table, I've probably put in about a hundred million from my own bank account, my own pocket.

I get asked a lot these days about why I did it, how I can bear to see that much money go out. They say, 'You're a wealthy man, but £100 million has got to hurt anyone.' We're not talking a lump sum, but it's still a fortune, yes. And the thing is, I know I'm never going to get it back. There are very few clubs in the world that make anything like a decent profit – Manchester United and Arsenal do in this country, but the rest of us struggle. I try to run Wigan as much like a business as I can, but every time I put money in I do it knowing I'm not going to see it again.

I'll be honest – I could never have done this when I was a younger man. When you're still trying to establish yourself in the world, still building, you have ambitions for yourself, for your wife and for your family. You want the nice house, a decent car, good holidays, then if you can have a property abroad, you'll get that. You want to make sure your kids are fine, and that they can continue to live in your lifestyle when you die and you're not passing it to the Government in taxes. All those things you have to think about. There's always something daft that you can spend money on like new cars you'll never drive or clothes you'll never wear, but really, when you've got everything you want you've got to help someone else. Whether that's a charity, whether you help kids or whatever, you have to do something with your money. I chose long ago to help football, and Wigan Athletic primarily. I have chosen to help them because everything I've got I owe to professional football so I intend to put back.

By buying Wigan Warriors I also did what I could for rugby as well. Saving the club from extinction wasn't the extent of my ambitions. Just as I'd made a promise to the fans of Wigan Athletic to get them into the Premier League, I also pledged to get Warriors back on to the top table of rugby. I wanted them winning the Super League and the Challenge Cup, getting back to being the very best – and more than anything I wanted them to beat St Helens, our fiercest rivals.

One of my first steps was putting Maurice Lindsay back in charge. He's a rugby man through and through and with him as chairman I thought we stood a very good chance of getting the success the town craved. As owner I still had my say, but he was in charge of the day-to-day running. When match day came around on a Friday night, however, we were just two normal fans urging the lads on.

Even though JJB was doing very well, with profits of sixty-odd million by then, Wigan football club was still run very much as a separate business. I backed my manager as best I could but we wouldn't throw silly money around, which, to be fair, John Deehan respected. In June 1998, however, he left us to join Steve Bruce at Sheffield United, which meant he would never see the new stadium, but he had done well for us so he went with my blessing. We were one step further up the ladder than when he'd arrived and I was grateful for that.

Ray Mathias was next in the hot seat. I'll be honest, he wasn't my choice. Even though I owned most of the shares, Brian Ashcroft, Phil Williams and John Winstanley were all directors of the club and they felt I was being domineering in my appointments, so I said, 'You can vote on the next one.' One of them had been here when Ray Mathias had been at the club before and so he argued like hell that we should bring Ray back. He came in during the summer.

Even though he'd been at great attacking sides like Liverpool and Tranmere he was a very, very defensive-minded guy. He used to play 5-4-1 if he possibly could, to protect his goal, but we did all right. The Auto Windscreen Shield was the big trophy for our division and Ray focused a lot of energy on that.

In the first round of the northern competition we had Rotherham at home and 1,225 people watched Stuart Barlow, Paul Warne and Stuart Balmer put three past them. Another 400 fans watched us beat Scarborough by the same score (Michael O'Neill, Graeme Jones and David Lee). We were away at Carlisle for the third round, and their crowd of 2,283 seemed huge by comparison, but we managed the same score: 3–0. Barlow was on the scoresheet again, and Simon Haworth and Ian Kilford. For the semi-final we were drawn away again, this time to Rochdale, but once again it was Barlow on target, this time with O'Neill. Suddenly we were in the final of the northern half of the competition, facing Wrexham over two legs. A record crowd of nearly 5,000 packed Springfield Park to see Barlow score in his third successive round on the way to a 2–0 advantage. Away we won 3–2, Haworth scoring twice. I couldn't believe it. Thirty-nine years after I'd been stretchered off the lush north London turf I was going back to Wembley.

What a feeling that is, seeing your team playing beneath the shadows of the Twin Towers. More than 55,000 people turned out on 18 April 1999 to watch us take on the winners of the southern competition, Millwall. Everywhere I looked there was the JJB logo. I couldn't have been happier – but then we kicked off and I was as nervous as a kid at his first game.

A cracking effort from Paul Rogers put us ahead though and we managed to cling on. We'd done it. We'd won the Auto Windscreen.

And I'd beaten the Wembley hoodoo.

As great as it was going back home with that Shield in our coach and memories of a Wembley victory in our heads, I would have swapped it for a win a month later. Often after a cup run you can lose a bit of momentum in the League, but somehow Ray Mathias galvanised the squad and we bounded into the play-offs for the first time.

'Is this our season?' I wondered.

We were drawn against Man City so I knew it would be tough. City had tumbled down the leagues but they still had great players on big wages – and the largest attendances in the division. The first leg, at our place, attracted 6,000 Wigan fans to see a 1–1 result. Maine Road, though, was heaving with 31,000 cheering their boys on. And it worked. We went down 1–0. That was it, our season over, and it felt terrible ending things like that. In a way you wish you didn't get into the play-offs because losing like that takes the edge off your summer. But it could have been worse. We could have lost in the final. And, as I knew to my cost, being on the losing side at Wembley is very, very hard to take.

As successful as he was, I have to admit I didn't take to Ray Mathias's style, which was too defence-minded for my tastes, so I called him in at the end of the season and told him I wanted to take the club in a different direction. He took it well and we parted on good terms. His replacement was John Benson. John had played for Man City and managed or coached at Maine Road, Bournemouth, Burnley and Norwich. When he became John Deehan's assistant in 1995 I couldn't have been happier. He was a man I had a lot of respect for – and still do. But would he do any better in the top job?

I was determined to give John the best opportunities I could – and that started with a decent stadium. The finishing touches at the Robin Park development took place during the summer and I have to say it looked amazing. Watching it grow was an inspiring experience. My office was only five minutes up the road so I was driving past every day and witnessing progress. By the time I came in towards the end and saw the name 'JJB' written in giant letters across the seats and along the stands it was perfect. It actually brought a lump to my throat looking out from the Chairman's Suite at the amazing green turf. Who couldn't be moved by a sight like that?

JJB, at my behest, signed a ten-year rights contract with the club, giving them shirt sponsorship during that period, but more importantly, they also owned the stadium's name. It would be known as the JJB – and overnight it became one of the most famous landmarks in Wigan.

It was a great triumph for me as a chairman and on a professional level I had no complaints. But there was someone I wish could have seen it happen.

My dad died before we floated JJB. He was around during my market days and he saw me retire a millionaire from the supermarkets. But he never saw my greatest triumphs – making old JJ Bradburn's one of the world's leading brands, and getting Wigan into the Premiership.

He had a happy life though and he always enjoyed himself. It was while he was enjoying himself, in fact, and after a few beers, that he fell down some uneven steps in Majorca and hit his head. We didn't realise then, but that accident introduced a tumour into his brain and two years later he died.

My mam stayed in the house I bought them in Poolstock for another fifteen years. I did buy them a lovely place in the posh end of Wigan, in Standish, but they hated it there. 'We don't belong here,' my dad used to say. 'We miss our old friends.' So back they came to the same area they'd lived all their married lives.

My mam died shortly after the stadium was finished. She had been looked after in a hospital for three months or so and was slowly deteriorating. It was just old age. You could see she was losing the will to carry on. The doctor rang me one day and said, 'I think you should come down now,' so I dropped everything and drove straight over there.

I'm so glad I did.

My two sisters were there when I arrived but before I even said hello to them, I rushed over and grabbed my mam's hand. A few seconds later I felt the life pass out of it and she was gone.

I don't know if she would have known I was there but the timing was perfect. It felt like she was waiting till I arrived. I'm glad I got there when I did.

Her funeral wasn't a big affair – only family – and I didn't do a reading. I couldn't face it. I've done it at other people's funerals but I couldn't at my mam's and I couldn't at my dad's. Funnily enough, I think my dad would have been disappointed with me over that, because he always said, 'When I die, remember I have had a really, really lovely life. I've had everything I want. I don't want you in mourning. I want you to get everybody a few drinks in them and have a laugh and celebrate that I have had a super life.'

I think if you've lived a good life, it should be celebrated. It's nice when they clap at football stadiums these days when someone has died. I prefer that to the minute's silence. These people have entertained, they have played football, and they loved it, so why not give them a cheer?

My parents are buried together at St Paul's Church in Wigan, but they'll never be forgotten as long as the JJB Stadium stands. Right next door to the Chairman's Suite in the corporate area is the Jimmy Whelan room. Even more importantly, just downstairs in the main stadium is the best Italian restaurant in Wigan. And what's it called? Rigaletto's, of course, in memory of the greatest tenor I ever saw.

Speaking of the greatest, now that the JJB was virtually finished I started thinking about a fitting opening ceremony.

'It needs to be something memorable,' I thought. 'It needs to be something big.'

In summer 1999 there was no one bigger in the game than Alex Ferguson. A few months earlier his Manchester United had pulled off an impossible feat, winning the FA Cup, the Premier League and the Champions League treble. I've known Alex through Sir Bobby for years, so I put a call in to him on the off chance that he might be free to bring a few players along.

'Dave,' he said, 'I'll bring the full squad. Just give me the date!'

On 4 August 1999, the Red Devils of Manchester United ran out on to the brand-new pitch of the JJB Stadium. Alex was as good as his word. Every single player on his bus was a household name and 13,428 people turned up to watch. I'd never seen a crowd in Wigan like it. He did us proud that day and there's a plaque up inside the stadium saying that he officially opened the building. It goes without saying that we didn't win, but what a way to start.

A month later, on 5 September, I watched as Wigan Warriors played their last match at Central Park. Fittingly they beat St Helens 28–20. Their next match began one of the most famous ground shares in sport. With the cooperation of both clubs' leagues, they play at the JJB on alternate weekends – Warriors on a Friday and Athletic on a Saturday or Sunday. I never miss a match for either team if I can help it and by and large it's been a very successful arrangement. It wouldn't be until 2008, in fact, that the first major hiccup would arrive.

Warriors' first match at the JJB wasn't a good one – we lost a Super League play-off to Castleford Tigers. For the first time in fifteen years there would be no trophy in the cabinet, so Maurice Lindsay decided to part company with the coach Andy Goodway. His replacement, Frank Endacott, lasted another two years before Stuart Raper, Mike Gregory, Ian Millward and Brian Noble all tried without luck to restore success to the club.

Meanwhile, the new man in charge of the football team, John Benson, got off to a flyer. He'd made some astute signings, with the Dutch defender Arjan de Zeeuw the pick of the crop. Arjan was a great addition for us and I even picked him up from the airport myself in the JJB helicopter. I needed to show the top players that we had Premier League ambitions and I think it worked. With him in the side the team quickly gelled. In fact it was nine games before we lost our first competitive match, 2–0 at Watford.

Going into the new year we looked very strong, but injuries began to take their toll and luck started turning against us. As the season drew to a close we began to slip down the table. I had really thought we were odds-on for automatic promotion but we had to settle for a second year in the play-offs. I just hoped we could do better than last time.

We'd already shared two draws with Millwall in the League, so no one could predict which way it would go over two legs in the play-offs. Predictably it was another draw at the Den, but back at ours we just nicked it with a winner from Darren Sheridan. We'd done it. For the second year running we had a date at Wembley in the final – this time against Gillingham.

We were so excited to be there again, especially in our first year at a new stadium. It just felt like we were meant to win. Unfortunately the referee didn't see it that way.

Our captain, De Zeeuw, was a great lad, and when I heard his dad was dying from cancer I said, 'He'll want to see you at Wembley then, won't he?' and I arranged for the JJB plane to bring him over from Holland for the day. He was so chuffed by that – and it was so perfect because he saw his son score a brilliant winning goal.

Unfortunately it wasn't given.

Arjan powered down this incredible header and their goalie, Bartram, had no chance of stopping it. It shot into the goal and hit Nicky Southall, who was standing a good eighteen inches behind the line. The ball shot straight back out again but that didn't matter, I thought, because we'd scored.

Except the linesman didn't give it and the referee Rob Styles wouldn't either.

I could not believe it. Every single person in that stadium knew the ball had crossed the line apart from that pair, and they were the ones who mattered. I've never felt so sick in a football match before. It was a disaster for us. It's bad enough losing at Wembley – but losing when you know you should have won is gutting. I felt shattered.

Our luck got worse after the match. The manager, John Benson, had had a heart flutter and he'd warned me he was considering his position. 'I mustn't have any pressure, Dave,' he told me. 'I'm stepping down.'

I couldn't let a good man like him go, and to this day John is still an important part of the club. He basically looks after all the manager's needs. He sorts out travel arrangements, he looks after new players when they come here, he's a scout and right-hand man for the boss. He's a jack of all trades and a master of them all. A very valuable man for us.

My next appointment had big shoes to fill. Bruce Rioch had managed Arsenal, QPR and Norwich before he came to us. He was known as 'the Sergeant Major' because people said he was tough. But our views on discipline were clearly quite different. Also he chose to keep his home in Norwich, so he was just travelling here two or three days a week. I don't think you can manage a team like that and I started to wonder what the hell he was doing.

We got round to February and then John Benson came to see me.

'Dave, if this fella is not gone by the end of the week, I'm off, sorry. I can't work with him any more.'

I said, 'Well, John, it has been on my mind and you've made the decision for me. He's going.'

I rang Bruce that day and said, 'Sorry, you are sacked.' He took it without any problem.

'Well, if that's what you think, that's what you have to do.'

He's done all right since with other clubs in Europe, even playing in the Champions League, so I think a lot of his problem was because he didn't move up here. Wigan is a long way from Norwich, and it was probably the wrong decision to take the job if he wasn't going to commit wholeheartedly and move.

I was in a bit of a fix by then. Our League position wasn't great and although I didn't think we could get sucked into relegation worries, you can't afford to leave anything to chance. I advertised the position and got a good crop of replies. The one that really stood out for me, though, was Steve Bruce, the old Man U defender – one of the greatest players never to get in the national side. He'd been out of work for a while so I said to him, 'I will give you a job on a month-to-month basis. Immediately I see you can do the job I will give you a two- or three-year contract.'

He said 'OK', and we both settled for that.

I shouldn't have been surprised, but Steve did really well for us. We had six games left to play and he won three and drew one. The players really responded to having a big name in charge. Don't forget, it was only five years since Steve had been wearing a Manchester United shirt so most of our lads, especially the defenders like De Zeeuw, respected him before he'd even stepped through the door. He had nothing to prove to them.

From the moment he got here I could tell he had it. It's his attitude, his commitment and his knowledge of the game, which is supreme. He knows what's what. So by the end of the season we were back in familiar territory – the play-offs.

We'd only taken a point off Reading in the League, but here they were at the JJB – in front of the biggest crowd of the season – for the first leg. We put the ball in the back of the net twice – but somehow the game ended 0–0. The ref said the first 'goal' had been cleared off the line – just like De Zeeuw's had been at Wembley – and the second was scored after the ball had been knocked illegally out of the goalie's hands. Ridiculous decisions.

The second leg was even more frustrating. It started well – a great free kick from Kevin Nicholls put us one up early on. An hour later we were still clinging on to that lead and I could tell the Wigan fans were dreaming of Wembley. Maybe one or two of the players were as well. Then out of nowhere Nicky Forster crossed from the left and Martin Butler equalised for Reading. Absolutely gutting, but at least we'd have extra time to put it right.

Things didn't work out like that.

That lad Forster caused the trouble again. When he went down in our area in the last minute the ref had no hesitation in pointing to the spot. Sitting there in the directors' box at the Madejski Stadium, I prayed that our keeper, Roy Carroll, would pull off a save.

And he did.

For a fraction of a second I thought all my Christmases had come at once.

So I couldn't believe it when Forster was there to collect the parried ball and put it past Roy. That was it. A few seconds later the whistle for full time went and our promotion hopes for another season went with it.

It was deeply depressing but a lot better than losing at Wembley. And in Steve I felt we had the man who, given a full season, could really make things happen for us.

I had seen how the players had responded to him in those few weeks – imagine how much he could get out of them over a whole season. We began to plot our next move. He agreed with me that the squad needed pruning for a serious attack next year and very efficiently set about letting players go. Once again I was impressed by the way he went about it. There was no room for sentiment or worrying about fans' favourites. He only looked at what was best for his team the next year.

My mind about Steve was finally made up. A few weeks into the close season I got him in and said, 'Right, I think you'll make a very good manager. I think you can do the job. I'll give you a three-year deal.'

I had never offered a manager this sort of long-term package before. It was a sign of how much I rated Steve. But it turned out I wasn't the only one.

He said, 'Chairman, I've been offered a deal at Crystal Palace. My wife wants to go and live in London and I fancy the challenge.'

That came out of the blue. I said, 'You have a big opportunity here.'

Steve shrugged. 'Yes, I know that, but I think I'm going to give it a bash.'

There is no use arguing over these things because you can't stand in the way of someone's progress, but I had to let him know he was out of order for not giving me any warning.

'It's not on, Steve. We're halfway through the summer and you should have let me know earlier so I could make preparations.'

I had a bit of a go at him, I must admit, and he did apologise, but we parted as friends. There's no point making enemies for the sake of it. You never know when you'll need people again – and it wouldn't be long before I needed Steve's help urgently.

Fourteen

I HAVEN'T DONE ANYTHING

There was a lot of unease in the country as the new millennium loomed, but as far as I was concerned, things had never been better. Wigan football club was heading in the right direction – and the very thing that allowed me to run it was doing even better.

Since floating, JJB had gone from strength to strength. After the success of the health clubs I'd looked at new avenues and in 1999 we opened our first Soccer Domes in Wigan and Manchester's Trafford Centre. These were an instant hit – all-weather synthetic six-a-side football pitches under a solid roof. And of course there was a superstore in each building as well. We launched a fully functioning website that year, and really started pushing whole ranges of new sporting equipment, in particular cycling and one of my favourite pursuits – golf.

Golf became a very big area for us. In fact, when the rights to the Slazenger Golf range became available a few years later , I immediately put in a bid. We now had a blue-riband brand in our stores so I thought it only fitting that we asked a blue-riband player to front our new direction.

Tony Jacklin is widely regarded as the best golfer of his generation. In 1969 he became the first British player in eighteen years to win the Open. A year later he became the first Brit since 1920 to win the US Open, and he is still a Ryder Cup legend. When I approached him about becoming the 'face' of JJB's Slazenger Golf range he couldn't have been more helpful and we went on to have a very fruitful relationship.

I'm happy to say we also became firm friends and one conversation we had early on has stayed with me to this day. We were discussing childhood and I confessed to Tony that I had actually been so cold as a kid that I'd peed on my hands to keep them warm. You never know how a person will react to that story, but Tony just shook his head and laughed.

'I used to do that as well!' he admitted.

'I can't believe you've ever been that cold,' I said.

'No, I wasn't. But when I started playing golf seriously my dad used to say, "If you don't want to get blisters, pee on your hands." So I did. And to this day I've never suffered a callus.'

I couldn't believe I'd finally found someone else who'd done it – even if it was for very different reasons.

By Christmas 1999 JJB were operating from 430 stores nationwide – more than three million square feet of retailing space. The only figure the City was interested in, though, was our profit. But that was impressive as well: £43.2 million, up nine million from the previous year.

Everything was getting bigger and better. We built a new 85,000-square-foot distribution centre next to our main office to cope with the greater demands from our web business and the old Sports Division stores. For the next two years we posted even better profits as a result: £74 million at the end of 2000 and £84.1 million twelve months later.

At the same time I celebrated my sixty-fifth birthday. I'd never been busier, but in the City's eyes I'd reached retirement age and it was time to put in place a succession plan for the company. There was only one person who even entered my mind as a possible heir – and that was my son-in-law Duncan Sharpe. In February 2001 he was promoted from managing director to chief executive.

While the superstores continued to replace smaller high-street premises, and health clubs and Soccer Domes grew, we were still interested in new acquisitions. When the TJ Hughes discount department store chain came up for sale in 2001 we leapt in. At £43.2 million it was good business.

In fact, 2001 was our best business year all round. The numbers were incredible. From 3,748,000 square feet of selling space we had a turnover of £739 million. But it's how much of that turnover you convert to profit that really counts. We're in a business with a lot of overheads and more than 12,000 staff. Had we done enough?

Yes we had. For the first time we'd broken another barrier and it was with great pride that in January 2002 JJB posted profits of £110.2 million.

We were the toast of the City. No sport retailer had ever got close to our success and people were desperate to share the good times if they could. Our share value soared and from a single shop JJB was now valued at £1 billion.

My world in 2002 was a wonderful place to be. We were on target for another bumper profit – down slightly at £90.3 million – and business was very good. Then something happened to put everything into perspective.

My daughter Jayne was with me in my office on 7 October when, just after midday, the phone rang. It was the police.

'We have some bad news, Mr Whelan. Your son-in-law, Duncan Sharpe, has been found hanging from a tree just outside Blackburn.'

What do you say to that?

Your brain isn't programmed to deal with information like that. My mind went blank and I listened in silence as the policeman spoke. As his words began to sink in I felt my heart go cold. Duncan had been a close friend of mine for so many years. He was an integral part of my business and he was mad for Wigan Athletic, just like his boys. But on top of all of that, he was family.

I looked over at Jayne as I hung up the phone. I wasn't looking forward to the next few minutes one bit. How do you tell your daughter that her husband – the father of their four children – has taken his own life?

I tried to stay calm as I spoke the words to Jayne, but it was a horrible situation and I knew I was about to break her heart. Watching your little girl get upset is a terrible thing for a father, however old she is, but I have to say she impressed me greatly with her reaction. She stood up and was counted like a woman. I was so proud of her. She listened to what I had to say, took it all in, then said, 'I've got to look after the children.'

I went to Blackburn that night to identify Duncan's body. The police have a morgue near the Royal Infirmary and it was with great sadness that

I entered that building. I took one look at the figure beneath a white sheet and nodded.

'Yes,' I said, 'that's him. That's Duncan.'

He was forty-three. That's no age for anyone to go.

The saddest part of all was that Duncan had been a man in decline for a while, although we'd all done our best to help him.

When you work closely with someone you see things in them. I'd noticed he had started saying some odd things, but as he was doing such a grand job for us you're likely to ignore this sort of thing. Shortly after we posted our record results, he said, 'I'm thinking of getting out of JJB. I've gone as high as I can and I need a new challenge.'

I will never stand in someone's way when they tell me that. It doesn't matter if it's a manager, a footballer or a chief executive. You have to do the best for you and them.

'What are your plans?' I asked him.

'Flashing lights that you can wear,' he announced. 'It's the new thing coming out of America. The kids in clubs will be mad for them.'

As he told me it was as though he had discovered fire. He thought this kid's toy, whatever it was, was the biggest thing he had ever seen in his life. I sat there in disbelief, literally scratching my head, wondering what had got into him. 'You're running the biggest sports company in the land – and you want to give it up for *that*?'

That's when I started monitoring him a bit more closely. I didn't like what I discovered. He'd started gambling. A little at first. Then like all punters, the numbers had got bigger and bigger and bigger.

To this day I can't tell what caused him to change, or what got him hooked, but something did. He was a good worker, he'd been at my side through a phenomenal rise in JJB, and together we'd overseen record profits. He was promoted because of it and I swear he loved his work. You could see it in his eyes.

But that wasn't a good enough story for the media. For weeks after Duncan's death we had to read countless newspaper articles speculating about it, raking over his past in a very unfair manner. No one wants to see in black and white accusations about their family like that, and the press overstepped the mark, in my opinion, when they started saying that I might have been partly responsible for Duncan's decline. I had put him under too much pressure, overworked him, bullied him – so much rubbish like that. It was unfair on me and my family and it made a hard time even worse.

Of course, when you're the chief exec of a successful PLC there's a certain amount of public glory that goes with that and people do react differently to fame. A bit of recognition can alter a person's thinking. I've seen it with footballers and it's the same for businessmen on a smaller scale. I don't know if this was the root of Duncan's troubles, but something definitely happened to push him off the rails.

One day he came to me and admitted he'd been stupid. 'I've done so many things,' he said. 'I've hurt people and I need to make it right.'

I gave him the best advice I could. 'We've all been stupid at times in our lives, Duncan. Calm down, get some fresh air then get back to work. You just need to take your mind off everything, stop the gambling and it'll be fine.'

For a while he seemed to be OK, but I realised he needed proper help. I even took him to a specialist hospital in Manchester. They kept him in for psychiatric tests for a week. I went in to see him a couple of times. But in the end it obviously wasn't enough.

The day before he died, Duncan had dropped out of sight for the entire day. He had left their house in Clitheroe in the morning and returned at eleven that night. He'd spent the entire day driving up and down the motorway – nothing else, just driving and driving.

The next morning he'd taken the kids to school early and not come back home. That's why Jayne had been in my office. She'd rung and said, 'Has Duncan come into work yet?'

I said, 'No,' and she filled me in on what had been going on. 'You'd better come over to the office. When he gets here we'll sit him down and get to the bottom of it.'

But he never did get there. Jayne had been there a quarter of an hour when the police rang.

It's so tragic to take your own life for no reason. He was a successful man, he had a great job, was well respected and his family loved him, really loved him. A switch had been pushed in his head though, and that was it. There was nothing anyone could do.

The funeral was a very difficult time for all Duncan's family and friends, but it was heart-warming to see how many people turned out. There were hundreds, from all over the country, including plenty of staff from JJB. He was so popular.

Because Duncan had been in charge of a public company, we were forced to make some very swift moves in the City. We brought forward profit announcements to make clear that there was nothing wrong at JJB – thousands of people's careers and investments hinged on this, so it was paramount we act fast. We also replaced Duncan with a respected City man called Tom Knight. Our investors seemed happy with the change, but I knew I had to back Tom to the hilt as well. He was filling the shoes of my son-in-law and a close friend – and that's got to be a tough challenge for anyone coming into a business, even at the best of times.

From a personal point of view, of course, it was difficult for me as well, going back to work knowing that after nineteen years of having Duncan around the place he wouldn't be there. But if there was one thing I knew about Duncan, it was that he would not want me to hold back because of him. Apart from his family, nothing gave him more pleasure than seeing JJB move forwards.

With that in mind, I decided to do just that. But it wasn't going to be so easy.

One morning I arrived at the office and the car park was swarming with cars I didn't recognise – and at least one police vehicle.

'What's going on here?' I demanded.

'You need to speak to this chap, Mr Whelan,' one of the officers said. 'He's in charge.'

A fella in a suit came over and introduced himself. 'I'm from the Office of Fair Trading and you are being investigated for price-fixing.'

I was stunned. All I could think was, 'Where's this come from?'

The OFT chap wouldn't tell me anything, so I was left to just stand and watch while they had accountants and all sorts swarm all over the offices, going through the computers, taking all the files and paperwork, poking into anything they wanted.

I've never been so angry in my life. It made me feel like a murder suspect.

'Whatever you're looking for, you won't find it!' I said. 'Because I haven't done anything!'

They spent all morning turning my office over before I was finally let back in. Even then I couldn't touch any of the computers or filing cabinets, but they let me use my phone and sit at my desk while a girl carried on going through everything.

Eventually I discovered what I was being investigated for. The OFT claimed that along with Manchester United, Umbro, the Football Association, Allsports and various other retailers we'd acted as an illegal 'cartel' and kept the prices of Manchester United and England shirts unnaturally high.

'What a load of rubbish!' I thought. 'I've made a career out of lowering prices – why the hell would I put them up as high as my competitors'?'

I was furious. Not because I was guilty – on the contrary, I knew I was innocent. I'd fought my corner in the courts before and won, and if need be, I'd do it again. But sorting this mess out would take time, and who knew what it would do to JJB's reputation and future sales? Football shirts, especially England and Manchester United's, were an important part of our business. Customers needed to know that they could trust us.

However, as the trial got closer, events took a worrying turn. All the other companies accused by the OFT pleaded guilty. The FA, Manchester United and Umbro all decided it was easier to take the punishment. 'How does that make us look if they're admitting it?' I thought. But I had to believe in the ability of the courts to get the right verdict.

When the trial started there were just two defendants left: JJB and Allsports.

The next three days in that London High Court were awful. I had to sit there as the case against us was sketched out by the opposition QC and listen as he assured us that we were guilty of price-fixing. This time I wasn't arguing with Boots about whether I had a shop or not – I was fighting to protect a billion-pound empire I'd built up from nothing, and the livelihoods of thousands of people.

At the end of the trial we were given a date by which a verdict would be delivered – by post – then there was nothing else to do but get back to work and wait.

Three months later, with the cloud of suspicion heavy over our heads, I went in to the office knowing that judgement day had arrived. The envelope was delivered with the rest of our mail. I opened it and couldn't believe what I was reading.

We'd been found guilty.

I was knocked sideways by that. Guilty? Of what? I cut my teeth on price-cutting. That's how I've always made my money – by being cheaper than the other fella. What part of that did those idiots in wigs not understand?

The verdict was bad enough, but the punishment almost blew it out of the water. We were fined £8.3 million for our part and Allsports had to pay £1.35 million. Shirt manufacturers Umbro were hit for £6.6 million, Man U for £1.65 million and the FA for £158,000. They weren't the only ones: Blacks (£197,000), Sports Soccer (£123,000), JD Sports (£73,000), Sports Connection (£20,000) and Sportsetail were all found guilty as well.

The letter said we had the right to appeal – but only the right to appeal against the fine, not against the decision. We put in an appeal the next day.

One of the companies not on that list was Mike Ashley's Sports Direct. In fact not only were they not found guilty, not only were they not even charged – it turned out it was them that put in the complaint about us!

The OFT's whistle-blower was Mike Ashley.

Since I'd first spotted his fledgeling business back in the late 80s, Ashley's rise had been spectacular. Ten years later those six shops had grown to more than a hundred and now his Sports Direct company has 400 stores, 20,000 staff and controls brands like Dunlop, Carlton and Slazenger – it was from him that I later purchased the Slazenger Golf line.

He's never lost sight of that supermarket policy: 'Pile it high, sell it cheap'. But he's also done some very clever things as well. He was one of the first to sell his own products alongside the name brands. He realised early on that if he was actually manufacturing the product he'd keep most of the profit as well. It might not sell for a hundred quid like an Adidas item, but when you're taking home ninety per cent of the profit you can flog it for a tenth of that and still get the same return. He led the way in sourcing materials directly from the Far East and, to be honest, JJB followed as fast as we could.

Without a doubt, some of the deals he'd done had had a huge effect on us – selling stuff cheap by the shopload, really going after our customers – but if there was one time I sincerely regretted not putting a stop to Mike Ashley's rise to success, it was right then after that verdict.

I wondered how I'd feel the next time I ran into Mike.

It wasn't long before I found out.

Over the next few months JJB fought like crazy through the courts to get the OFT verdict overturned, and I have to admit it was a big distraction. Market conditions were also getting tighter and we never repeated our high of £110 million profit, so my workload was growing, not shrinking. In 2005, approaching my sixty-ninth birthday, I took a very hard decision. I thought, 'I'm not getting any younger and I can't be everywhere at once.' I was needed in the City, in Wigan and at shops all over the country at the same time, and it just wasn't possible – even with a helicopter.

'I'm standing down as chairman.'

Just writing those words now makes me reflect once more on the magnitude of my decision. When you've built something up from next to nothing and turned it into a world-beater, it's very hard to let go of the reins. But I had to do it.

'I'll still be on the board and I'll still have the majority shareholding,' I thought. 'It's not as though I'm selling up.' But I knew really that it was the end of an era.

If I was honest with myself, though, even if I wanted to take back full day-to-day control in the future, it would be hard for me because I had another very pressing demand on my time – and I could not have been happier.

Ten years after I had bought Wigan Athletic Football Club they had done what I'd dreamed and what I'd promised.

They had reached the Premier League.

Now the hard work really began.

Fifteen

HAVE A PIE, MR ABRAMOVICH

It had started with Paul Jewell.

I had no manager when Steve Bruce left. I wasn't happy that he told me so late, but it's no use falling out with people just because they want to go somewhere else. I advertised the post as usual and we got some very strong candidates. Even though we were in League One – the old Third Division – people could see that because of our stadium and our set-up there were good possibilities here. Dave Jones, who is at Cardiff now, was one of the big names, but in the end I went with an old Wigan striker.

Paul Jewell had been with Bradford and he got them into the top flight and kept them there, but he didn't feel he could work with their chairman, he said, and at the end of the season he walked away. He went to Sheffield Wednesday after that and then applied to us. If you think about it, this was a man who had walked away from a Premier League club and he wanted to come to us two divisions down. That shows you how far we'd come when we could attract that calibre of candidate.

An interview for a football manager is exactly the same as for any other member of staff. They come to the JJB, they see the building, look at the organisation, then walk into one of the offices. They'll be suited and booted with a collar and tie, just like any other prospective employee, and they'll sit down and I'll ask them questions. What are your thoughts on football? Do you like 4-4-2? What is your training routine? What's your opinion on discipline? You can ask what you want, but you still won't find out what they are like until you actually get them on board. Unless somebody has worked under them and can tell you, there's only so much you can learn.

I have just as many big questions to ask myself when I look at a new appointment: Has he got the bottle? Has he got the knowledge? Has he got the enthusiasm? Is he a workaholic? Will he let the boys take liberties or will he be the boss? Football is a harsh game for lads taking the mickey. If players think they can get away with it, they can be toxic, so you have to stamp down on that early and show them who's in charge. The manager doesn't need to have been the best player in the world but he has got to understand players and their attitudes and what they believe in. It does help if you have played at the highest level, no question – but it's no guarantee of success.

Bryan Robson is the biggest example. He was one of the best midfield players I've ever seen, and as a footballer he had everything. So why hasn't he done it as a manager? But he'll always get another chance because chairmen are like fans and they live in awe of reputations. I don't think you can do that. A chairman has got to look at so many other things.

Footballers are not like the average worker. Some of them have very strange ideas about who they are, what they are, what they should be doing in training. Some are very religious and some are just superstitious, so before a match you'll get some saying prayers and others touching all kinds of things before they step on to the field.

Your manager has got to accept all those things, be aware of them, and not let anything get out of hand. He needs to let you go so far and then clamp down and say, 'This is what you're doing.' And Paul was tough. I could see that as soon as I met him.

The press had a bit of fun when he joined because they said, 'He has a tortoise named Trotsky and the chairman is a major donor to the Conservative Party – how are they going to get on?' But we did. Politics, religion and colour should never come up in football. That's a wipe-out. Football is sport. It is in your blood and you live, eat and breathe it, and nothing else matters.

In their own time, players can believe in what they like. As my father used to say: religion is like beer – there are no bad ones, just different ones.

I never socialise with my managers or players anyway, so personalities shouldn't really come into it at all. It is a business relationship. I go out with the boss if we've got a dinner or a charity event, but normally the managers are quite a lot younger than their chairman and they want to do different things. I have my life and he has his.

Paul didn't move here. He stayed where he was living on the Yorkshire Moors, but unlike Bruce Rioch he used to travel in every day. I could tell right from the start that he was a good manager, although I wasn't so happy with his staff while he was here. He brought in Chris Hutchings, who is a brilliant football coach, as good as they come, but some of the others didn't impress me. I didn't like his scouting system or his assistant coaches, and his keep-fit team weren't as good as he was either.

Picking the right team around you is crucial. It's true of a manager but it's true of a chairman too. I've had some absolutely quality people with me at Wigan for years now. Brenda Spencer, the club's chief exec, has been here longer than I have, and she handles all contracts and runs the business side. Then there's our old manager, John Benson, who takes care of everything the new manager shouldn't have to worry about. Logistics, training, scouting – you name it, John does it and does it very well.

I'm not an interfering chairman, but because I've played the game I do like to see what's going on with the players, so I go down to the training ground to keep an eye on things. Football's like any business: it's good to make sure the lads know you're about. You have to rely on your manager to be the boss but I think it can help if his players know you're right behind him. They see that you're interested and that's a positive. The other thing I do, and I've always done, is that I will have a meeting with the manager on the Monday after a match, just ten minutes, just to catch up. I give him my opinion and say I thought the number nine did well, or so-and-so was a bit off the pace, whatever I've observed from up in the stands. It's the manager's opinion that counts, of course, so I like to know what he thinks.

After about six or seven games I knew I'd backed the right man. I thought, 'This lad is tough enough to do it. He is absolutely straight down the line, he tells you what he thinks, he tells you what he wants you to do.' For us he was a super manager, absolutely brilliant.

Paul's first season didn't really go anywhere for us and Arjan de Zeeuw left for Portsmouth in the summer. But we got the keeper John Filan, an Australian lad, from Blackburn and Nathan Ellington was another good buy. He was a lovely player, but watching him take a penalty terrified me. It's very peculiar how he takes them. He strolls up to the ball and I don't know how he does it but he always sends the keeper the wrong way. Then he just strokes the ball in. My heart was always in my mouth when I saw him put the ball on the spot, but I've never seen him miss one.

The next year there was a real buzz around the place. We had Leighton Baines at left back and Jimmy Bullard in the middle of the park. Jimmy has the record for the most consecutive appearances in a Wigan shirt, and he was a brilliant lad to have around, both in the team and in the dressing room. He's fantastic, never stops talking, full of jokes, nothing gets him down. On the pitch he will run and run and run until he drops. Up front Nathan and Jason Roberts were the leading goalscorers for the club and the league. As the season went on I thought, 'We can do this.' And sure enough we did – and in style. Twelve thousand fans saw us beat Barnsley on the last day of the season. We had a record 100 points, we were champions of League One – and that was cause for celebration.

Over the years the Wigan rugby team have had a dozen parades around the town to show off their silverware, but it was unusual for Athletic to do the same. That year, though, we had the full open-top bus ride around Wigan and thousands of fans turned out to wave us on. It ended with a great reception at the town hall. It was a marvellous day, and so nice to share it with our fans. It was the first time I'd ever done it, and so far it was the last. I don't believe in having a parade if you're a runner-up. Celebrations are for winners.

As we drove around the streets that day I was interviewed a dozen times and I always said the same thing: 'My dream of the Premiership doesn't look so daft now, does it?'

But plenty of teams have got close to the Holy Grail and fallen away. We still had a whole lot of work to take care of.

The next season went very well and towards the end the play-offs looked very achievable. In the end, all we had to do was beat West Ham at home on the final day and we were in the mix. Two minutes from the end of the match and everything was going to plan. I think there were only thirty seconds on the clock when Michael Carrick knocked the ball over to Brian Deane and he headed it past Filan.

Heartbreaking.

I know it was only for a place in the play-offs, but that was our route to the promised land and I honestly thought we were going to do it. I sat in the directors' box for about five minutes after the game absolutely devastated. Then I told myself, 'Right, that was last season and it's over. It's my job to rally the troops downstairs for next season.'

Picking football players up is no small task. When I was a player I wouldn't talk for the rest of the day if we'd lost – Pat and the kids soon learnt not to bother speaking to me. I couldn't think about anything else but that defeat. Paul Jewell is even worse. He was no use to anyone for two days if we'd lost. I bet he's still the same now. His wife would come in, complaining that he was in a grumpy mood after a bad result, and I know how it feels but that is exactly how I would want it. You know you've got a good team if you go into the dressing room after a loss and it's silent. Talking after a defeat? I don't like that. And if anyone dares laugh or have a joke then they fall off my Christmas card list. Win – and the team should go through the roof. Lose – you feel like rubbish. And that's how it should be – and that's what I was facing that day.

Coming seventh in our first year in what is now the Championship was no mean feat. Looking back I would much rather have lost that game and not gone into the play-offs than to have lost at Wembley. That is devastating, as we knew to our cost. It's like losing an FA Cup final, and it killed us a bit at the time. But we bounced back then. And now we had to bounce back again.

Once again it was Ellington and Roberts doing the business for us up front in 2004, but Lee McCulloch got plenty as well and the whole team really worked for the manager. By Christmas I was thinking once again about the play-offs – but this time I had an incentive for the lads. I got the entire squad together and said, 'If you get us to the Premier this year, I'm taking the whole lot of you to Barbados. You can all come out with me and teach the kids over there how to play!'

I don't know if that played a part but our form into 2005 was excellent. We were in a play-off place for most of it, but by the end of the season we had the chance to go one better. We had Reading at the JJB. They needed a win to get into the play-offs – and we needed a win to come second in the league.

The JJB was packed that day. From just over a thousand fans when I'd first watched the club to twenty times that in May 2005 – we'd given the town a stadium worth going to and a club worth supporting – and they'd responded. And like me, they all had their hearts in their mouths that day. For the ninety minutes that a match is on you're powerless. I was nervous as hell watching, because we'd come close so many times before and something always seemed to get in the way. Last-minute headers or disallowed goals can't be predicted. If we lost the match then we'd still qualify for the play-offs – but given our previous experiences I didn't fancy our chances. 'No,' I thought. 'We have to win. We have to keep our fate in our own hands.'

It was a tense affair. There was so much riding on the game for both clubs that it was hard to enjoy. But then Jason Roberts scored on eighteen minutes and I began to settle in my seat. When Lee McCulloch added another three minutes later I even managed a smile. By the time Nathan Ellington hit our third I was laughing. I didn't even care that Steve Sidwell had scraped a last-minute consolation goal. I was already celebrating.

I wasn't the only one. Fans poured on to the pitch the second the final whistle blew. The players ran for their lives, but they were mobbed by jubilant well-wishers and I couldn't wait to get down and join in. I lost track of the number of people who shook my hand or patted me on the back and said, 'Well done, Dave.' But I'll never forget the sight of one banner unfurled from the stands. It said: 'Whelan is God.' That's how much winning meant to that fan – and that's how much it meant to me.

It took ages to clear the stadium that afternoon because no one was in any hurry to leave. For a club that had only been in the Football League for a quarter of a century to reach the Premier League was a modern-day miracle – and we all knew it. The longer I stayed out on the pitch the more faces I recognised. Old players from the past were there, lads I'd come to watch. I saw Les Campbell, one of my old mates from Wigan Boys Club, and I had to go over and say hello. He was as thrilled as I was. Everyone was. This was exactly what I'd promised the town.

A decade earlier I'd said I wanted Wigan in the Premier League and people had laughed. But we'd done it. We were runners-up to Mick McCarthy's Sunderland. We were joining the big boys now.

Home advantage in front of that passionate Wigan crowd had been crucial. Yet we'd almost had to play the match without them. Imagine my shock when, a week before the big day, I got this message from the chief of Manchester police:

'You're playing that game behind closed doors. No fans allowed.'

The problem had started after we'd played a match against Leeds in the Championship. We'd had 16,000 fans here and the police charged £42,000 for policing. Preston played Leeds and paid £4,500, Burnley played them and paid £4,000 police costs. How could they justify that difference? I told the police I wanted a reduction and they said, 'If you don't pay, we won't police your matches. You'll have to play behind closed doors.'

What could I do? I've never wanted to fight something so hard, but when you've got so much riding on a match you have to be sensible. I paid the bill under protest so the match could go ahead – and braced myself for legal proceedings.

It was a problem that had been bubbling underneath for a while.

When we first arrived in the Championship we were paying £4,000 or £5,000 for policing of our home games. Then when a new Assistant Chief Constable of Greater Manchester Police came in, we started getting bills for £14-15,000 instead. The new guy took the view that football clubs should pay for all policing on match days, whether those coppers are at the stadium or at the railway station or moving traffic along. Every policeman who was on duty was billed to us.

I totally disagreed with this. We already pay the police through our rates. It's their job to look after the public on public land. It's only my responsibility if supporters are on my private land, so I said I would only pay what we'd been used to paying. Instead of £15,000 or £42,000, we paid £7,000.

By the end of the season the police said we owed around £300,000 in unpaid charges, so they took us to court. I went through all the evidence with the lawyers, saying the JJB is a modern ground, we've got video cameras, proper safety, proper exits – it's obvious we're being overcharged. All logic said we should win.

However, the judge at the High Court in London ruled we were liable for the whole fee. He said, 'I don't care what the police charge Burnley or Preston. They have charged you £300,000. That is what you have to pay.'

I was disgusted by that outcome and we went straight into appeal. In December 2008 the Appeal Court verdict came back. By this time we'd spent a lot of money on barristers but it was the principle of the argument. It was something I believed in passionately. I would be mortified if I lost again.

I didn't. The judge ruled in our favour. The police were ordered to pay all our money back plus five per cent interest – and they had to do it within 48 hours.

More important, though, it set precedents for policing. Number one, all policing for football matches has to be agreed between clubs and police beforehand. And number two, the judge ruled that clubs only have to pay the police for working on their private land. For any policing on public highways we do not have to pay because we're all ratepayers.

If you think that Newcastle get charged something like £110,000 when Sunderland come to play, and that the stadium is surrounded by public roads, that club should be looking to be compensated by thousands. This case has been a landmark – and they all have us to thank.

But beating Reading in the Championship was way more important.

When I walked through the dressing-room door after the match I heard the lads singing, 'We're going to Barbados!' and I thought, 'They remembered!' Now we were going to celebrate in style.

Pat and I have had a house in Barbados for a few years and we love going there, especially when it's cold at home. Whenever I'm over I like to do a bit with the local football academies and schools, so I thought, 'They'll be made up when they see the whole team over here.' Of course, the team would not be so thrilled when they learnt they'd be working for their break in the sun.

It wasn't just the team that went, though. The whole squad came – physios, coaches, everyone. I had them all over to the house for a few lunches and dinners and we also did a few mornings training with the local kids. It was a proper busman's holiday for everyone, but I heard no complaints. It's an eye-opener seeing professional players coaching youngsters. These lads get such a bad press sometimes, but a lot of them will do anything to help if they can.

While we were over there I had a few games of tennis, as I usually do, but the players don't like going up against me. They don't dare say it, but no professional sportsman likes being beaten by a pensioner!

I came to the sport late, when I was in my forties, but I took to it immediately. I remember going into the dressing room and hearing the boys talking about tennis. I was sixty-three at the time but I said how much I enjoyed it.

'Don't tell me you're still playing.'

'Watch your tongue. Not only am I still playing but I could beat any of you lot.'

The noise when I said that! Youngsters always think the older generation has got nothing to teach them – I was exactly the same. So, I said, 'Who are your best players? I'll take them on.'

David Lowe, our centre forward, stepped up first and so that afternoon the whole squad was at the local courts waiting to see me take a pasting.

'How much do you want on it?' I asked him.

'Don't worry, Chairman, we don't want to take your money.'

In the end we agreed on a fiver.

That was one of the most satisfying fivers I have ever earned! I gave David a right hiding and his mates could not stop laughing at him. After the match I turned to the rest of them and said, 'Well, who's next?'

Funnily enough, everybody kept their mouth shut after that.

I met a true legend of the sport when I was playing golf in Barbados once. A couple of lads were behind me and my partner so I called them over to play a round of fours. They came over and I thought, 'Blimey, it's Jimmy Connors.'

He turned out to be such a nice fella, a real gentleman, and we played golf with him about four or five times that week. There's a little bar near the golf course called Groots, named after its owner Hans Groots, which does the best fish and chips. I'm a regular in there and in fact there's a picture of me on the wall alongside photos of all the other sportsmen who've been in. When I walked in with Jimmy Connors one day, we happened to hear a couple of guys looking for a game of doubles.

'What do you reckon, Jimmy?' I said.

'Why not?'

So we went over and said hello and a few minutes later the four of us were heading over to the courts. I couldn't help smiling. 'How can this pair know about tennis and they haven't recognised this Wimbledon champion!'

They noticed him soon enough though! Jimmy's first serve flew past at 120 miles per hour.

Ace.

'Have you played before?' one of the lads said.

'I've played a bit,' Jimmy said, and sent down another missile.

30-love.

We had a few games and it was a whitewash. Our opponents didn't score a point and it actually became embarrassing. Laughing too much to continue, I called the guys over. 'Do you not recognise who this is?'

They stared at him and then the penny dropped. You can imagine the swearing – they were so embarrassed at not noticing before.

Jimmy put them straight at ease. 'Look, guys, if it makes you feel any better, I'll play with a golf club.'

I thought he was joking, but he got hold of a nine iron, tossed a ball up and *whack* – another ace. Absolutely incredible. When you see the cream of a sport like him, you can't help be impressed. But what a lovely fella as well.

*

Speaking of the cream of sport, in August 2005, Wigan Athletic were up against the best team in football at the time. For our first match in the Premiership we were drawn against José Mourinho's Chelsea. Talk about a baptism of fire.

The press were out in numbers for that match. There wasn't a person in the land who expected us to get anything from the game. Most people were saying we'd get a kicking that day and drop straight back down at the end of the season. I wasn't so sure. From the moment we'd clinched promotion, that's when the work behind the scenes had started. We already had a Premier-quality stadium and I had complete faith in all my staff. Most importantly we also had some decent players. Arjan de Zeeuw returned as skipper, but there was also Henri Camara, David Connolly, Stéphane Henchoz, Josip Skoko and Michael Pollitt. I felt confident we wouldn't be embarrassed – especially as our wage bill had suddenly rocketed from about £3 million to £30 million.

There are so many qualities you need to be successful in football and I've had them all at various times. But to do well in the Premier League you must have all three at once. You have to have luck, you have to have players who will fight, who have spirit and who will roll up their sleeves. And you have to have the right manager. West Brom, who have just been relegated, have the last two. They've just been short on luck.

'I will know as soon as our first game kicks off how many of the three I've got,' I thought.

A few days before the match we got a call from Chelsea saying that Roman Abramovich's security team wanted to come up to check out where his helicopter could land. I told them it was OK – he could land at the JJB offices just over the road from the stadium. But no, they insisted on coming up to check it out for themselves.

When they'd approved that, I said to the chief exec at Stamford Bridge, Peter Kenyon, who I knew from his days at Umbro, 'We'll pick Roman up when he lands. Don't worry about that.'

'Oh no, that won't do,' he said. 'He'll travel in his own car.'

'But I thought he was flying up?'

'He is.'

Can you believe it? He flew up with three bodyguards in a helicopter and by the time he arrived, his bulletproof limousine, with another three guards in there, was waiting for him. Just to get to a stadium that's 400 yards away!

I always welcome visiting owners and managers, so I had Roman and his boys in my suite at the stadium and he was nice enough. He speaks a bit of broken English – you know, 'Hello' when he came in, 'Goodbye' when he was going, 'Good match' after the game – that sort of thing. But the funniest thing about him was that he wouldn't have a drink of tea or water or wine while he was here. Absolutely nothing. He wouldn't have a bite to eat either.

I said, 'Have a Wigan pie, Mr Abramovich. Have a pie!'

But he said no to everything and I thought, 'What a way to live.'

One of my other guests that day said, 'Now, that is a man with enemies.' I don't know the facts, of course, but you would think so from the way he behaves.

Just before the game someone had told me that I was the first person in the country to have played in all four divisions and then gone on to be chairman of a football club in all four divisions as well. That had never struck me, but it's a record I don't think will ever be equalled.

The tension in the JJB before kick-off was incredible but once the game got going I could relax. Chelsea were awesome but Paul had us organised so well that I even started thinking we could nick it. After ninety minutes we'd held the champions to a draw – or so I thought. We had a glorious chance at the end to snatch the points but it was saved. Then in the ninety-fourth minute Hernan Crespo hit a rocket of a shot straight into the top corner. There was nothing anyone could do. We were sunk. But what a game. What a welcome to the big time.

José Mourinho was the first to say that we didn't deserve to lose, and he wasn't the last either. We won a lot of friends that day and as the weeks went by we surprised a lot more people. By November we were second in the League. Absolutely amazing.

We also started doing well in the League Cup. Bournemouth, Watford, Newcastle and Bolton all came and went and then we were in the semi-final against Arsenal. The first leg at our place was cagey but Paul Scharner nicked it for us. Down at Highbury it was a different story. Arsène Wenger had a few of his younger players in the team as usual, but on the night it was enough to make us look a bit slow. They were winning 2–0 with five minutes to go when suddenly that man Scharner popped up and squared it back for Jason Roberts to stick it in.

I was out of my seat with the rest of the Wigan fans. 'Brilliant,' I thought. 'That takes us to extra time.'

But I was wrong.

I'd forgotten the away goals rule. The aggregate score was 2–2, but because we'd got a goal at Arsenal we were winners. When the ref blew for full time after ninety minutes it took me a while to realise we'd won – but what an absolutely fantastic feeling it was then.

Arsenal were really good to us. Their chairman came into our dressing room with a full case of champagne and said, 'We can't drink this now – you take it back with you.' Even though they were so disappointed they still had a lot of class.

To be honest, everything about that club is classy, starting with the manager. You see people on television and you get a certain impression of them, but Arsène Wenger is a fantastic gentleman and a very, very nice man. He hates losing, of course he does, but if you don't then you shouldn't be in the game. I always go in and say hello to him before or after a match, but if I don't get the time he always makes a point of hunting me out.

In fact I always make a point of tracking down the opposition manager before a game if I can to wish them well – for later. 'Good luck – next week!'

I think it's important to be hospitable at home but just as crucial to be polite when we're on the road. Wherever I go I never forget I'm representing Wigan Athletic and I'm usually treated very well. Crowds at Blackburn are very nice to me, obviously, but they're the same at Newcastle, Bolton and City – places where the fans respect what I've done for my club. Whenever I go to those places I get people saying, 'I wish you were our chairman, Dave.'

Most of the managers are a decent bunch. People like Arsène, Alex, or Harry Redknapp – they're just some of the biggest gentlemen you'll ever meet in your life. You always get a few personality clashes. For some reason

Mark Hughes won't talk to Steve Bruce, not since some falling out they had back in their Manchester United days, and Rafa Benítez seems to have got under the skin of a few people recently.

I follow my team all around the country, but you'll never see Sheikh Mansour bin Zayed Al Nahyan, the new owner of Man City, at other grounds. He certainly hasn't been to our place. It's the same with the Americans at Liverpool. I've seen George Gillett and Tom Hicks once at Anfield but they didn't dine with us like a lot of the owners do, which was a shame. Someone who does go out of his way, though, is Sunderland's Niall Quinn. They've got a good one there. A great ambassador for the club and for the game. Just what a chairman should be.

You won't find a nicer manager, of course, than Sir Alex Ferguson. A lot of opposition fans would disagree with that, but if they forgot their rivalries for a moment they'd find him a true gentleman. And it was Sir Alex that we lined up against for the League Cup final. The build-up to that day was absolutely amazing and all of Wigan was buzzing. It was a shame not to be at Wembley, of course, but the Millennium Stadium in Cardiff is an awesome venue.

When you get to a final there's so much you need to think of. Someone recommended a good hotel for us, because we'd never been before, but then they said, 'Have you got your suits made?'

All teams wear new suits at cup finals, don't they, so we got a couple of dozen made with the JJB logo on so I was doubly proud watching the team walk out for the photocall before the match.

But I wasn't the only person taking an interest in what the lads were wearing that day. Do you know that two years after that final, I got a letter from the Inland Revenue saying that by giving the players new suits we had paid them 'benefits in kind'. In other words by not declaring those new togs they had all broken the law and would have to pay tax on them!

I was stunned. I still am. How petty can you get? For the sake of 120 quid a suit they go to all this trouble.

At the time, we were oblivious and just concentrated on getting the most from the day. In the end United were too strong. We went a goal down then missed a good chance in the second half that might have changed the whole course of the game, but Man U responded with another three.

There were a lot of miserable faces back at the hotel, led by the manager, but after a while I wanted them cheered up. 'It was an incredible achievement getting to this final in our first year in the division,' I said. 'Tomorrow we have to concentrate on the League – but tonight we will have a damn good party!'

And we did.

Sod's law, our first match after that was against United, and once again they beat us, but it was a much closer game. I was impressed that all the players responded and we finished the season in a very creditable tenth.

Nobody from outside the club had seen that coming.

While Athletic were going from strength to strength and making good on all my predictions for the club, the news from Wigan Warriors wasn't so rosy. Silverware still hadn't been forthcoming, and far from reclaiming our spot as the team to beat, we'd actually faced relegation in 2006. Even worse – we were docked points three years in a row for breaking the salary cap. It was a sorry state for a proud institution.

In my opinion the salary cap in rugby league has killed the game. Yes, you have a more even playing field. But what about quality? If one team is prepared to invest in its players, why not let them? Instead you have this budget of £1.6 million for your entire team – there are plenty of footballers who earn double that on their own. It's a ridiculous state of affairs.

I'm not the only one in the game who thinks this. All the clubs have done their best to find a way around it – believe me, if they can top up a player's wages with a bit of cash, then they do. The only problem is where to get the cash in an age where so much is done with plastic. At Wigan we have a state-of-the-art stadium. No one comes into the JJB without being recorded. There's a paper trail for every penny, but it's not like that everywhere. Even in this day and age there are plenty of stadiums that still have the old manual turnstiles. Those clubs can announce they've had 10,000 fans, but really another 5,000 have bought tickets with cash. It's that cash that finds its way into the pockets of the club's star players.

Maurice Lindsay took certain decisions on our behalf – the same decisions that other clubs have taken – but perhaps he didn't disguise them as well as the rest do and we were penalised. As a result, in 2007 Maurice announced that he would step down. Soon after, when Harlequins' chairman and Wigan fan, Ian Lenagan, made me an offer for the club, I decided to leave as well. It was a sad day saying goodbye to the club I had saved from extinction, but for as long as the Warriors play at the JJB – and they have a fifty-year deal – I'll be watching and supporting.

Wigan Athletic's second season in the Premier League was a lot more demanding than the first. All of the teams were familiar with us now and nobody arrived thinking we'd be a walkover. We lost a lot of games by the odd goal and Lady Luck was definitely absent during a few matches. It wasn't long before we found ourselves in the bottom three. I had absolute faith in Paul Jewell to get us out, but I thought, 'It's time to roll our sleeves up. We're in a real fight now.'

Our final game of the season was against Sheffield United at Bramall Lane. There could not have been more riding on our match. We needed a win to stay up. Assuming West Ham lost at Old Trafford at the same time, then the Blades would stay up too, on superior goal difference. But if the Hammers were to get a point then Sheffield needed the win. In other words if we won we stayed up. If we lost, the Blades stayed up. It really was a fight to the finish.

Our form going into that match had been terrible. We'd lost the last three games and failed to score in any of them. Our record signing Emile Heskey had been on fire earlier in the season and I was praying he'd find some form again. It was a horrible match to build up to. The media followed us every inch of the journey and every paper I opened had the various permutations of all the potential results. It was even worse in the stadium. Every single person there had so much to lose. And I was one of them.

When I woke up that morning I honestly felt, 'This is it. We're going down.' But by the time I'd showered and dressed those thoughts were pushed out of my mind. This was a day for positive thinking. Even so, as Pat and I drove to Sheffield for the match, it was a tense time. We never talk about a game before kick-off and on this occasion we didn't have to. We both knew we had a big day ahead of us.

The United chairman, Kevin McCabe, welcomed all the Wigan directors as usual and we ate a nice meal in their boardroom. Everyone was pleasant. I don't honestly think Sheffield United thought they were going down. For a start, nobody expected much from West Ham against Manchester United. Secondly, Neil Warnock and his team had home advantage. That's all any club could ask for going into the last game.

The directors' box in any stadium is right in the middle of the home supporters, so I was aware, as I took my seat, that we were surrounded by 32,000 optimistic Blades fans desperate to support their club. Three thousand Wigan fans completely filled our quota, and I could hear them making a noise. There's no question, though, which set of fans were more anxious – and me among them.

I've never been more uncomfortable at a football match. As an ex-player you feel so useless sitting there in the stand knowing there's nothing you can do. But it's the same for everyone. You can't enjoy a match like that.

We started well, which settled my nerves. Then in the fifteenth minute we got a break. Kevin Kilbane's pass was met by Paul Scharner. Bang – we were a goal up and 3,000 Wigan fans were going crazy.

The rest of the stadium was silent. The fans all knew that West Ham were still level with Man U. As things stood, we were staying up – and Sheffield United were going down.

The tension didn't get any better from there. A single kick can change the course of an entire game – as Chelsea found out to their cost when they lost their Champions League semi-final to Barcelona in injury time in May 2009. I knew I was not going to relax till it was all over.

I was right to be worried. Twenty-five minutes later, Phil Jagielka put in a cross from the left and Jon Stead slotted it home. Bramall Lane erupted but my heart sank. The word from Old Trafford was that Fergie's men were still being held by West Ham. Now it was Wigan on the cliff's edge. 'Come on, Man U,' I willed.

Things got worse a few minutes later. News from Manchester was that Carlos Tevez had scored for the visitors. Now only a win would save us.

On the stroke of half-time our fortunes changed. Jagielka handled in the box and we had a penalty. If I was suffering, imagine how David

Unsworth felt as he stepped up to take the spot kick. When the season started he'd been a Blades player. Now he had the chance to put the knife into the club that had worshipped him. Talk about pressure.

But his shot went in and everything changed again. We were staying up. Our hosts were looking at the drop.

The entire second half was unbearable. When Lee McCulloch was sent off in the seventieth minute, however, it just got worse. Sheffield threw everything at us and suddenly we were defending for our lives. I've never been so tense watching sport – and I wasn't the only one. My wife shut her eyes as McCulloch went off and I don't think she opened them again until the final whistle.

With no change in the score from Old Trafford, everyone at Bramall Lane knew what was happening. If United scored, they stayed up. If we held them off then the next season's final Premier League spot was ours.

We won.

I felt like jumping for joy after the final whistle, but there was no way we could celebrate with United in despair around us. Almost the entire stadium was in floods of tears so we couldn't get out of there quickly enough.

On my way out of the Bramall Lane tunnel the microphone from Sky Sports was thrust under my nose. The interviewer wanted to know how I felt, obviously, but there was more to it than that. As calmly as I could, I said, 'Yes, I'm delighted we've stayed up, but my sorrow is with Sheffield United at this moment.'

I paused – there was something else I wanted to say, but did I really want to get into this now?

But yes, it was only right, so I continued: 'Sheffield United should never, ever have gone down today. It's West Ham who should not be in the Premier League next year.'

It wasn't just the emotion of the day getting to me. In my view West Ham really had survived at Sheffield's expense. The goal that Tevez had scored to win their game against Manchester United – just as he'd scored against several other clubs in the last few months – had kept them in the League. But I don't believe he should have been playing for the club to begin with.

Premier League rules state that no player can be owned by a third party and when Tevez had signed for the Hammers he was owned by a group led by Kia Joorabchian. I was one of several chairmen who had opposed this flouting of the rules and West Ham had subsequently been found guilty in April 2007. The Premier League had fined the club a record £5.5 million and West Ham had stated that they'd torn up their agreement with Joorabchian's Media Sports Investment (MSI) company – who also happened to be the owners of Tevez's previous club, Brazil's Corinthians.

But something about West Ham's statement didn't ring true. One party can't just tear up an agreement, not unilaterally. If you could do that we would all walk out of our mortgages. 'I know I've signed an agreement but I've changed my mind and I'm keeping my house. Goodbye!' I smelt a rat.

After the verdict I sent emails to the boss of the Premier League, Richard Scudamore, saying there was no way West Ham could just tear up a contract. Both parties had to have agreed it – surely? I asked, 'Can I see the contract that West Ham have torn up?' But he didn't reply. I knew that if we had that response in black and white it would be the end of the matter. I sent that request three times but never received an answer.

I raised the point at the next Premier League meeting and still nothing was done about it.

The directors at West Ham swore blind that they now owned Tevez. But I just couldn't see how that was possible. This was a player worth £30 million and they hadn't paid that for him. And when he left for Manchester United that summer West Ham didn't receive the loan fee for him. If that doesn't prove it, I don't know what does.

Up to that point no club had ever been found guilty of breaking the third party rule. So there was no precedent for West Ham's punishment. The commission set up by the Premier League had certainly handed down a massive fine, but when they found the Hammers guilty I was shocked that they hadn't decided to deduct points as well. Several reasons were given for this: one, it was late in the season; two, it would mean certain relegation; three, it was unfair on the supporters.

What a load of rubbish!

We could have been relegated as a result of that decision. What about *our* supporters? I felt, as did many others, that the Premier League had bottled it – and I was willing to say so.

I backed Sheffield United's chairman, Kevin McCabe, all the way to get justice. Tevez wasn't eligible to play before the commission ruled on it – but he certainly shouldn't have been afterwards. What had changed? It was Tevez who ran the team when they beat us 3–0 at the JJB that April. He was sensational. If he hadn't been playing we might have won. That would have put us further up the table, out of relegation's way, and in line for a bigger reward from the Premiership's purse at the end of the season. Instead the Premier League registered him at noon that Saturday and he lined up against us. And it wasn't just Wigan and Sheffield, all the teams turned over by West Ham that year had a right to be aggrieved.

Sadly our protests didn't stop the Blades going down – but Kevin McCabe didn't give up and a ruling at the Court of Arbitration later found in his club's favour. They said that West Ham should compensate Sheffield United to reflect the loss of earnings that relegation had imposed – that figure has been estimated at between £20 million and £30 million, although the parties involved have kept it secret.

But I still believe Sheffield United should have kept their place.

The Premier League wanted the matter finished with, but it's still going on. The FA are running with it now. They want to get to the bottom of the statements made by West Ham. And there are plenty of other people with legitimate claims, in my opinion, against the club. All those Sheffield United players should have been on Premiership wages – but they all took cuts when they were relegated. Neil Warnock resigned his job because of it. It's messy. They all have claims and this could run and run and run.

At the time a lot of the media and other clubs were saying 'Drop it', but you can't. That could have been us in Sheffield's position, or Fulham. And where will it end? Maybe you could parachute players in for an FA Cup final and say, 'Oh, we own them, they're eligible.' It's ridiculous.

It's sad when football matters have to be resolved in the courts but one thing was evident at the end of the 2006/7 season – we had made it on our own merits. Through our own grit and determination and skill and everything else you need in a successful football club, we had clung on to our League status. We would be in the Premier for one more season.

But we would have to do it without Paul Jewell.

Sixteen

AN OFFER I COULDN'T REFUSE

There was no way we could celebrate our victory over Sheffield United while we were still in their stadium, so we got out of there as quickly as possible. The players had their own party while the directors all had dinner with their partners at my Wrightington hotel. Even though spirits were high there was something on my mind. It was something the manager had said to me as we were leaving Bramall Lane.

'Dave, can I have a meeting with you on Monday?' he'd asked. Of course, I said yes. This was the man who had kept us in the top division for another year. I would have agreed to anything he wanted. But as I ate my celebration meal, I had no idea what that was.

On Monday I found out. I could tell immediately from Paul's voice that something was up.

'Dave,' he said, 'I'm stepping down.'

He convinced me that nothing was wrong with his health. He just felt that he'd done as much as he could with the club and he needed a break.

'Look, it's just the pressure of that match,' I said. 'You know that's a one-off. Why don't you take your family to our house in Barbados for two or three weeks, get a complete rest from the game? Then tell me your decision then.'

But he wouldn't think about it.

'I'm sorry, it's nothing to do with the pressure. I've just had enough.'

We still disagree to this day about his reasons, but I maintain that the pressure got to him in the end. And I don't for one minute blame him. In our first season we got to the Carling Cup final and finished halfway up the League. We had a fantastic year. Everybody was backing Wigan to go straight back down, but we defied all the odds. The second season was harder, though. You can't be a Premier League manager unless you've got your coaching badges, and Paul had to do his that summer. For several weeks when he should have been signing players and working at the club he was doing exercises with security men, schoolteachers and other pure amateur coaches, which is absolutely wrong in my opinion. Then he had to have a holiday with the family, so he was away for five weeks. By the time he was back at the JJB we needed to make some signings fast, and I think a few of them were slightly panic buys. Then, right from the start, the pressure began to mount. On me, on Paul and on the players. And to come down to the last game of the season where we had to beat Sheffield United to stay in the League, for the sake of £30 million, it was just too much to handle, I think.

At the time a lot of people thought Paul had another job lined up. But he said to me he wanted to have a break till Christmas, and he did.

Then one day I got a call from him saying he'd been offered the manager's job at Derby. Paul had a clause in his contract that stipulated he had to pay £750,000 if he signed for anybody else, so he said, 'Are you going to hold me to that if I take this job at Derby?'

'Of course I'm not, no. You've done such a fantastic job for us, I'm not going to take a penny off you.'

He was happy with that, obviously, and so was I. A few weeks later, though, my mood changed.

Within a few days of Paul's new job starting, about six of our staff disappeared up to Pride Park with him – scouts, physios, even our PR lad. He took them all.

I thought, 'This is a bit steep.'

I don't like falling out with friends, but I honestly felt Paul was taking the mickey, so I sent him a letter. In it I said, 'I agreed to you going there without paying me any money, but what you have done by poaching our staff is wrong. You never rang me for permission. Your chairman never rang either. You've just taken them so I'm sending you a bill for the £750,000.'

That riled him up a bit! He was straight on the phone, but I knew he could see he was in the wrong. Eventually he apologised and before you knew it, all had been forgotten. I didn't want the money – that wasn't the point. But I didn't want to be taken for a mug, either. As soon as he apologised that was the end of it. I can't fall out with Paul Jewell. He's done too much for this club.

While Paul was saying goodbye to Wigan I had some big decisions to make for myself at JJB. When I'd stepped down as chairman two years earlier I hadn't realised how hard it would be to take a back seat in the company I had grown from scratch. I was still the majority shareholder and a powerful voice on the board. A lot of the key people in the business were my appointments, like the chairman, Roger Lane Smith, a personal friend of many years. But I wasn't in charge any more and, perhaps inevitably, certain decisions were made that I didn't approve of.

For instance, deals were agreed with Adidas that gave them access to our stores – which is something I would never have done. You do not give one of your suppliers preference over another – so I said as much.

A bit later the company had to prepare a P&L – profit and loss forecast. It's something you have to do for the City twice a year. I looked at it and thought, 'This is being a little bit generous, predicting £44 million.' Again, I spoke up: 'The forecast needs to start with a "three". £38 million would be closer to the mark.'

Then a meeting was called to discuss it and things got worse. Two or three of the non-executive directors said they didn't like the forecast either – but they wanted it to be bigger!

'We want it to start with a five – £50 million or so.'

I said, 'That is impossible.'

The market had got a lot tougher and there was no way we would make anything like that profit. You can forecast all you like but you have to have some chance of meeting it.

There was another meeting, this time in London with UBS, our City advisers. The same forecast was brought out again and I said, 'You cannot put that out to our shareholders.'

All hell broke loose then, but I stood firm.

'I will not put my name to that document.'

So then, of course, I was seen as a divisive influence within the company. Things started being said about me and naturally I heard every one of them.

'He's losing his way.'

'His eye isn't on the ball.'

'He's too old.'

It felt as if I was being stabbed in the back by some of the very people I had once employed. There wasn't one of them who hadn't made a lot of money because of me, but that wasn't enough for them to give me their loyalty now.

I realised a stark truth. I either had to get out of JJB altogether – or sack the entire board and take control again.

I weighed up both options.

My relationship with JJB was very strong – it still is. But significant figures on the board, men who were very well respected in the City, were against my involvement. And my good friend Roger, and my son-in-law's replacement as chief exec Tom Knight, were among them – which was their right, of course. 'These are business decisions,' I admitted to myself.

It would have been very difficult to overthrow them and I have never seen it done before. The founder of a company like JJB takes it to the market, floats it, stands down as chairman – and then sacks the whole board? It was a daunting prospect and I knew it would cause a massive, possibly very damaging reaction in the City.

But there was another reason for not wanting a fight. I was seventy years old and unbeknown to any of my colleagues, I was ill.

For about six months I'd felt myself slowing down. Not obviously at first, just small things like being tired all the time. Of course I put it down to my age. 'You're not getting any younger,' I told myself.

As the weeks went by I realised my health was fading rapidly. I've never been the earliest riser, but by half eight in the morning I'd always be ready to leave for the office. But Pat was having to shout at me to get me out of bed before ten – and that was with more than twelve hours' sleep. I had had a full check-up barely six months earlier so I knew there was nothing wrong with me. There was only one other explanation.

'This is it,' I thought. 'Old age. My time's coming to an end.'

I didn't discuss it with Pat and she never mentioned it to me but we both knew what was happening.

I suppose I was resigned to it and mentally began to prepare for slowing down. But one day I went to see the club's head of medicine, Dr Ansar Zaman. He is a brilliant physician who I've worked with for twenty-five years, first when he was Wigan and Great Britain's rugby league doctor, and for the last ten years with Wigan Athletic. I told him what I'd been going through.

'When did you first start feeling tired?' he asked me.

'I suppose it's gradually crept up on me over the last six months.'

'Right – it's a blood test for you.'

He did a pinprick test and when he told me the results I was completely shocked.

'For some reason your body is producing an excess of iron,' he said. 'The last time we checked your reading was 327. Today it's 1257. No wonder you're feeling tired – the upper limit for a healthy person is 400.'

He sent me straight to a liver specialist in Manchester called Dr Warne, who confirmed my blood was producing too much iron.

'We don't know why it happens but we think we know how to reverse it – if we're lucky.'

'And what if we're not?' I asked.

'You will be dead within six months. Your liver is encased in iron and before long you won't be able to get oxygen in or out. If we don't act immediately you will die.'

That's frightening. Imagine if I had never mentioned it to Doc Zaman.

'So what do I have to do?'

'You have to have all your blood taken out and replaced by new blood.'

I pictured a transfusion. But that wasn't Dr Warne's plan.

'It's no good giving you someone else's blood,' he explained. 'You've got to make your own.'

My mind was swimming when I left Dr Warne's office. It was uplifting to learn I wasn't dying of old age – but I was dying of something much worse and the treatment had no guarantees. All I could do was follow the doctor's instructions to the letter and hope.

Every ten days for the next three months I went to the doctor's and had a packet of blood taken out – just like a blood donor would have done, except my blood was thrown away. After every fourth visit my blood was tested. I can't say there was an immediate improvement but gradually I realised I felt a little bit better.

After ten packets had come out Dr Warne checked me over again. 'You seem to be replenishing the supply OK,' he said. 'I think after two more visits you should be back to yourself.'

And I was.

Dr Warne rang me with the good news a few weeks later. 'Dave, your iron level is back down to 327. You're going to be fine.' I couldn't thank him enough for saving my life, but I already knew it had worked because I had all my old energy back. It had returned as slowly as it had vanished. Now, half a year after thinking my number was up, I was as good as new and raring to go.

And totally regretting the decisions I had made six months earlier.

When I thought that I was dying I had decided not to put the shareholders of JJB through the distress of a boardroom power struggle. That left me with one other option.

In January 2007 I shocked the market by selling £50 million of my shares in the company. Business commentators had their own thoughts but they all missed the point. It wasn't a random sale – in offloading that amount of shares it brought my personal holding down to 29.9 per cent. That's a crucial figure in the City because it's the maximum you can buy of a company without being obliged to make a bid for the rest of it. I knew what I was doing. I was putting it out as bait.

I knew that somebody would come along for that 29.9 per cent because they would control the company but with no pressure to buy the rest of it.

It worked just as I expected. But I didn't predict who the buyer would be.

I don't have a secretary screening my phone – if someone wants to get through to me, they can. And about a year after the OFT trial I took a call that made me sit bolt upright.

'Hello, Dave. It's Mike Ashley.'

I could think of a few things I'd have liked to say to him but instead, through gritted teeth, I said, 'Hello, Mike. What can I do for you?',

'I'd like to have a meeting.'

That came as a shock, and as I flew to the Midlands in the JJB helicopter to meet him, I wondered if I was wise to be going at all.

We met at a big country house with lovely gardens and a terrific stable block. I'm a keen rider myself and I could tell this set-up was owned by someone who really cared about their horses.

Ashley was dressed as he always is, in jeans and a casual shirt, and his manner was the same as ever. He acts like he doesn't have a care in the world – and maybe he doesn't. By contrast, I was wary of him to the point of frostiness.

But Ashley is a very shrewd operator – I knew I wouldn't be there without good reason, so we chatted for a few minutes. Then he got down to business.

'Dave, I want to buy your shares in JJB.'

I was taken aback. I don't know if he thought I'd become tired of the business, especially after the OFT verdict, but he couldn't have been more wrong. I may have been in my sixties, but at that time I felt as hungry to grow JJB as I ever had.

I said, 'You'd have to make me a very good offer to sell.'

But he couldn't and so we parted.

Then six months later, he approached me again. This time we met at the Wrightington Country Club, my hotel where I'd signed the Three Amigos, and after the sandwiches and the talk about Wigan and Spurs, he came out with another proposition. This offer was more to my liking, but I still rejected it, albeit for another reason.

'Mike, if you try to buy JJB the OFT will be swarming all over you. The monopolies commission will never allow it. There's no point in going forward.'

I must have had about six approaches from him over a couple of years and each time my answer was the same. The only time I came close to wavering was when he suggested I keep the fitness centres – the aspect of the business I cared most passionately about. But still I said 'no'.

And then one day in June 2007, after I'd turned seventy and I really thought I was on my way out, I got an offer that I couldn't refuse. But this time it wasn't from Ashley. Not quite. It was from Chris Ronnie.

I'd first encountered Ronnie when he was a buyer at Tom Hunter's Sports Division. Subsequently he'd gone to Umbro, before becoming Ashley's right-hand man at Sports Direct. But it now turned out he'd quit Sports Direct and, he claimed, had put together his offer with personal backing from the Icelandic bank Kaupthing.

I was interested, but thought, 'If I go ahead with this I will need guarantees that Ashley is not involved.' I could not afford the OFT to think I was conspiring to break their rules.

First, though, Ronnie had to come up with a price that suited me. To my astonishment, he did. He said, 'How much per share do you want?' I gave him a figure and he came back and said, 'I'll give you 270p.'

And that is what I took. I kept the dividend, which was 7p, so I got 277p per share. We did it all face to face at the Wrightington. Then everything moved very quickly. They did due diligence over a period of fourteen days, then we met in London and signed it off.

At that point some of the big manufacturers started getting jittery. They were scared Mike Ashley was secretly backing Ronnie and understandably didn't want the creation of a company that would effectively control the entire British sports market. So to put their minds at rest, Chris Ronnie provided me with documentation stating that his old boss was not involved in any way, shape or form, and Roger Lane Smith counter-signed it.

Telling Roger in the first place hadn't been easy, but, I said, it was for the best. 'I've got to sell now or I'm going to fall out with you and everyone else on the board. I've known you too long to do that, so I'm just going to walk away now.'

And that was it. With £193 million in my pocket I walked away from the company that had been so much of my life for twenty-nine years.

When I retired from the supermarkets at the age of forty I didn't have anything else to do. That's how Pat had tricked me into shopping five days in a row. But this time it was different. I was busy. I had a new venture, Viz-Wear, which supplies safety clothing. That's going to be a growth industry in the next few years with new European guidelines coming into force in the transport business. And I'd even bought a pie company – Pooles of Wigan. But my biggest distraction, of course, is Wigan Athletic – a fact that a lot of people used as a weapon against me in September 2008.

It began when Wigan Warriors drew a thrilling match with St Helens 16–16 to earn a home tie in the play-offs. No one had seen that coming. With four matches to play, Warrington were odds-on to grab fourth spot. But with them suffering a run of unexpected losses, Wigan suddenly had a chance. Their play-off match against Bradford was scheduled for the next Friday. Unfortunately, Wigan Athletic were due to play Sunderland at 3 p.m. the next afternoon.

I had a dilemma – could both matches be played on the same ground in such a short space of time?

To be honest, we'd done it before. But as the 2007/8 Premiership season had closed, I'd been hammered in the media for the sorry state of the JJB's pitch. With our fourth top-flight season under way, I didn't want to go through that again.

Then there was a more practical argument. Yes, we'd managed to host both clubs in quick succession before – but each time it was touch-and-go. Cleaning the stadium, repairing the turf and changing all the markings takes time. If you can avoid it, you should. And as owner of the stadium, that was my priority.

I contacted Ian Lenagan and said, 'Sorry, you can't play here. If you can get your play-off moved a day earlier, that will be fine. But at such short notice I can't get the Sunderland match delayed.'

Of course the story was picked up by the media and soon there were angry letters in the Wigan press – and even calls for a boycott of future matches at the JJB. Warriors fans started saying, 'Maybe we should get our own ground.' And that's fair enough. Fans are passionate people. I've been around for a long time and I can take criticism.

I've done a lot for both clubs over the years, but when pushed, Wigan is still a rugby town at heart, and a lot of people let me know it.

*

Things at Wigan Athletic weren't going so smoothly at the time either. When Paul Jewell left I looked around as usual for new managers but I thought, 'We've got a really good fella here already.' That's why I promoted Chris Hutchings from assistant manager to Number One.

We got off to a flyer, but things quickly took a downturn. I don't think injuries to players like Heskey helped, but I could see the problem was deeper than that. Chris is a brilliant coach and he has a super attitude, but in my opinion he is not tough enough with the players. There is nobody better equipped than Chris to be a manager but he just hasn't got the killer instinct that puts his thumb on a player and says, 'You – you are not trying.'

It was about four weeks before Christmas, and we were going down. We'd just lost our sixth game in a row and I knew I had to act. I went downstairs after the match and said, 'Bad luck lads, come on, if we can get some spirit back that's all we need.

'By the way, Chris, come and see me before you go.'

He came upstairs later and I said, 'Chris, sorry, I've got to cancel your contract.'

He took it like the gentleman he is. We shook hands and he said, 'I wish you all the best for the rest of the season.'

He knows everything about the game but he couldn't put that little bit of fire into the bellies. Fergie does it, Wenger does it – and so, I knew from experience, does Steve Bruce.

When I put the word out for our vacancy we got about fourteen very good names in immediately. But one name in particular caught John Benson's eye and he rang me straight away in Barbados.

'Dave, Steve Bruce has put his name forward.'

'Right, he's the man. I don't care who else is on the list – tell him I want to speak to him.'

I knew how good Steve was – I'd been gutted when he'd left us before – so I didn't need to see him in person. He was being messed around over his contract by Birmingham at the time so I spoke to him by phone and we did the deal with us thousands of miles apart. I had to pay a fortune in compensation to the Blues but I knew it would be money well spent. Steve Bruce was worth every penny – and he had to be to keep us in the division.

The transformation under Steve was immediate. We'd lost our previous eight League games, conceding twenty goals, but in Steve's first game in charge, at home against Sven-Göran Eriksson's Man City, we stopped the rot with a 1–1 draw. We then lost to Bolton but a week later put five past my old club Blackburn. If there's one club I don't like to see suffer, it's Rovers, but I couldn't have been happier with that win. It was just the same when we met Derby at Pride Park. I knew a loss for them would be another blow for Paul Jewell, but we needed the points as much as they did. We won that day, just as we later did at home. Paul got a terrific reception on his return to the JJB – but I know he would have preferred the three points.

I knew it would take Steve a bit of time to impose some consistency on the side, but I could already see he had the dressing room behind him. Players want to play for him. They give that extra ten per cent that makes the difference between drawing and losing, winning and drawing. Footballers respect the way he works. He doesn't shout and rave. He tells them what he expects and lets them get on with it. And it works.

The good results kept coming and a month later Steve masterminded a 1–1 at Anfield. Wigan had never taken a point from Liverpool or any of the other 'Big Four' clubs in the League before, but that Titus Bramble goal, his second in two games, put an end to that statistic. We then did the same against Arsenal and Chelsea – the latter at Stamford Bridge, in a match that some said ended Chelsea's dream of the title.

Going into the last few matches of the season, though, it was still very tight. Paul's Derby were gone but the other two spots were still available – and we could very easily fill one of them if things didn't go our way. I don't know if it is because of what we went through the year before or because of how I saw Steve work, but I wasn't as worried as some other chairmen. I had every faith that he would pull us through.

April was very good to us. A win over Steve's old club Birmingham was followed by three draws – a string of results that could not be bettered by the teams around us. When we beat Aston Villa 2–0 at Villa Park we finally secured safety with a game to spare – which was just as well, because our last game of the season was against Man U. We lost in the end to a wonderful Giggs goal, but we made a lot of friends along the way with our passing and technique. That is what football is about. And that is what Steve Bruce's teams are about. From staring down the jaws of relegation for so long, we somehow finished the season in fourteenth position. An absolutely amazing turnaround considering where we had been in November.

The following season was even better. As I took my seat in the directors' area for the opening game of the season against West Ham I had a big smile on my face. I knew I was looking at the best Wigan Athletic team there had ever been. Steve had brought in wonderful players like Amr Zaki (who scored that day) and Wilson Palacios and suddenly the press were talking about us for footballing reasons again.

We had a good, solid back four and a tremendous midfield. Palacios is brilliant all over the park, Lee Cattermole is fantastic and Antonio Valencia formed such a potent partnership with our right back. Then up front we had Emile Heskey. What can I say about Emile? He is one absolute gentleman and I was sad to see him go in the January transfer window. His contract was up at the end of the season – that was the only reason. I would love to have kept him because he is a special lad, he's a nice guy and a team player. As soon as he joined this club he went up to Brenda, our chief exec, and said, 'I'd like to buy a box for my family.' He didn't want free tickets and he didn't even ask for a discount. You don't see that too much in professional footballers, but he is an awesome lad and a terrific player. He plays hard and he plays to win. Just like me.

It's a measure of how much Steve Bruce improved the club that I was actually a bit disappointed with our start to the season. Not the quality of the football, which was the best I have ever seen at the JJB, but the points on the board. For our first home match we played Chelsea, live on Setanta, and actually felt unlucky to lose 1–0. I sensed that everyone at the club was upset by that result and I knew that the players were itching to get their revenge. It came against poor Notts County in the next game. We won that League Cup match 4–0, then destroyed Premiership new boys Hull, 5–0 at the KC Stadium. That was more like it, I thought. That was the sort of score our performances warranted.

By the time we reached Anfield in October we were flying. The goals from Zaki were going in from every angle and I had a good feeling as Pat and I sat down in the directors' area. 'Don't get overawed by your surroundings,' I urged the players. 'This team is good enough to win here.'

Seventy minutes later I knew I was right. Zaki had scored on the half-hour, Dirk Kuyt equalised, but then our lad put us ahead on the stroke of half-time. What a feeling, knowing that Steve Bruce's team talk was about how to maintain a lead at Anfield!

When the match restarted I hoped the team wouldn't get nervous, but their response was first-class. It was Liverpool who didn't know what to do and as the game entered the last fifteen minutes we looked, if anything, like we would get a third or fourth.

'We're going to do this,' I thought. 'Our first-ever victory against the Big Four.'

I've been around football a long time and I know that mistakes happen. But the moment Alan Wiley pulled out a second yellow and then a red card for Antonio Valencia in the seventy-fifth minute I lost a lot of faith in referees. I won't see two decisions as bad as that for the next ten years; it was diabolical. Antonio got a ridiculous booking for a very, very soft tackle. Then, while the Liverpool players were climbing all over us, he was pulled up for encroaching on a free kick. The rules say you can move once the ball has rotated fully once. That ball had turned three or four times when he ran forwards. It was a joke.

Everything changed after that. Rafa Benítez threw attackers forward and Riera scored five minutes later. Kuyt won it for them five minutes from time and I felt absolutely sick. When I saw Steve he said we'd been robbed, and that's exactly how it felt.

A few days later I smiled when I remembered that match. Going to Anfield and being disappointed not to win was unheard of for Wigan. 'Look how far we've come,' I thought.

When Villa came in for Emile in the transfer window we took Mido on loan from Middlesbrough and Hugo Rodallega from Colombia. We also swapped our free-kick specialist, Ryan Taylor, for Newcastle's Charles N'Zogbia, and I couldn't say no when Harry Redknapp offered us £14 million for Wilson Palacios. I'm afraid we're not the kind of club who can turn that kind of money down and Steve knew that. For a while everything just clicked. Past the halfway point of the season we went up to seventh, ahead of the likes of Spurs, Newcastle, Sunderland and many other clubs with much bigger budgets than ours. More importantly, we'd acquired forty-one points in the League – the magical target which most seasons is enough to guarantee another year of Premiership football.

That should have been a reason for celebration, but actually I don't think it helped us that much. I have to admit we had a very disappointing end to the season. There was an obvious dip in form – and, more worrying, a dip in effort as well. You can get away with not giving a hundred per cent if you're a brilliant player, but honestly, how many of those can you name in the Premier League? I've played in all four divisions and I've brought Wigan up through the leagues as well and I know that you need fight and desire – and if I'm honest, as soon as my team reached that safety zone and knew they couldn't be relegated, they stopped trying. By the time you read this I expect we'll have changed half a dozen players. I know that has got to happen. The manager knows it too.

In our last ten games of the season there was only one match where we showed what we were capable of. Once again it was against one of the Big Four – in fact it was the biggest of them all. For the second season in a row we had the opportunity to play a critical role in deciding where the League trophy was heading. With three games to go, United needed only four points. If they lost, it would give Liverpool a genuine shot at their first title in years. As much as I admire Sir Alex and for all the happy years Steve spent under him at Old Trafford, nothing would have given us more pleasure than to put a spanner in the works. But in the form we were in, I wasn't holding my breath.

As it turned out, I was really proud of the players that night. They ran the game from the first whistle and it was no surprise when we took the lead through Rodallega. Even when Tevez equalised half an hour later I still fancied our chances of nicking a winner – or at the very least holding on for a draw. But this is United, of course. If one of their strikers doesn't score then they have so many other players who can. On that Wednesday night in May it was Michael Carrick who stuck the knife into us on eighty-six minutes. Typical United but even so I was proud of my team. They proved again that they have the ability to go toe-to-toe with anyone in the League.

We ended the season strongly with a good home win over Portsmouth. Nearly 18,000 fans saw Rodallega score the winner and like me I'm sure they were delighted that it secured us eleventh place in the League – our second highest position ever.

I'm sure I wasn't alone, however, in thinking of what might have been if we'd played to our capabilities for a whole season instead of just over half of it. If the team had continued to play after Christmas to the same standard as they'd played before it then we would have finished in the top seven, without a doubt.

But football fans never look back for long and even at the end of May, with the team still doing a lap of honour on the pitch, I could hear a buzz around the stadium as supporters started to imagine us doing even better next season. Everyone wanted to know who we were going to buy, who we were going to sell and who we were going to replace Antonio Valencia with if Man U came in with their rumoured bid for him.

I love that sort of conversation as much as anyone, but there was one question I was relieved that no one was asking: 'Will Steve Bruce leave us for Newcastle?' For all the run-ins I've had with Mike Ashley, it gave me no pleasure seeing that great club get into trouble. With about ten games to go, however, I started hearing whispers in the press that Steve had been identified as the man to save them. I had no doubts that he could do it – he'd done it for us, after all. The thing that seemed to swing it for the media, of course, was the fact that coming from Northumberland he was a bit of a local hero. In the end it was another Geordie legend who got the call from Ashley – Alan Shearer. Sadly he was unable to stop the club from sliding down the table. On the day Wigan secured eleventh spot in the League, Newcastle were actually relegated to the Championship.

A lot of people who know my history with Ashley say, 'You must have had a smile on your face when you heard the news?' But nothing could be further from the truth. I honestly believe the man went into Newcastle with good intentions. He didn't realise how difficult it was going to be – a lot of people from outside the game have no idea what it's really like. But Ashley aside, it's the fifty or so thousand people who pack St James' Park every match who I feel desperately sorry for. There are no better supporters of a football club in the world. They are so loyal to that club it's unreal.

The one positive to come from Newcastle going down is that I genuinely thought I'd hold on to Steve for another year. That man has the potential to manage a top four club, no question. In fact, I'd not be at all surprised if David Gill hasn't already marked him out as a potential successor to Fergie when – or if! – he retires. Newcastle were genuinely the only other club I thought could possibly lure him. When your family are staunch Geordies, like Steve's are, you'd have to be mad not to consider it. And, let's be honest, with the right leadership that club has the potential to be among the very best.

But I'm pretty sure Steve wouldn't want to work in the Championship again so, when Newcastle went down, I breathed a sigh of relief.

But then I got a phone call I didn't expect. It was from Brenda Spencer, Wigan's chief exec.

'Dave,' she said. 'I've just had a call from Niall Quinn. He wants permission to talk to Steve.'

Was I surprised by the call from the Sunderland chairman? Yes. Was I disappointed to think that Steve might leave us again? Absolutely. But did I consider saying 'no' to Niall's request? Of course not. You know by now that I won't stand in someone's way. Make a manager, a player – anyone – work for you against their will and you'll never get their best out of them. That's not my policy and it never will be.

Of course, I already knew what Steve's answer would be. Niall would never have rung us if he hadn't already sounded him out. That's how everyone works in football. It's not tapping up – it's just saying, 'If I were to ask for permission to talk to you, would you be interested in listening?' What's the point of making a fuss through official channels if your attentions are unwanted? It only gets into the press and upsets people.

That was on the Monday.

On the Tuesday I spoke to Steve – I already knew what he was going to say.

'I've had a brilliant time here, Dave, but I've got the opportunity to go to a bigger club with bigger budgets and a more realistic chance of success.'

I knew his mind was made up – you don't take the job of managing your dad's most despised team lightly.

'Well, you leave with my blessing, Steve. Thanks for all you've done. And I'll see you for a beer when you're on holiday in France in the summer.'

Shortly after that conversation, the press got hold of the story and I began to read about all the managers I was considering to replace him. Darren Ferguson was in the running according to one paper. Paul Jewell was coming back I heard from somewhere else. In reality, though, there was only one name on my list. Just like Niall Quinn had almost certainly done a few days earlier, I picked up the phone and contacted my target.

'Hello. Roberto. It's Dave Whelan. Have you got a minute for a chat?'

Since coming to Wigan as one of my 'Three Amigos' when we were in the old Fourth Division and utterly impressing everyone who saw him, Roberto Martínez had gone on to play for a number of clubs before really finding promotion success as captain of Swansea City, then returning later as manager. What a transformation he brought to that club. They won promotion to the Championship – with a record points tally – narrowly lost the Johnstone's Paint Trophy at Wembley – on penalties – and really caught the eye of neutrals when they knocked Portsmouth out of the FA Cup live on television in 2009 and took Fulham to a replay.

I thought, 'He's young, he's super-talented and the people of Wigan love him. He's the perfect man for us.'

But was he interested?

Luckily for me he was. That's when I spoke to Brenda and we put the official wheels in motion.

Not only does Roberto have wonderful memories of Wigan but he can see the potential in the club. There's money to spend on players and there are some very good people already here. Steve Bruce did some great things for this club but we did great things for him – that's why he was chosen by Sunderland when they announced they were looking for a 'big name'. Wigan made him into that big name as a manager. We can do the same for Roberto, I'm sure.

If Roberto is half as much of a breath of fresh air as a manager as he was a player, we'll have a tremendous next few years. Apart from his obvious ability to get the most out of his players and his excellent tactical skills, I know for a fact that he has incredible contacts in Spain. Steve Bruce set the bar very high for us, with some of his brilliant 'unknown' signings – but if anyone can match them it's Roberto. I can't wait for the 2009/10 season to get started now to find out!

While the fortunes of Wigan Athletic go from strength to strength, the rest of the world has taken a bit of a beating. Like everyone else, I watched in horror in autumn 2008 as the 'credit crunch' took its toll on companies all over the world. But one company had been in trouble before the international recession hit – and that company was JJB.

Every day I opened a newspaper there seemed to be more bad news. Stores were being closed – they shut eighty just like that, but still had to pay rent on them even when there was no income coming in. Good staff, who I had employed, were being sacked. And they'd bought some very bad businesses: Qube from Tom Hunter, for a pound, and the Original Shoe Company from Ashley. Those two alone were losing £16 million a year when Chris Ronnie agreed to buy them. Why on earth would he do that? Worst of all, in my opinion, he struck a deal with Ashley to stock Sports Direct's own brands from China.

It appeared the market didn't like the way the company was going either and the share price plummeted to 12p. It was an awful thing to see happen. A once proud company, and an important employer in Wigan, was going to the wall. I wished there was something I could do.

And then one day Chris Ronnie rang me with an offer, which again I couldn't refuse.

When I first did the deal to sell my shares to him, I'd said, 'If you ever decide to get rid of the health clubs, I would like first option on them.' I never really expected that call, but here it was. Unfortunately I wasn't given an exclusive option and there were a number of other interested parties – Ashley, of course, was one. But I'd seen enough of *my* company being destroyed – if there was a chance I could save just a part of it, I'd do everything I could.

But I had a problem. The money I needed to make the deal was in a bank in Iceland – and that bank was just about to go into receivership.

Because Ronnie had borrowed the money from Kaupthing to buy my shares, I decided to leave £76 million in one of their fixed-term high-interest deposit accounts. In 2008 I took out £20 million. The remainder had been due to be released the week after the bank stopped trading. What could I do?

I have to say, the next few days and weeks were very uncomfortable. Like everyone else, I was watching the banks in America get into trouble and wondering where it would all end. Then suddenly it looked like Kaupthing was going down – and there was nothing I could do to get my money out.

To say I was worried is an understatement. But as the confusion of the first few days eased I tried to be phlegmatic. Yes, I was about to lose an awful lot of money. But there were people worse off than me. My problem wasn't life-threatening – and if I'm honest, I could live without that money.

Fortunately our Government guaranteed all UK depositors that we would get our savings back. I can still remember the relief of hearing that news. Even though it was my money in the first place, it felt like I had won the Lottery.

I filled in a claim form and waited for my deposit to be returned. And waited and waited. By the time the offer for the health clubs came up I was still £56 million short of the £76 million, plus stock at value, that I'd agreed to pay – and JJB were in dire need of that cash. The bank had refused to renegotiate a £60 million loan. Things were looking very bleak indeed – especially for Ronnie, who found himself parting company with the business he'd run.

That's when I decided to get our local MP, Neil Turner, involved. He didn't need asking twice. It wasn't just a case of one rich man wanting his savings back. He knew that what I intended to do with my money could help secure hundreds of jobs in Wigan. He got straight on to the Chancellor and things started happening instantly. My money arrived from the Treasury ten days later.

A few days after that I was the proud owner of fifty-four of the best health clubs in Britain – all part of the brand new DW Sport and Fitness company. I couldn't have been happier.

There was one other complication in buying the fitness business, however. They were all located on property leased for a JJB store. But if, as was looking increasingly likely, JJB ever went into receivership, then those leases would revert to the landlords. JJB would lose their shops – and I would lose my gyms. There was only one way around it. If I was serious about securing the health clubs then I had to buy the shops as well. I have to admit, it was a means to an end, nothing more. I honestly thought I was finished with the sports retail business, but it seems that I'm not. As I write today, more than thirty years after I founded JJB, I am once again the owner of fifty-one sports superstores and the employer of 1,500 people all over the country.

And I can't wait to get started.

Epilogue

WHELAN OF WIGAN

Even when JJB was booming in the 80s and 90s and professionally I had everything I could dream of, there was still something missing. A life needs balance and I needed to have a sporting outlet that challenged me. Football had given me a buzz that no sport – not tennis, sailing, skiing or golf – had ever come close to replacing. That hit of adrenalin when you wait for the three o'clock whistle is irreplaceable. That's why so many footballers walk away from the sport when their careers are over. They can't bear to watch others play when they can't. And they definitely don't like paying for the privilege.

Then a good friend of mine, the industrialist Arthur Snipe, introduced me to the world of hunting with horses – and I was hooked from the start. What really attracted me at first was the battle of wills, me against this giant horse. But once I'd learnt to ride it was the electric feeling I got taking jump after jump as part of the hunt that fired my enthusiasm. I couldn't get enough of it and I took part in hunts twice a week.

There are a lot of misconceptions about hunters. The truth is the one thing we all have in common is we love to ride. Yes, you get rich land-owners enjoying the sport, but you also get just as many blacksmiths, farmers, students, housewives – anyone who loves the country and loves horses.

Speaking of misconceptions, I met a fella one day who blew me out of the water with his fearless riding.

I was out with the Cheshire Hunt and we'd gathered at the house of the master, Sebastian de Ferranti. Like Arthur he had also made his money through engineering, and this house was extraordinary – every single stone had been imported from Italy. I was enjoying the views when the chap who looked after my horses at his stables, Mark Chambers, came across and said, 'Prince Charles is riding today.'

I looked over and saw six riders chatting. Everyone was wrapped up well because it was December and the sleet was falling and I could tell they were all freezing. I thought, 'I've got just the thing.' I clicked my heels and my horse, Banker, jogged over to join them. As soon as we pulled up, Prince Charles said, 'Good morning.'

'Morning, sir. Would you like a drink to warm you up?'

I pulled out a little flask of whisky and Drambuie that hunters carry on cold mornings, and his face lit up.

'What's your name?' he asked as he took a swig.

'It's Whelan, sir.'

'Where do you come from?'

'Wigan.'

'Ah, Whelan of Wigan. Thank you for the drink. Most warming.'

When we got going I was sent with the Prince and one other fella to watch for the fox in the cover. If we saw it, we'd holler and the pack would come steaming over. There were other groups watching elsewhere.

Suddenly we heard the horn. The fox was away and the pack was heading out.

The Prince looked at me. 'Which is the best way?'

I pointed towards a path that had a five-bar gate at the end. Before Charles could say anything, the other rider said, 'The Prince doesn't want to be going over blind jumps. We'll go the long way round.'

But he was wrong. HRH just kicked his heels and he was off. I set off after him but he was really flying. He got to the gate and just soared over it like he'd jumped it every day of his life.

I knew then that this man could ride. But more importantly, he had nerves of steel. I rode with him for four hours that day and he just impressed me more and more. Sometimes I led because I knew the short cuts, but then I thought, 'I'll stay behind him for a bit to see if he has any bottle,' but I already knew the answer from that first gate. He did not flinch at anything. Hedge after hedge, gate after gate, he just powered over them all.

At the end of the day the Prince came over and said, 'Whelan of Wigan, will you join us for tea?' and I couldn't say no. He even tried to buy my horse, but I wouldn't part with him.

The press call Charles all kinds of names now, but one thing you have to say about him is he has got bottle. I like to think I have the same quality. I've enjoyed a lot of good fortune in my life but I've had to work for it – and I've had my share of knocks along the way.

Yes, I broke my leg in a cup final and yes, I was on the losing side. But I don't like to think about that. I had one dream as a boy, and that was to play in the FA Cup final at Wembley. And I did that. To this day it remains the greatest achievement of my life.

Things could have turned out differently for me. In those days, before you were chosen to play for England you were selected to join the Football League team to take on the Scottish Football League team. I was chosen – and then I pulled my hamstring against Preston and Jimmy Armfield was given my place. He was the one who took the step up to play for England after that, not me. But I know I was knocking on the door.

Maybe without my injuries I would never have gone on to the markets. And then I would never have founded JJB and I wouldn't be sitting here today as the owner and chairman of DW Sport and Fitness. I have so many plans for this company and I'm just as excited now as I was thirty years ago. The health clubs are going to grow and grow and the stores will be the best in the land. We're going to stock the top brands – Adidas, Nike, Puma, etc. – but also offer our own cheaper lines as well. If you are serious about sport, you'll come to DW Sport and Fitness – just like you used to come to JJB.

And best of all for me, it's going to be a family business. My new son-in-law, Scott, will oversee the health clubs while three of my grandchildren, Matthew, David and Laura, are all working on buying and importing for the company. I couldn't be happier. By the time the credit crunch is over, we'll be ready. And it will come to an end. Young people might not realise that, but I've lived and worked through two recessions and this one might be worse than the others, but it's following the same patterns. In any downturn the first area to suffer is retail and I've always managed to keep trading. But I think things have bottomed out now. By spring 2010 we'll see green shoots and an upturn. And DW will be ready, fully stocked and trading online and in our brand-new shops.

People in Wigan will be seeing a lot of my new venture, because the naming rights at the football stadium are up for renewal at the end of the 2008/9 season – and guess who its new sponsor is going to be. Where it says 'JJB' on all the seats at the moment, it will now say 'DW'. The stadium's name will change as well. On the one hand it's the end of an era – but on the other it's an exciting new dawn, for me and for Wigan and the club.

With my health scare a few years ago I began to think about the future of Wigan Athletic. I knew that I needed to have things in place to ensure the club's future. But then I started looking at the finances of other clubs – and that doesn't make for easy viewing.

Before the huge Sky money started pouring into the Premier League, most clubs had manageable debt. Then the prize for winning started getting greater and owners began to take bigger risks. And that is wrong.

At Wigan we have an overdraft facility of £21 million. We're currently running at around £15 million in the red, but that's OK. When money comes in from transfers – Spurs still owe about £6 million on Wilson Palacios – that will go down. Then in July we will get a proportion of the annual £36 million TV money that is our due, so that debt will be wiped out completely. But I will always cap our debt at £21 million. That's a figure that I know that I could pay back if the banks suddenly called in their loans. But how many clubs' owners could do that?

If you look at the way Liverpool and Man U are financed, it's disgusting. The Glazer family borrowed millions to buy up all the United shares – and then they said to the club, '*You* have to pay that back.' I've never seen that done before. Man U make huge profits, but because of their owners they owe nearly £1 billion to the banks, so in reality they are now losing money. It's the same way Hicks and Gillett managed to finance the purchase of Liverpool. There are even potential problems at Chelsea. Mr Abramovich is a wealthy lad, but all the debt of that club is in Chelsea's name – not his. If he walks away, they have a terrible balance sheet.

I think that FIFA, UEFA and the Premier League need to act on this and I am actually leading the way with my plans for Wigan. I am going to turn the £21 million that I'm prepared to cover the club with into shares – equity. That way the club doesn't owe me and if I sell the shares, it won't affect the club. That's how it should be at every club. An owner should not be able to saddle a great footballing institution with an unserviceable debt. It doesn't make sense on any level and it's not fair on the fans who have to pay for it through increased ticket prices and restrictions in the transfer market.

Those are my long-term plans for Wigan. A lot of Premier League chairmen don't agree with them because it would affect their own club – you'll never get the 'top four' to vote to ban debt, obviously. But my immediate aims for Wigan are a lot more straightforward. I only have one ambition: and that is to stay in the Premier League. That was my promise to the town when I bought the club and that is all I want to see. If Roberto Martínez can get us into Europe then you will not see a happier man than me. But if he guarantees me seventeenth place for the next ten years I'll be just as delighted. To this day, the greatest moment of my Wigan life has been watching us beat Reading knowing that it would take us to the Promised Land. I will never, ever forget that feeling – and neither will thousands of Wiganers.

I always knew we would make it because I'm an optimist by nature. Just occasionally, though, I allow my mind to wander. What if, God forbid, my father had never returned from the war? What if I'd never known his guiding hand? What if he'd never taken me to Wigan Boys Club to straighten me out? It sends a chill through me just thinking about it. Without Mr Gibson and the Boys Club I would never have been noticed by Blackburn Rovers and I would never have received such preferential treatment in the Army. Perhaps I would have been dispatched to one of the world's danger spots, like Korea, where the war had only just ended. Perhaps I would have been posted to the other side of Europe and never given the chance to get to know Pat.

There is a very good chance I would have stayed in a factory all my life. There's nothing wrong with that, and thousands of men and women have done it and still do it. But to think of never working on the markets or having my own chain of supermarkets or running the country's most successful sports retail enterprise chastens me. That's when I realise how much I really owe to Wigan Boys Club. They gave me the opportunities to try wonderful new sports and a whole range of experiences that I could so easily have missed out on. I absolutely threw myself into everything on offer, just like thousands of other lads in those days. I know it was the making of me.

Like me, Steve Bruce says he owes his sporting career to his time at Newcastle Boys Club. Other towns still have them. These days Bolton's Lads and Girls Club is the most successful in the country. They get 3,000 kids through their doors every week – and that's exactly what I want to see in Wigan.

And that's why I'm doing something about it.

Myself and two other Wigan men, Martin Ainscough and Bill Ainscough, have privately raised £3 million, and construction of a state-of-the-art centre for young people is going to become a reality. This is a facility for all Wigan kids, aged twelve to twenty, that will open 364 days a year from 9 a.m. to 10 p.m. It will have everything a boy or girl could want in the way of sport. Gym equipment, all-weather floodlit football pitches, badminton halls, rock climbing walls – you name it, if the youth of Wigan would benefit from it, then we will be including it.

And I can promise this: everything we have in there will be of the highest quality. Too many people are guilty of thinking, 'Oh it's only for kids – the cheapest thing will do.' That's not what we think. That's not what youngsters deserve. And that's not what they will get.

As I write we're entering the planning stages, but crucially the local authority is already fully on board with the project. They've assigned a perfect piece of real estate in the centre of Wigan and, more importantly, agreed to co-fund the club. Bolton's club receives forty per cent of its income from the council; the rest it makes from the private sector in the form of donations, charges or charity work. That's exactly the split we've agreed with Wigan Council. Like us, they want to help a new generation of children to explore their potential with as many new experiences as possible; to find some point to their lives and keep them off the streets. Basically, we want to give these children the opportunities that we had as kids. When I think of how much pleasure my trombone playing still gives me today, I just wish every child in the country could experience the same, and through the Wigan Boys and Girls Club we'll be making a great start.

I think I've achieved a lot in my life, thanks first of all to my father, who took me to Wigan Boys Club and through that my career in football and beyond. Not only could I not have done it alone, but I would not have enjoyed it on my own either. Fortunately, I've been lucky enough to have a wonderful family to share every adventure with. That is why there was not a prouder man on earth in 2006 when Wigan Council bestowed on me the honour of Freeman of the Borough of Wigan. I'm grateful Pat was there to enjoy the moment with me because I could not have done it without her.

But I did have a moment of reflection, thinking of two other people who had shaped my life – my mam and dad.

As I accepted the award I couldn't help thinking, 'From peeing on my hands to Whelan of Wigan. They would have been so proud.'

ACKNOWLEDGEMENTS

I would like to thank the following people for their friendship and support.

My wife Pat; Scott, Jayne, Paul and my grandchildren Laura, Matthew, David, Paul and James; Brenda Spencer – Chief Executive of Wigan Athletic; Dr Zaman – lifesaver, friend and brilliant physician; Roger Lane Smith – long time lawyer, friend and advisor; David Fairhurst – long time friend, accountant and advisor; my sisters Elsie and Pauline.

For helping to bring this book to life, Bill McCreadie and Sam Harrison from Aurum Press; my agent David Riding; and Jeff Hudson.

In memory of people no longer with us: Mr James Gibson – the leader of Wigan Boys Club; Mr William Haydock – the conductor of Wigan Boys Club Brass Band; my brother Jimmy.

And, of course, my Mam and Dad.

INDEX

Bruce, Steve 1–5, 104, 238–40, 264, 282–3, 284–5, 298
Buchanan, Jock 76
Bullard, Jimmy 254
Burke, Dr 122, 141
Burnley 52, 114–16
Busby, Matt 80, 86, 93
Busby, Sandy 86–7, 93–4
Byrne, Roger 86

Camara, Henri 261
Campbell, Les 257
Cantwell, Noel 64
Carey, John 53–4, 55, 58, 60, 61, 64, 72, 78, 85, 92, 94, 95, 99, 112
Carroll, Roy 239
Cattermole, Lee 5, 284
Chamberlain, Trevor 88
Charles, Prince 294–5
Charlton Athletic 88
Charlton, Bobby 75, 79–80, 81, 86–7, 206
Chelsea 261–2, 284
Chimbonda, Pascal 137
Clamp, Eddie 130
Clayton, Ron 58, 62, 63, 65–6, 78, 85, 91, 92, 95, 96, 98, 127, 128, 136, 137, 147, 152
Clough, Brian 111
Colman, Eddie 79, 80, 86
Connolly, David 261
Connolly, John 115
Connors, Jimmy 260

Coventry City 154
Crespo, Hernan 262
Crewe Alexandra 149–50, 151–6, 164–6, 167–8
Cruz, Roque Santa 3
Crystal Palace 2
Cullis, Stan 53, 138
Curry, Bill 92

de Zeeuw, Arjan 236, 237, 239, 254, 261
Deaks, Willie 40
Dean, Bill 33, 49, 129
Deehan, John 227, 228, 231–2
Deeley, Norman 130, 131, 133, 135, 138
Diaz, Isidro 226
Dick, John 64, 65
Dobing, Peter 58, 62, 85, 89, 92, 115, 127
Dougan, Derek 99–101, 116, 119, 123, 125, 126, 127, 128–9, 130, 135, 136, 137, 145
Douglas, Bryan 58, 62, 85, 89, 92, 96, 97, 103, 115, 127, 136, 147
Duncan, Dally 94, 95, 99, 100, 106, 112, 113, 118, 121, 123, 125, 126, 128, 138
Dunn, Barry 202, 205, 211, 214, 217
Dutton, Len 157, 158–9, 170
Dwight, Roy 125

second season in the Premier
    League 266–8
sends out scouts to Wigan Boys
    Club 47
and Steve Bruce 238–40,
    282–3, 284–5, 288–9
and 'The Three Amigos' 226
tries to sign up DW 54–5
Wigan Boys Club 37–46
Wigan Warriors 228–31, 236,
    265–6, 281

Williams, Phil 232
Winstanley, John 232
Wolverhampton Wanderers
    53, 111, 119, 129–31,
    137–8
Woods, Matt 85, 97, 114,
    127
Wright, George 64

Zaki, Amr 284, 285
Zaman, Ansar 277